Post-Celtic Tiger Ireland and Contemporary Women's Writing

Post-Celtic Tiger Ireland and Contemporary Women's Writing: Feminist Interventions and Imaginings analyzes and explores women's writing of the post-Tiger period and reflects on the social, cultural, and economic conditions of this writing's production.

The Post-Celtic Tiger period (2008–) in Ireland marks an important moment in the history of women's writing. It is a time of increased visibility and publication, dynamic feminist activism, and collective projects, as well as a significant garnering of public recognition to a degree that has never been seen before. The collection is framed by interviews with Claire Kilroy and Melatu Uche Okorie—two leading figures in the field—and closes with Okorie's landmark short story on Direct Provision, "This Hostel Life." The book features the work of leading scholars in the field of contemporary literature, with essays on Anu Productions, Emma Donoghue, Grace Dyas, Anne Enright, Rita Ann Higgins, Marian Keyes, Claire Kilroy, Eimear McBride, Rosaleen McDonagh, Belinda McKeon, Melatu Uche Okorie, Louise O'Neill, and Waking The Feminists. Reflecting on all the successes and achievements of women's writing in the contemporary period, this book also considers marginalization and exclusions in the field, especially considering the politics of race, class, gender, sexuality, ethnicity, nationality, and ability.

The chapters in this book were originally published in the journal *LIT: Literature Interpretation Theory*.

Claire Bracken is Associate Professor in the English Department at Union College, New York, USA, where she teaches courses on Irish literature and film. She has published articles on Irish women's writing, feminist criticism, and Irish cultural studies. She is co-editor of *Anne Enright* (Irish Academic Press, 2011) and *Viewpoints: Theoretical Perspectives on Irish Visual Texts* (Cork University Press, 2013). Her book, *Irish Feminist Futures* (2016), was published by Routledge as part of the Transformation series.

Tara Harney-Mahajan is Assistant Professor of English at Caldwell University, New Jersey, USA, where she teaches courses on Irish literature and Global Anglophone literature. Her research specializes in contemporary Irish and South Asian literature, and her scholarship has been published in journals such as *Women's Studies* and *New Hibernia Review*. In the *Palgrave Studies in Adaptation and Visual Culture* series, she has a chapter forthcoming on representations of Ireland's architecture of containment in recent films. She is also co-editor of the literary studies journal *LIT: Literature Interpretation Theory*.

Post-Celtic Tiger Ireland and Contemporary Women's Writing

Feminist Interventions and Imaginings

Edited by
Claire Bracken and Tara Harney-Mahajan

Routledge
Taylor & Francis Group

LONDON AND NEW YORK

First published 2021
by Routledge
2 Park Square, Milton Park, Abingdon, Oxon, OX14 4RN

and by Routledge
605 Third Avenue, New York, NY 10158

Routledge is an imprint of the Taylor & Francis Group, an informa business

British Library Cataloguing-in-Publication Data
A catalogue record for this book is available from the British Library

ISBN13: 978-0-367-46517-9 (hbk)
ISBN13: 978-1-032-00980-3 (pbk)
ISBN13: 978-1-003-02924-3 (ebk)

Typeset in Minion Pro
by codeMantra

Publisher's Note
The publisher accepts responsibility for any inconsistencies that may have arisen during the conversion of this book from journal articles to book chapters, namely the inclusion of journal terminology.

Disclaimer
Every effort has been made to contact copyright holders for their permission to reprint material in this book. The publishers would be grateful to hear from any copyright holder who is not here acknowledged and will undertake to rectify any errors or omissions in future editions of this book.

Contents

Citation Information

The following chapters were originally published in *LIT: Literature Interpretation Theory*, volume 28, issue 1 and 2 (November 2017). When citing this material, please use the original page numbering for each article, as follows:

Chapter 2
Claire Kilroy: An Overview and an Interview
Mary Burke
LIT: Literature Interpretation Theory, volume 28, issue 1 (November 2017). pp. 13–33

Chapter 3
"no difference between the different kinds of yesterday:" The Neoliberal Present in The Green Road, The Devil I Know, *and* The Lives of Women
Mary McGlynn
LIT: Literature Interpretation Theory, volume 28, issue 1 (November 2017). pp. 34–54

Chapter 4
Transformative Tales for Recessionary Times: Emma Donoghue's Room *and Marian Keyes'* The Brightest Star in the Sky
Margaret O'Neill
LIT: Literature Interpretation Theory, volume 28, issue 1 (November 2017). pp. 55–74

Chapter 5
Queer Possession and the Celtic Tiger: Affect and Economics in Belinda McKeon's Tender
Patrick Mullen
LIT: Literature Interpretation Theory, volume 28, issue 1 (November 2017). pp. 75–95

Chapter 6
Gina and the Kryptonite: Mortgage Shagging in Anne Enright's The Forgotten Waltz
Rachael Lynch
LIT: Literature Interpretation Theory, volume 28, issue 2 (November 2017). pp. 115–133

Chapter 7
Waking the Feminists: Re-imagining the Space of the National Theatre in the Era of the Celtic Phoenix
Emer O'Toole
LIT: Literature Interpretation Theory, volume 28, issue 2 (November 2017). pp. 134–152

For any permission-related enquiries please visit:
http://www.tandfonline.com/page/help/permissions

Contributors

Claire Bracken is Associate Professor in the English Department at Union College, New York, USA, where she teaches courses on Irish literature and film. She has published articles on Irish women's writing, feminist criticism, and Irish cultural studies. She is co-editor of *Anne Enright* (Irish Academic Press, 2011) and *Viewpoints: Theoretical Perspectives on Irish Visual Texts* (Cork University Press, 2013). Her book, *Irish Feminist Futures* (2016), was published by Routledge as part of the Transformation series.

Mary Burke is Professor of English at the University of Connecticut, USA. The author of *"Tinkers": Synge and the Cultural History of the Irish Traveller* (Oxford), her scholarly and creative contributions on Irish culture have placed with *JJQ*, NPR, the *Irish Times*, RTÉ, and Faber, among other venues. She is a former NEH Keough-Naughton Fellow at the University of Notre Dame.

Susan Cahill, Ph.D., is a writer and former Associate Professor in the School of Irish Studies, Concordia University, Montréal. Her creative non-fiction essays have appeared in *Winter Papers* and *The Puritan*. Her monograph, *Irish Literature in the Celtic Tiger Years: Gender, Bodies, Memory*, was published by Continuum in 2011. She has also published two collections of essays on contemporary Irish writers: *Anne Enright* (edited with Claire Bracken) and *This Side of Brightness: Essays on the Fiction of Colum McCann* (edited with Eoin Flannery). She has published numerous book chapters and journal articles on subjects such as gender and the body in contemporary Irish fiction, historical children's literature, fairytale cinema, and Irish literary girlhood. She is currently working on her first novel.

Tara Harney-Mahajan is Assistant Professor of English at Caldwell University, New Jersey, USA, where she teaches courses on Irish literature and Global Anglophone literature. Her research specializes in contemporary Irish and South Asian literature, and her scholarship has been published in journals such as *Women's Studies* and *New Hibernia Review*. In the *Palgrave Studies in Adaptation and Visual Culture* series, she has a chapter forthcoming on representations of Ireland's architecture of containment in recent films. She is also co-editor of the literary studies journal *LIT: Literature Interpretation Theory*.

Rachael Sealy Lynch works and teaches in the field of contemporary Irish literature and culture, with a focus on women's fiction. She is Associate Professor of English at the University of Connecticut, USA. She is currently working on fictional representations of tuberculosis in Irish literature.

Sara Martín-Ruiz is a Ph.D. candidate at the University of the Balearic Islands, Spain. Her research focuses on contemporary Irish fiction written by immigrant female authors, with a special interest in the intersection of race, gender, and class. Her publications include "'The way the Irish asylum system turns people into un-human is my problem': An Interview with Ifedinma Dimbo" (*Estudios Irlandeses*, 2015), and "Literature and Dissidence under Direct Provision: Melatu Okorie and Ifedinma Dimbo" (*Irishness on the Margins: Minority and Dissident Identities*, 2018, Ed. Pilar Villar-Argáiz). She is currently co-editing, with Seán Kennedy and Joseph Valente, a volume titled *Irish Shame*.

Mary McGlynn is Associate Professor of English at Baruch College, CUNY, New York, USA. She writes about contemporary English, Scottish, and Irish fiction, and also about film, country music, and cultural studies. She is the author of *Narratives of Class in New Irish and Scottish Literature* (2008).

Patrick Mullen is Associate Professor of English at Northeastern University, Boston, USA. He is the author of *The Poor Bugger's Tool: Irish Modernism, Queer Labor, and Postcolonial History* (Oxford, 2012). He has also published on Roger Casement, James Joyce, and Edith Wharton. He has a queer reading of James Joyce's *The Dead* forthcoming in *The New Joyce Studies* (Cambridge) and is working on a book manuscript about queer sexuality in contemporary Irish literature and film.

Melatu Uche Okorie has published award-winning fiction in a range of publications, including *Being Various: New Irish Short Stories* (Ed. Lucy Caldwell) and *The Art of the Glimpse: 100 Irish Short Stories* (Ed. Sinéad Gleeson). Her collection of short stories *This Hostel Life* was published by Skein Press in 2018. This collection was then published by Virago Press in 2019.

Margaret O'Neill is a Postdoctoral Researcher at the Irish Centre for Social Gerontology and the Huston School of Film at NUI Galway, Ireland. Her research interests focus on social and cultural representations of ageing, and contemporary Irish writing. She has published widely in this area, most recently co-editing the collections *Ageing Women in Literature and Visual Culture: Reflections, Refractions, Reimaginings* (Palgrave Macmillan, 2017), a special issue of *Nordic Irish Studies*, entitled *Women and Ageing in Irish Writing, Drama and Film* (2018) and *Women and Ageing: Private Meaning, Social Lives* (Routledge, 2020).

Emer O'Toole is Associate Professor of Irish Performance Studies at the School of Irish Studies, Concordia University, Montréal. Her current research, funded by the Fonds de Recherche de Quebec and by the Social Sciences and Humanities Research Council of Canada, examines the relationship between aesthetics and activism in contemporary Irish theatre. She is the author of the book *Girls Will Be Girls* and co-editor of the collection *Ethical Exchanges in Translation, Adaptation and Dramaturgy*. She is also a contributor to publications including *The Guardian*, *The Irish Times*, and *The Independent*.

A Continuum of Women's Writing: Reflections on the Post-Celtic Tiger Era

Claire Bracken and Tara Harney-Mahajan

Post-Celtic Tiger Ireland and Contemporary Women's Writing: Feminist Inter-ventions and Imaginings was first published as a double special issue, "Reces-sionary Imaginings: Post-Celtic Tiger Ireland and Contemporary Women's Writing," in the journal *LIT: Literature Interpretation Theory* in 2017. This book compiles the double special issue, but it has been updated to combine our two introductions, and it now also includes a postscript by Mary Burke to her in-terview with Claire Kilroy and an update by Sara Martín-Ruiz to her interview with Melatu Uche Okorie. All of the other contents and details of the book stay true to the time period reflected in the double special issue and are time-stamped as of its publication in 2017. The premise of this work is that women's literary voices play a significant role in the questioning and interrogation of the neoliberal value systems that continue to structure, post-boom, the austerity and recovery policies of the Post-Celtic Tiger period. Ireland's economic boom period, popularly known as the Celtic Tiger, began in the 1990s and came to a spectacular end in 2008 with the wholesale collapse of the property industry and the destabilization of the banking and financial sectors. In the subsequent years of recession, austerity measures dominated the discursive and political landscape. These measures were used as neoliberal tools to protect the inter-ests of late capitalism, which inflicts its severities on ordinary citizens, espe-cially those most disadvantaged in Irish society. The prioritization of *individual* responsibility (over, for example, state or corporate responsibility) was rendered most explicitly in a number of controversial policies of the post-Tiger period, including the 2008 bank guarantee, the 2010 bailout, the implementation of home property taxes, and the water charges. While officially Ireland was said to be out of the recessionary period in 2013, austerity measures have continued to shape much of Ireland's economic and fiscal policies.[1] And it is the severity of these policies that generated a significant shift in public attitudes to the rhetoric of the neoliberal so revered in the Tiger period. Notwithstanding its continued dominance in the shaping and governing of Irish lives in the post-Tiger period, there is much more suspicion towards neoliberalism in the wake of austerity measures.

Contemporary women's writing in the recessionary and post-recessionary periods is a powerful site of neoliberal critique. Despite the fact that funding for the arts has been cut roughly 40% since 2008,[2] the literary field is currently marked by a burst of creative energy. In a 2015 *Guardian* article about the current state of Irish writing and its relationship to boom and bust, Anne Enright makes the point that "[i]t was hard to write in Ireland during the Tiger times—there was a sense of 'Get with the programme, you're off message,'" noting that "[t]he boom was also estranging—the whole dance of it" (Jordan). What we see in the post-boom period is a paradox of explosive literary activity in the face of austerity's structural project of paring back. In the interview with Mary Burke, Claire Kilroy explains that the economic climate of the post-Tiger period itself has fostered the production of creative work:

> There weren't many significant literary debuts during the boom, other than Kevin Barry, but since the collapse, there has been enormous activity and the big prizes and advances have returned to Irish literary fiction. It's happening because in recent years it was acceptable to not be in 'gainful' employment, so people had permission to write again. (21)

And writing by women has been especially vibrant throughout the post-Tiger period, functioning as an important place from which to explore critically the temperatures of the time. As feminist theorists Avtar Brah, Ioana Szeman, and Irene Gedalof have identified: "in recovery or crisis, neoliberal economics and politics have proved deeply destructive to most women, and have exacerbated the intersecting divides of gender, race, ethnicity, sexuality, and class" (7). Especially given the ways in which Irish recessionary culture locates the feminine as a site of blame for the excesses of the Tiger period, women's writing represents an important intervention into gendered constructions of late capitalism. While women became increasingly disempowered by and subsumed under the ethos of materialist consumerism, there was correspondingly a rise in the language of faux feminism in pursuit of late capitalist neoliberal ideology. The subsequent economic crash of the Tiger ushered in an altered, yet still heteronormative, gendered economy of representation, enfolding a masculinity in crisis with more traditional and domestic representations of the feminine (Negra).

The post-Tiger period thus points to an important moment in the history of women's writing. It is a time of increased visibility and publication, dynamic activism, and collective engagements, as well as a significant garnering of public recognition to a degree that has never been seen before. Anne Enright was the esteemed inaugural Laureate for Irish Fiction (2015–2018), Paula Meehan and Eiléan Ní Chuilleanáin were consecutive Chairs of Irish Poetry (2013–2016; 2016–2019), and Siobhán Parkinson and Niamh Sharkey held the Laureate na Óg—the Laureate of Children's Fiction—from its inauguration in 2010 to 2014. In theater, the Waking the Feminists (WTF) movement, which identified major elisions of women dramatists and systemic gender bias in the field, garnered massive support and gained traction in the implementation of positive and hopeful change. Independent publishers and journals, such as New Island Books, Tramp Press, New Liberties Press, *Banshee*, and *The Stinging Fly*,[3] are all leading the way in publishing exciting new voices, with work by Sara Baume, June Caldwell, Catriona Lally, and Danielle McLaughlin being released through these venues. In poetry, we see writers such as Sarah Clancy and Elaine Feeney shaping the terrains and aspects of an increasingly influential genre of performance poetry, something which is also evident in Sarah Maria Griffin's poem, "We Face This Land," powerfully orated by a group of women in a 2016 video directed by Dave Tynan in support of the Repeal the 8th campaign. Two collections of women's short fiction, *The Long Gaze Back: An Anthology of Irish Women Writers* and *The Glass Shore: Short Stories by Women Writers from the North of Ireland*, won the Best Irish Published Book at the Irish Book Awards in 2015 and 2016 successively. Both edited by Sinéad Gleeson, these collections of short stories bring together contemporary work with writers of the past. Their recognition by the Irish Book Awards judges indicates an important and necessary visibility for women's writing in Ireland. This non-exhaustive, preliminary sketch of the current landscape provides the rationale for this book, which charts the extraordinary dynamism of contemporary women's writing, a literary affective atmosphere of willful desire[4] that critiques the post-boom economic landscape.

The reasons for this current literary momentum are manifold, not least of which are decades of work by women writers and feminist scholars establishing trajectories of literary genealogies, a vibrant and ever-developing (non)tradition. There is undoubtedly, as Sinéad Gleeson identifies, an extraordinary "exuberance and confidence" to contemporary women's writing. While this energy is palpable, we must tread carefully in our consideration of this contemporary moment: it is not happening in an ahistorical vacuum. Therefore, as we celebrate the current level of creative output by women writers, this work must also be placed in a temporal and spatial continuum of women's writing, remembering its differences, histories, activities, and voices, which of course is part of the project of the monumental *Field Day Vols. IV and V*.[5] It is crucial to be aware of how cycles of forgetting have functioned in the Irish literary tradition, propelling the elision of women's voices, stories, and words, positioning major happenings in women's writing as discrete, unconnected events.[6] Thus, any exploration of the energies of the current moment of women's writing should keep in view a continuum of its pasts and histories. Women's writing in Ireland needs to be thought of, again and again, in terms of its connections, its linkages, its contradictions, and its traversals over time. Doing so stages a resistance to paradigmatic, generational structures that repeat the time and again of elision.

Our conceptualization of a continuum therefore rejects traditional literary movements motivated by linear succession. It draws upon Adrienne Rich's powerfully articulated "lesbian continuum" which dislodges any notion of successive progression, instead focusing on its spatial and temporal possibilities:

to include a range—through each woman's life and throughout history—of women-identified experience…to embrace many more forms of primary intensity between and among women, including the sharing of a rich inner life, the bonding against male tyranny, the giving and receiving of practical and political support…. (27)[7]

Engaging a similar figuration in *Nomadic Theory*, Rosi Braidotti gives shape to a "time continuum," "the fleeting copresence of multiple time zones" (209), that enables "the simultaneity of our being in the world together" (210). Rich and Braidotti's conception of continuum calls forth the OED's definition as "a continuous body or thing…a continuous series of elements passing into each other." While Rich and Braidotti focus on the continuum as it relates to subjecthood and subjectivity, the usefulness of this theoretical tool for our purposes is how it allows for non-linear creative exchange between moments of time in women's writing. Our drawing of the continuum here as spatially and temporally fluid operates as a queer, willful counter-measure to an Irish literary tradition that marginalizes women's writing across many decades.[8] The envisaging of women's writing in Ireland in terms of a continuum is first and foremost about establishing non-homogenous connections, highlighting both continuities and divergences across time and place. Thus, rather than seeing this current burst of women's literary activity as a discrete event, an exceptional moment in time, we would point instead to the continuum between the Field Day controversy and the Waking the Feminists campaign, between the dynamism of women's poetry in the 1980s and 1990s[9] and the current short story form written by women, between a world in 1960s Ireland when Edna O'Brien could not identify any literary foremothers to the landscape today where women writers occupy major literary positions in twenty-first-century Ireland.

Post-Celtic Tiger Ireland and Contemporary Women's Writing: Feminist Interventions and Imaginings follows the fluid logic of a continuum as a guiding frame for its structure. In addition to focusing on the recent varying intersections of activism, ethics, and women's writing, the essays included also analyze how contemporary women's writing critiques neoliberal economic and political ideology and explore the Tiger period through the lens of post-Tiger austerity. Many of the chapters critique the power of neoliberalism, focusing on representations of the Tiger and post-Tiger periods through the lens of post-Tiger austerity. Women's fiction is perfectly positioned to conduct the work of looking back, to provide an accounting of and for the Tiger period in the post-Tiger era. This is because a major contextual setting in contemporary women's fiction is transversal, exploring the space between the Tiger and post-Tiger moments with the knowingness of austerity and "set against a material landscape of intense financialization" (Negra and Tasker 9). As such, chapters two through five reveal and underscore linkages and tensions staged between the novel and the economic sphere, between aesthetic and neoliberal ideologies, between the politics of finance and the politics of art, while the subsequent chapters reflect on the many exclusions and marginalizations that have been exacerbated in the post-Tiger era, especially in the context of gender, race, class, sexuality, ethnicity, and dis/ability. As the recession is deemed to be over, it is crucial to underscore that despite the economic upheavals of the last two decades, a portion of the population experienced neither the boom nor the bust—for many, things were bad, and then they were worse. Like the willful voices of women's writing represented in chapters two through five, the writers featured in the later chapters radically interrogate these landscapes, focusing especially on the material realities of precarious forms of living in twenty-first-century Ireland.

The Essays

This book is focused largely on fiction and first-person accounts from key writers in the field, except for one chapter on the Waking the Feminists movement and our analysis later in this chapter, which considers poetry, drama, and short fiction. While in some part this reflects the submissions we received to the initial cfp, the end result is a book where the lion's share of the focus is on fiction and we recognize this as a strength of the book, as the essays are in receptive and open dialogue throughout, but also of course a limitation. If space permitted, we would have loved to capture in more detail the vital developments happening in non-fiction, poetry, drama, film, and the visual arts. So while in this introduction we chart the vibrancy of women's writing across genres and provide a sketch of some of the current trends, it must be stressed that myriad fields are producing important work and we look forward to engaging with scholarship which considers these movements.

The book takes a unique approach, in that it opens and closes with first-person accounts and interviews from writers in the field—Claire Kilroy and Melatu Uche Okorie. The first piece, "Claire Kilroy: An Overview and an Interview" by Mary Burke, places each of Kilroy's novels in the affective atmosphere in which it was wrought and provides a reading of her oeuvre to date. The interview that follows Burke's preface stages a radical intervention into sanitized exchanges between interviewer and author, as Burke and Kilroy retained the complicated logistics and constant interruptions involved with scheduling and conducting an interview when both participants are juggling the often conflicting demands between motherhood and careers. Amid the din of small children, Kilroy, prompted by Burke, offers a brave, gut-wrenching account of her experiences of early motherhood, which Burke then presciently reads as the foundation for the next major turn in Kilroy's literary career. Mary McGlynn's essay, "'no difference between the different kinds of yesterday:' The Neoliberal Present in *The Green Road*, *The Devil I Know*, and *The Lives of Women*," explores Claire Kilroy's fiction alongside novels by Anne Enright and Christine Dwyer Hickey. Illuminating a shared tracing in these three novels of neo-gothic themes and globalized representations of "non-place," McGlynn places these post-Tiger novels as engaging in a "robust" critique—both formally and thematically—with neoliberal ideologies of progress and teleology. Central to McGlynn's powerful argument is that a tension exists between the official neoliberal narrative of development and its vernacular embrace of a space-time compression, which necessarily constructs a temporality of presentness, of the ongoing and eternal. The third chapter, Margaret O'Neill's "Transformative Tales for Recessionary Times: Emma Donoghue's *Room* and Marian Keyes' *The Brightest Star in the Sky*," continues the discussion of home and domestic space and also considers the neo-gothic as a structuring paradigm of the post-Tiger novel. It presents a comparative reading between one of Ireland's best-selling and critically acclaimed novelists—Emma Donoghue—and one of Ireland's most successful writers of popular fiction, Marian Keyes. O'Neill's reading of Keyes interrogates the genre known as "Chick Lit," a label that Keyes herself would reject, and the essay demonstrates how both novels are intently preoccupied with critiquing how neoliberal ideology and economic austerity dominate Irish lives and structure gendered bodies. Patrick Mullen's "Queer Possession and the Celtic Tiger: Affect and Economics in Belinda McKeon's *Tender*" also considers the intricate intersections of economics and sexuality in the Tiger period through an astute close reading of Belinda McKeon's novel *Tender*. Drawing on Eve Sedgwick's theories of the closet, Mullen persuasively reads McKeon's novel as an indictment of the Tiger period and argues that *Tender* configures an aesthetic sensibility that sets the stage for queer reflection, critique, and ethical possibility, all of which is configured—given the novel's publication in the post-Tiger period—from a recessionary-era lens.

Rachael Lynch's chapter "Gina and the Kryptonite: Mortgage Shagging in Anne Enright's *The Forgotten Waltz*" offers an insightful reappraisal of Enright's fifth novel by situating it within the Tiger years and the first few years of the crash. Lynch argues for the power of Enright's novel as a critique of what she sees as a Tiger posthumanism, replacing it instead with an "ethical post-Tiger post-humanity," embodied in the non-normative familial bond between Gina and Evie (118). Emer O'Toole's "Waking the Feminists: Re-imagining the Space of the National Theatre in the Era of the Celtic Phoenix" investigates the radical potential of the Waking the Feminists movement specifically in the context of "the raucous…spectacle" that was held at the Abbey Theatre, arguing that the Waking the Feminists movement might "permanently transform the space of the national theatre, if not the nation" (141). O'Toole moves to an analysis of THEATREclub's Heroin (2010), directed by Grace Dyas, and ANU Productions' Laundry (2011), directed by Lisa Lowe, productions which speak to the "presence of visionary female theatremakers" (149) and concludes by speaking to the relationship between protest and performance and the exciting developments that are transforming Irish theatre. Susan Cahill also harnesses the idea of feminist protest in a captivating analysis of the literary representation of girlhood in post-Tiger culture. Her chapter "A Girl is a Half-formed Thing?: Girlhood, Trauma, and Resistance in Post-Tiger Irish Literature" identifies trauma as a marked configuration of the girl in twentieth-century Irish literature. These traumatic markings, she argues, continue as fundamental elements in post-Tiger women's writing, evident in two important—and indeed very different—contemporary fiction writers: Eimear McBride and Louise O'Neill. Cahill cogently traces the connections between the two writers, both of whom figure the precarity of girls' bodies violated by sexual assault, abuse, and rape. Moreover, she argues, what is at stake across the work is a feminist articulation of rage, an outpouring of critique at the maligning of girls' subjectivities and bodies in the postfeminist and neoliberal climate of post-Tiger culture. The last section of the book focuses on the work of the award-winning writer Melatu Uche Okorie.[10] In "Melatu Uche Okorie: An Introduction to Her Work and a Conversation with the Author" Sara Martín-Ruiz provides an overview of Okorie's published work to date, noting the ways in which she interrogates both "traditional" modes of life in Nigeria and lived experiences of deprivation in contemporary Ireland. Martín-Ruiz demonstrates why it is "high time that the literary voices of immigrants themselves are finally heard" (176). Following this preface is a compelling interview with the author and the book then concludes with a short story by Okorie entitled "This Hostel Life,"[11] which centers on a community of women that develops within the depredations of Ireland's Direct Provision system.[12] Publishing a piece of creative writing was a first for *LIT: Literature Interpretation Theory*, and this story and the essays that precede it connect to Sara Ahmed's observation about the current "buildup of a momentum around feminism" and demonstrate the new potentialities that are being crafted in literature and literary criticism (*Living a Feminist Life* 109). Together, these pieces continue the formation of "a willful archive," contributing to the material sinews of the continuum of women's writing (Ahmed, *Willful Subjects* 12).

Trends in the Field

All together, these articles represent a snapshot of the interventions women's writing is staging into some key concerns of contemporary Ireland. And yet, it would be remiss of us not to mention some of the writers not discussed in this book, mostly because their work is so recent. We are thinking here of the writings of Sara Baume, June Caldwell, Alvy Carragher, Lisa McInerney, Doireann Ní Ghríofa, Danielle McLaughlin, and Laoisa Sexton. Women writers in Northern Ireland are also gaining greater visibility in the current moment, as evidenced in the recent publication of the aforementioned *The Glass Shore*. While increased visibility is without a doubt a notable feature of this contemporary landscape of women's writing, this is not all encompassing, with many exclusions and marginalizations, especially in the context of race and class, with access to publication venues remaining a key challenge. Self-publishing is one possible avenue, one that Ifedinma Dimbo, Jane Ovbude, Ebun Akpoveta, and J. B. Rehnstrom have all engaged in producing their work. However, the visibility of these texts to the general readership is limited at best, as they are not available in libraries and bookshops, and if available online, the cost can be prohibitive for the average reader.

Ifedinma Dimbo's 2012 novel *She Was Foolish?* and Ebun Akpoteva's *Trapped: Prison Without Walls* (2013) both engage the difficult themes of sexual violence, rape, and assault in the context of an experience of immigration, something which we can identify as a trend in post-Tiger women's writing. Louise O'Neill's YA fiction also treats the traumatic subject of rape, as does the poet Alvy Carragher in her YouTube released poem "Numb" (2014). Carragher's work is interesting in its hybridity, its mixing of media and aesthetic forms, a hybridity that is a marked feature of an aforementioned important facet of contemporary women's poetry in Ireland: performance poetry. Similarly, the poet dramatist Ursula Rani Sarma's plays experiment with a sort of verse drama, while Claire-Louise Bennett's *Pond* (2015) advertises itself as a collection of short stories, but in its sustained, unconventional first-person perspective, might just as easily be categorized as a hybrid form—a short story-novel.

Indeed, experimentation is an important aspect of contemporary women's writing, where it is deployed to take on themes of immense social importance—implicating, in particular, gendered bodies. For example, the horrifying effects of the Eighth Amendment, which equated the life of the fetus to that of the mother, are interrogated in June Caldwell's short story "SOMAT." Written from the perspective of a fetus, the story recounts how a mother's dead body is artificially kept alive, so that the fetus might be successfully harvested. "SOMAT" powerfully comments on the "gorgeous filthy" ironies that abound in such a situation, that is, unfortunately, not at all impossible in contemporary Ireland (237). Lucy Caldwell's 2016 "Mayday" also takes on the subject of reproductive rights in a story of a young woman taking abortion pills in Northern Ireland and her fears and anxieties regarding a society that renders her choice for bodily autonomy an illegal act. Well-known writer Anne Devlin, after a hiatus of many years, returns to the short story with "Winter Journey (The Apparitions)" and "Cornucopia." Known for her riveting plays from the 1980s and 1990s, Devlin experiments here with a first- and third-person perspective to embrace a time-space continuum between the 1970s and the present, moving between Northern Ireland, England, and Europe.[13] And of course we must conclude with the forerunner for this recent explosion in experimentalism, Eimear McBride's novel *A Girl Is a Half-Formed Thing* which powerfully harnesses experimental form to take stock of the harrowing traumas of sexual abuse.

Sinéad Kennedy notes how the 2010 Bailout "locked Ireland into a very specific neoliberal economic model dominated by policies that have imposed immense hardship on working people, communities, the poorest and most vulnerable sections of society" (90). The work of contemporary women's writing has been particularly attentive to processes of social and economic marginalization in the recessionary period, something brilliantly explored in Lisa McInerney's novel *The Glorious Heresies*, winner of the 2016 Bailey Award and Rita Ann Higgins' poetry collection *Ireland Is Changing Mother* (2011). Moreover, as the essays in this book demonstrate, representations of the domestic and of the home are paramount, moving from a cultural Tiger context when, as Mary McGlynn perceptively notes, "a house was less a home than it was untapped capital" to a post-Tiger one where the home becomes a locus of debt and negative equity (54). In addition to Enright and Kilroy, whose recent work substantially engages with the house motif, we can also see it figured in the ghost estates of Tana French's crime fiction and in the intense meditation on "home" in the context of the ongoing humanitarian migrant crisis in Edna O'Brien's *Little Red Chairs* (2015).

Women's writing in the post-Tiger period defies the logic of austerity as it uses the recessionary (and post-recessionary) vantage point to stage a reckoning into the past, and therefore, into the present. Despite the fact that austerity "trains us to expect less and less" (Bhattacharyya 4), contemporary women's writing excess and energy interrupts the paring back of austerity's reductions by its very abundance. As we mentioned at the outset of this chapter, this book is time stamped at the moment of the double special issue's publication in 2017. However, publishing this now in book format, it is vital to mention how this creative energy has continued to grow and expand the boundaries of women's writing, particularly in light of Emilie Pine and Sinéad Gleeson's groundbreaking creative non-fiction books *Notes to Self: Essays* (2019) and *Constellations: Reflections from Life* (2019), Anna Burns' Booker Prize winning novel *Milkman* (2018), and Sally Rooney's explosive career with *Conversations with Friends* (2017) and *Normal People* (2018). As these most recent developments demonstrate, working with texts in the present always involves negotiating a moving terrain, a shifting landscape of potential and change. One of the exciting possibilities for this book is that it plays a role in the continued shaping of the continuum of women's writing in Ireland, connecting to the past and to the future in a field that is ever shaping anew.

Considering the Politics of Representation: Rita Ann Higgins, Rosaleen McDonagh, and Melatu Uche Okorie

In what follows, we provide a preliminary analysis of three exceptional literary voices—Rita Ann Higgins, Rosaleen McDonagh, and Melatu Uche Okorie—all of which engage in a critique of the precarious conditions of post-Tiger Ireland, ultimately raising questions about the politics of representation. In the post-Tiger period, especially in the recessionary moment, we have seen the political implementation of austerity measures that have rendered those at the margins of sociocultural life even more vulnerable. One of the consequences of this austerity regime in Ireland has been the normalization of precarity as a way of living. As Judith Butler notes, precarity is a lived condition of embodiment, structured by social, economic, and material differences (as Isabell Lorey insists "[n]ot every precarious body is the same"), but it is also produced by a process of "precaritization," a ubiquitous, hierarchy-inducing force, a "power without a subject" (173, 169).[14] While Higgins's 2011 *Ireland Is Changing Mother* specifically considers the affects of austerity, McDonagh's play *Mainstream* (2016)[15] and Okorie's "This Hostel Life" (2017) interrogate the lived experience of intersecting forms of discrimination and the Direct Provision system respectively. Higgins's poetry has always been preoccupied by the economic inequities rife throughout Irish society (regardless of "boom" or "bust"), and in this collection she scathingly unearths the contemporary economic post-Tiger landscape, engaging incisive class and gendered critiques of abject processes of marginalization.[16] *Mainstream* takes non-intersectional feminist agendas to task for continuing to ignore Traveller rights and rights for individuals who have disabilities, powerfully exploring the ethical imperatives of intersectional thinking for a fuller understanding of precarity. McDonagh also unearths the amnesia surrounding the institutionalization of children from Traveller communities during her own lifetime.[17] And Okorie's short story "This Hostel Life" reveals the ways in which the culture of institutionalization continues in the present day with the Direct Provision system of inhumane, perpetual incarceration.

These three writers explore the relationship between a lived experience of precarity and the powerful forces of economic and social precaritization that continue in post-Tiger neoliberal Ireland. If an atmosphere of "inescapable precariousness" is affectively built into Ireland's austerity program, the work of these writers crucially disrupts the before-after narrative that this implies, troubling the very distinctions between "boom" and "bust" in their poignant accounts (Bhattacharyya 100). Moreover, while these texts reveal the ways in which certain lives have always been rendered precarious—perpetually institutionalized and marginalized—they also demonstrate how, in this contemporary moment, existence is figured all the more precarious in the unknowability of what is to come. During both the recession and recovery periods, homelessness rates increased and the percentage of people experiencing enforced economic deprivation reached new heights.[18] Thus, these writers stage crucial interventions into representations of precarious life and underscore an intersectional feminist politics that we see as vital to the continual shaping of the continuum of women's writing.[19] Their work therefore provides a scaffolding of survival and resilience in the face of radical social uncertainty and the extremities of precarity.

Rita Ann Higgins Ireland Is Changing…Mother?

In her 2011 collection *Ireland Is Changing Mother*, Rita Ann Higgins interweaves gender with the economic so as to provide a piercing satire on sexuality, race, and class in Tiger and post-Tiger Ireland. In the opening poem "Ireland

Is Changing Mother," which shares its title with the collection overall, Higgins deconstructs the seemingly dated iconography of Mother Ireland, devastatingly dragging its clichés into the twenty-first century by playfully directing each stanza to "mother" and repeating the phrase "Ireland is changing mother" in the third and fifth stanzas. This grammatical ambivalence confronts the reader as both a declaration and a question: is Ireland changing, mother? or is Ireland indeed a changing mother? In both instances, Higgins interrogates the othering and fetishization of racial difference, and the poem serves as a satirical commentary on xenophobic and racist discourses on a "changing" Ireland. Moreover, Higgins locates the distanced positionality and objectification of female desire and sexuality in this poem by mentioning "local girls [who] wet themselves" and the aggressive, predatory "seizing" of "Cynthia's hips" (9–10). This is a "changing" world in which, Higgins seems to say, female desire and sexuality remain obfuscated, unexpressed, and unknowable.

Higgins's work overtly reflects on the inequities of late capitalist Ireland, underscoring important continuities between the Tiger and post-Tiger periods, interrogating the conglomerates, banks, and upwardly mobile middle-classes who funded the entire enterprise. In "The Builder's Mess," as in "Ireland Is Changing Mother," sexualized language is engaged to interrogate the phallocentrism and toxic masculinity endemic to the post-boom period. Perhaps one of the bleakest assessments of the crash and its casualties, this is a damning account of a masculinized "mess" with descriptions of construction masking striking language about misplaced ejaculations ("…the bubble's burst mother" "deposits in their pockets"), cavernous vaginas ("Some were completed and vacant / some were found to be occupied / some were found to be empty and occupied / all at the same time mother"), and unreleased sperm ("few finished, loads unfinished") (28). The speaker's unrelenting, dystopic vision of the Irish post-boom landscape in terms of failed sexual conquest blames a generalized, beleaguered "mother," as Higgins calls into stark relief the Oedipal dynamics that underpin the Irish cultural imaginary:

> All those estates
> six hundred and twenty, maybe more,
> few finished, loads unfinished.
> unsightly and neglected
> dirty-faced and dour mother
> toxic and tired mother. (29)

The abused nature of the Mother Ireland configuration is revealed in these lines, with the negative gendering clearly at stake in the adjectives that are, once again, purposely not separated by a comma: "unsightly and neglected / dirty-faced and dour mother / toxic and tired mother." This abjected representation figuratively connects to the goading questions repeated at the end of the poem in the last two final stanzas as the "sons and daughters / of the Celtic tiger" press "mother" for an answer (30).[20] Instead of a response from "mother," they call the "mess," with manufactured outrage, "a travesty mother" (30). This facile response drips with hypocrisy as a "homeless guy," voiced in an earlier stanza, responds that the ghost estates are "a crying shame mother," but is left unheard and unheeded (29). The poem seems to suggest that "The Builder's Mess" is not a "travesty" or "phenomenon," as both these descriptors imply an absolving of accountability and responsibility, but, as the man cries out, a "shame," a deep-seated societal "mess" that indicts bankers, builders, and conspicuous consumers (29–30). And while ghost estates resonate with the aura of dispossession, this poem's ethical center is directed more towards the intensification of precarity for the most vulnerable in society, those for whom "shelter" is denied: "The homeless guy who is barred / from the homeless shelter / for urinating in a doorway" (29). In this trenchant poetic critique, Higgins provocatively disassembles post-Tiger discourses about building, property, and homemaking, disrupting a framing of the crash in terms of middle-class loss, asking the reader instead to face and see the material realities of homelessness and the dispossessed.

Higgins continues to focus on the collapse of the building industry in "No One Mentioned the Roofer" (59) and "Where Have All Our Scullions Gone?" (54–57), as she foregrounds those complicit in the real estate bubble while also insisting on naming the dispossessed material lives of the workers. In "Scullions," Higgins purposely uses only the title to remind us of those nameless faces enrolled in the actual construction of buildings, while in "No One Mentioned the Roofer" the speaker searches for the worker who has been made invisible in public discourse about the collapse. While the tone in "Scullions" and "Roofer" is not as desolate as "Mess," Higgins's objective here is to consider lives on the margins of an already precarious recessionary culture. Higgins's poetry, as Moynagh Sullivan incisively writes, operates on the "threshold" "between conflicted public and private spaces" (131), and this collection in particular foregrounds marginalized figures in the Tiger and Post-Tiger periods in order to point to a politics of representation that continues to keep these lives outside public debates about recession and "recovery."

Moving to the ways in which austerity policies are perversely maintained in a post-recessionary climate, Higgins continues to focus on marginalized individuals in "Burden of Proof" and "His Brazen Hair," recalling Judith Butler's formulation: "When the bodies of those deemed 'disposable' assemble in public view, they are saying, 'We have not slipped quietly into the shadows of public life; we have not become the glaring absence that structures your public life'" (168). In "Burden of Proof" the callous ticket agent insists that the theatre-goer find "proof" that he/she is "human and unemployed" in order to obtain a reduced-price ticket (12). In "His Brazen Hair," the reverse happens: The speaker of the poem is visiting an exhibition and encounters a man "collapsed on the ground" in front of the gallery (17). While in "Burden of Proof," the theatre-goer is subjected to verbal abuse— "your mongrel mouth" "you snivelling git" (12–13)—in "His Brazen Hair," the police "poked him with the blue gloves," dehumanizing him in a description as "a body on the ground" (17). In both poems, the bodies of the theatre-goer and the man passed out on the street transgress the so-called respectability of aesthetic spaces such as the theatre and the gallery. Their bodies are misbehaving and unruly—exceeding and disrupting social spaces reserved for consuming aesthetic works of art. The critique is primarily directed at border control: the borders of bodies and the structural borders of civil society. By writing poems about these borders and the bodies that press upon them, Higgins reveals that the neoliberal systems controlling society through abjection in fact produce the very dimensions of precarity itself.

Rosaleen McDonagh and the "Burden of Representation"

In a plenary talk given at the 2016 IASIL conference at University College Cork, Anne Mulhall challenges the contemporary Irish poetic establishment for its resistance to "political poetry," connecting this resistance to "a neoliberal project" with "an extant investment of the lyric as a space of intimate revelation that has universal import [...] that somehow cuts across all differences and divides." Identifying Rita Ann Higgins, Elaine Feeney, Sarah Clancy, Abby Olivera, Connie Roberts, and Alvy Carragher as poets that "confront such delusions head-on," Mulhall makes the insightful point that "[f]or truly political poets the point is not to make a political poem, but to make a change to the political situation with the tools that they have." Higgins's collection *Ireland Is Changing Mother* does just this, engaging powerful and direct confrontations with the neoliberal logic of Tiger and post-Tiger culture so as to intervene and disrupt a politics of representation that privileges upper- and middle-class narratives and voices. Like the collapsed edifices of the building industry that the collection charts, all pretenses to universality are systematically unraveled. Playwright Rosaleen McDonagh shares a similar deconstructive approach in relation to what she terms the "burden of representation." A leading feminist activist within the Traveller community and in the area of disability rights, McDonagh is the author of many plays including *The Baby Doll Project* (2003),[21] *Stuck* (2007), *Rings* (2010), and *She's Not Mine* (2012). In a 2013 interview, she discusses the "ever present" "burden of representation" that both fuels and antagonizes her work. McDonagh explains further that this burden manifests itself in terms of

> [t]he pressure internally to encapsulate elements of the Traveller aesthetic while honouring disability culture. The binary position. If I write about Travellers or disabled people mainstream critics say I'm insular. While my instinct to encompass characters with impairments is strong, I attempt badly to ignore this urge. Then audiences and critics from the disability community reprimand me. Nobody told me that representation is such a critical part of theatre.[22]

McDonagh takes on these complex questions regarding the politics of representation in *Mainstream* (2016) both in its casting and in the concerns of the play itself. As she writes in the playwright's note, "[t]he burden of representation and resistance is ever present," as McDonagh negotiates her commitment as an activist with her vision as an artist, admitting that a compromise had to be struck given that "[c]asting all Traveller and/or disabled actors was not possible." But while McDonagh indicates that she had to cede her ideal casting wishes, her production of the play succeeds in addressing the "glaring deficit" in "Irish theatre" regarding "[d]iversity, accessibility, and opportunity" and its misappropriation—and indeed, caricature—of "Traveller identity." McDonagh's concern about being misappropriated by the "mainstream" in the play is palpable. On the one hand, McDonagh is compelled to address the misrepresentation and misperceptions about Traveller communities and individuals with disabilities rife throughout Irish society, and she wants to underscore the integrity of the Traveller community, in particular, which has experienced extreme discrimination for most of the twentieth and twenty-first centuries. The play is therefore a challenge to the "mainstream" about what it means to be accepted within this normative and limiting cultural construct, which historically for Traveller communities has translated to the decimation of their families and livelihoods. On the other hand, McDonagh wants to redefine the concept of what it means to belong to the "mainstream," arguing that this play is as representative of Irish life as anything that might be regularly staged at the Abbey Theatre. McDonagh's analysis of the "mainstream" thus pivots on two interrelated concerns: the failures of non-intersectional feminism, particularly from the viewpoint of women and children from the Traveller community who have disabilities, and the widespread institutionalization and abuse that many Traveller children suffered, without so much as an investigation, in the 1970s, 1980s, and 1990s.

In the play, McDonagh stages a complex, intergenerational debate between the characters Mary-Anne and Eleanor. Mary-Anne, a Traveller woman with a disability in her "mid-thirties," is in a long-term, troubled relationship with Jack. She is also a pseudo-mother to Eoin, a Traveller man who is gay,[23] and the connections between them were all forged during the many years they spent in the "care" of the state (2). Eleanor, in her "early twenties," is involved in producing a documentary film about members of the Traveller community who had been institutionalized by the state as children and teenagers (2). The documentary serves as the impetus for the play: the documentary producers, and by extension Eleanor, ruthlessly require a reality-TV-style story, and Eleanor manipulates Eoin into involving Jack, and then finally, Mary-Anne (Eleanor in fact sleeps with Jack in order to gain access to Mary-Anne). But Eleanor is no match for Mary-Anne; while the play establishes some similarities between the two, these moments are complicated by the fact that Eleanor is settled, was never institutionalized, and grew-up, in fact, quite privileged. Indeed, her rare, undiagnosable condition is in its early stages, so while in a few years she may need the wheelchair that Mary-Anne increasingly relies on, at this stage she repeatedly insists that she doesn't "identify" as "having a disability" (16, 26).[24] Throughout their conversation, Eleanor's tenuous, immature, misguided, and privileged version of selfhood is systematically dismantled by Mary-Anne:

> All sorts of women are caught in a compromise. It's not right. It's not fair but at least try and understand that our lives are complicated. I'm a Traveller woman. What I call liberation doesn't mean turning my back on the values I was reared with. (35)

A few moments later, Mary-Anne also admits that "the biggest liberalization of all, for any women—Traveller … Disabled … Muslim—is going against her family" (39). Mary-Anne's sense of her own intersectional subject position necessitates these productive, inextricable contradictions—they are not meant, she seems to say, to be separated into individual parts. In a dialogic exchange full of reversals, McDonagh ultimately allows Mary-Anne and Eleanor to find common cause, despite their obvious differences. Bringing to mind feminist theorist Isabell Lorey, who acknowledges that "[w]e are different in our common precariousness. Not every precarious body is the same…" (173), the play facilitates the representation of a shared togetherness with the two women, all the while carefully identifying the dividual lines of class and privilege and critiquing a strand of intractable, insular, non-intersectional feminism that ignores key elements of society.

In the acknowledgments to *Mainstream*, McDonagh dedicates the play "to the Traveller women, and men, who were in the care of the state, honoring particularly those who were in Derralossary House and Trudder House."[25] Honoring—representing, in fact—the lives of young Travellers in institutional care is a vital act of remembrance. In a 2011 Amnesty International report, Carole Holohan identifies how "the failure of government to complete and publish a report that investigated the grave abuses of Traveller children in Trudder House indicates how Travellers continue to be a low priority" (199–200). This is a forgetting of a very recent history—Trudder House was established as a care facility for Traveller boys in 1975 and Derralossary House for Traveller girls in 1983—and the play seeks to redress the betrayals of a widespread cultural amnesia that disposes certain narratives of the past.

Institutionalization is therefore a key focus of the play, with the narrative's traumatic center focusing on the abuse suffered by Traveller children in institutional care. The play culminates with Mary-Anne, Eoin, and Jack revealing traumatic memories of their institutionalized past. Eoin states,

> that time of my life, it's over. It's been over for many years yet I remember so many things. Even the noises. The eeriness of the place. There were sounds of dead voices, a mixture between a playground and a graveyard of all the children that had died over the years. (47)

In a moment that uncannily evokes the horrifying specter of the Tuam Mother and Baby home, McDonagh's play identifies the extreme vulnerability of Traveller children's lives.[26] Liminally occupying a precarious state between life and death, between the "playground" and the "graveyard," Eoin's memory of the "eeriness of the place" summons an atmosphere where the bodies of children are gravely treated as disposable objects marked by neglect and abuse. Mary-Anne remembers the bruises on their friend Michael's "body from the care-workers. All over his arms, his chest, his legs. It used to break my heart. He had no way of defending himself" (48). In the play's last scene, Jack, after a lifetime of withholding, releases an intensely hidden memory of his sexual abuse at the home:

> After the verbal abuse, he put Michael to bed and then came to me...I was already in bed. He pulled down the covers. The only thing I remember him saying was, 'You're drunk, you won't feel this'... The next time he was on, he told me I was too old for what he wanted.... (57)

These harrowing final lines of the play, spoken in a direct address by Jack to the audience, highlight not only the intense vulnerability of his body but also its disposability as no longer needed or required. While the lines refer to a past event, their affective charge and haunting horror make the past viscerally present and the audience leaves with this lived experience made temporally real. If we consider Eleanor's observation that "maybe our bodies are our histories" in light of Eoin's point about certain bodies not counting as "human," then the play asks important questions not only about the precarious existence enforced on forms of marginalized identities in Irish culture but also about the precarity of historical narrative itself (40, 17). There is therefore a relationship here between the vulnerability of bodies and the abjection of certain histories, and *Mainstream* navigates the contradictions of an ethically imperative intersectionality as well as the emotional resonances of a not-too-distant, institutionalized past.

Melatu Uche Okorie and "This Hostel Life"

It is impossible not to see the overt parallels between Ireland's history of institutionalizing women, "illegitimate" children, and Traveller children—bodies forced into seclusion because they transgressed the socio-cultural borders put in place by state and church collusion—and its modern-day counterpart, Direct Provision. As Anne Mulhall and Gavan Titley note, Ireland's Department of Justice "sees direct provision as part of a system of national defence," and when people seeking asylum describe the Direct Provision centers as "'open prisons,'" they speak to its deleterious effects. Direct Provision is designed to cordon off and make invisible racialized, othered individuals. Indeed, public and civil society is made complicit by their tacit participation in this farce of concealment.

In 2006, Melatu Uche Okorie came to Ireland from Nigeria, and she is one of a number of writers directly representing the experience of migrating to Ireland and then navigating the dehumanizing, punitive system of Direct Provision. In an interview with Sara Martín-Ruiz in this book, Okorie reveals that "[p]ublication has definitely been harder for immigrant women," further sharing that "some part of that difficulty comes from some people feeling that if you're not a certain way, look a certain way and speak a certain way, then automatically, your writing is poor" (180). Okorie's words powerfully connect a privileging of sameness—"a certain way"—with the politics of race, ethnicity, nationality, gender, and class, making evident not only the difficulty of publication she has encountered as an immigrant woman of color in Ireland but also significantly pointing to a vital concern in her thinking about the politics of representation itself. In this same interview she importantly discusses how the lived experience of a person seeking asylum in Ireland does not necessarily register the boom and bust narrative, as she discloses: "I think recession is a normal way of life for women like myself. During the Celtic Tiger years, we were left on the sideline, we were hearing of this new prosperity, but we never partook of it" (179–180).

Okorie's short story "This Hostel Life" is the concluding piece in this book.[27] In the short story, Okorie represents a community of asylum-seeking women navigating the absurdities of Direct Provision on a Monday morning (set between 10:26 am and 12:01 pm). Okorie tells the story from the perspective of Beverléé, a Congolese woman who arrives last to collect her provisions for the week. (187) The hostel is packed with "everybody" as Beverléé explains the rules, at least in this hostel, for obtaining provisions:

> For my last hostel, dey give you provision any day, but it's gonna be one month since you collect last. So if you get toilet paper today, it's gonna be one month before you get another. Dat is why me I happy when dey give me every week for here, but now, me I don feel happy again. Dis direct provision business is all the same, you see, because even if you collect provision for every week or you collect for every month, it is still somebody dat is give you the provision. Nothing is better than when you for decide something for yourself! (189)

Beverléé must first get a ticket in order to collect her weekly provisions, a process ostensibly designed to ensure that each person gets their provisions in an orderly manner, although it is this process that Okorie is most heavily invested in critiquing as a form of biocontrol. But before the breakdown over the distribution of provisions, Okorie provides us with a glimpse of a local, transnational community of women. It is a paradox of Direct Provision, Okorie seems to say, that it is one of the most heterogeneous multi-racial, multi-class, and transnational spaces in Ireland despite the fact (or because of the fact) that it is a system designed to enforce racialized national boundaries. Indeed, in a story with a deliberately brief timespan, the following countries and regions are represented: the Congo, Nigeria, Benin, Cameroon, Somalia, Zimbabwe,

Kenya, Uganda, South Africa, Eastern Europe, and, of course, Ireland. The story, therefore, functions as a radical affirmation of life in a system designed to eradicate it.

The heterogeneity characterizing this community of women is also central to the story's style and the linguistic fibers of its experimental voice. In the interview with Martín-Ruiz, Okorie provides an account of the language deployed by her first-person narrator.

> The language of the story is a completely made up one; by this, I mean the voice of the main character, Beverlée. It may come across to the reader as Pidgin English, but a study of the West African Pidgin English will show that the language of the story is different, and does not fit the construct of the Pidgin English, if there's any such thing! When writing the story I considered the fact that the main character, Beverlée, was Congolese, with little French and even less English. I needed to give her the right tool of communication. To do this, I had to coin out what I'll call a mixture of Englishes… (184)

Describing Beverlée's use of words as a "mixture of Englishes," Okorie's character functions in many ways as a transnational connector within a diverse community of women. Although she is warned by other Congolese people in the hostel to "Be careful of Nigerias; do not make friends with Nigerias; Nigerias like to make trouble and fight too much; the management don't like Nigerias," she knows "no one is good complete" and "Now, all Congolese people come to me and start to say, 'Please Beverlée,' for connect dem to my Nigeria friends" (190). Beverlée is thus a highly connected and connectable subject, and throughout the story we witness her reaching out to those around her. Empathy is a central attribute of her character, something which is in particular effect when she apprehends the isolation of another. For example, Beverlée comes to the aid of her best friend Ngozi, a Nigerian woman, when she perceives that none of the other women are listening to her story and she redirects the conversation to safeguard Ngozi's inclusion. In another moment, she even feels sympathy for the center's security guard, as she tries to help him call out the ticket numbers. Therefore, even in the context of powerful systems of control, her empathy connectively spreads. As she says, "no one is good complete," and with this statement Beverlée refuses the exclusionary logic that enforces the boundaries of homogenous culture and resists the stereotypes upon which that logic rests. She insists instead on individuals (and the nationalities to which they ostensibly belong) as being in process—and the unfinished and the incomplete become a hallmark of her ethical empathic landscape.

In many ways, a sense of the unfinished speaks to the asylum process itself, as people in the process of seeking asylum experience a constant state of waiting. The story picks up the tension explored by Anne Mulhall in her essay "Dead Time: Queer Temporalities and the Deportation Regime" between "stasis of dead time, time served waiting in the shadow of deportation" and moments when "the incarcerated is not entirely contained by the regime that would annihilate that force." As Mulhall debates this question in her essay, she references the work of activist and artist Vukasin Nedeljkovic, creator of the powerful digital art installation *Asylum Archive* and author of a companion book also called *Asylum Archive*. As Mulhall quotes in her article, Nedeljković has written about collective resistance in the face of extreme institutionalization:

> I created a home with my fellow asylum seekers within the walls of direct provision. Together we resisted institutionalism, poverty, social exclusion … Direct provision centers are not only sites of incarceration. They are sites where different nationalities have existed and persisted, collectively sharing the same locality and resisting national policy.[28]

And while Nedeljković here speaks to the persistence of collective resistance efforts, Okorie's short story represents the challenges of resistance in sites of incarceration. The denouement of the short story is a struggle over provisions: a battle over why, as Ngozi puts it, "staff not give everybody the same because everybody for equal" (194).

     After Ngozi's number is called and she collects her provisions for the week, she observes another person coming from the provision window with a jar of honey. It is at this moment that Ngozi attempts to stage an intervention into the Direct Provision system. She approaches the provision window, and while we don't hear the exchange, it is clear that Ngozi is asking about the inequitable distribution of provisions. In the next piece of dialogue we hear the "staff shout for Ngozi" saying "Who do you think you are?" (195). As the situation escalates to the manager, Ngozi's request is refused with two different and incompatible excuses as her anger is neither registered nor heard. Rather, the manager closes the windows (and the provision office) in order to stymie Ngozi's protest. This protest is about more than the acquisition of honey as Ngozi rails against the lies, the evasions, and the half-truths of an indifferent and seemingly impervious system of control.[29] In this respect, we can read her in terms of Ahmed's conceptualization of a willful subject, where "[w]illfulness could be thought of as political art, a practical craft that is acquired through involvement in political struggle, whether that struggle is a struggle to exist or to transform an existence" (*Willful Subjects* 133). However, once everybody realizes that the office is not going to reopen, the people voice their frustrations first to the manager: "You can't just lock up because of one person. We've been waiting here for long. What do you mean?" (196). When there is no response from the manager, they direct their frustrations about and to Ngozi:

> If there's no honey, why not take sugar?
> Is sugar and honey not the same thing?
> All these women that like to make trouble. (196)

Ngozi, therefore, protests alone, and the potential for collective resistance is not realized. The story poignantly signals the insidious domination of the Direct Provision system and its ability to maintain biopolitical control. Okorie suggests that the reader might applaud Ngozi's willfulness, but at the time she raises crucial questions about the efficacy of protest within the Direct Provision system. Okorie seems to point to both the futility and the necessity of Ngozi's lonely protest while underscoring that the wholesale dismantling of Direct Provision is the only way to secure meaningful change.

The final few lines of the story point to this contradiction: Beverlée emits an unspoken yet empathic desire to form a collective response to the injustices of the Direct Provision system. As the story concludes, the perspective shifts back to Beverlée's first-person point of view:

> I take my empty buggy and open the dining room door. I am quiet and sad as I go. Ngozi is my best friend for dis hostel but I have to leave her. From the window outside, me I can still see her stand alone for the dining room, fighting for her honey. (196)

These final lines stage a tension between Beverlée's inability to stand with Ngozi ("I have to leave her") and her empathy toward her. Although this moment of resistance is therefore seemingly foreclosed—and indeed women in general are indicted for their willfulness, their tendency to "make trouble"—Okorie harnesses this willfulness too in order to create a space for women that dominates the story prior to the incident with the honey. That the text accomplishes both of these feats—it represents a transnational collectivity and it registers the difficulties of staging a meaningful protest—speaks not only to the complexities of surviving within the Direct Provision system but also to Okorie's exceptional skills as a writer.

Conclusion: An Embodied Edifice of Contemporary Women's Writing

Our reading of Okorie's nuanced representation of individual protest within the Direct Provision system is not in any way to suggest that collective protest is futile. In 2014, the inhabitants of asylum residences nationwide engaged in collective resistance against the inhumane system of Direct Provision.[30] These willful collective protests in the face of an enforced precarious existence speak to the indefatigability of a character like Ngozi. As noted by Ahmed:

> Disturbance can be creative: not as what we aim for, not as what grounds our action, but as the effect of action: disturbance as what is created by the very effort of reaching, of reaching up, of reaching out, of reaching for something that is not present, something that appears only as a shimmer, a horizon of possibility.

When the arms refuse to support and carry, they reach. We do not know what the arms can reach. (*Willful Subjects* 204)

Ngozi's reaching for the honey, "for something that is not present," marks the creative disturbance of her "fight" and provides a glimpse toward a "horizon of possibility" in the face of extreme marginalization. This willfulness, in the midst of the extremities of precarity, pervades the work of Higgins and McDonagh. Consider, for example, Higgins's representations of classed subjects whose bodies press upon the borders of their enforced marginalization and her poetic speakers' persistent voicing of lives rendered invisible in post-boom Ireland or, in *Mainstream*, Mary-Anne's willful refusal of neoliberal exploitation of Traveller "lives," "bodies," and "identit[ies]" in the very face of systemic ableist, cultural, and ethnic prejudice (47). These voices underscore how precarity as a form of vulnerable existence is now fully enmeshed into the structures of late capitalist living and being. Moreover, they demonstrate ways of "reaching up" and "reaching out" amid the biopolitical control mechanisms effected on women's bodies in the post-Tiger landscape. The collation of scholarship on women's writing assembled in this book contributes to a form of "feminist criticism" that, as Gerardine Meaney declares, is part of a "broad coalition of social movements for social and cultural change" (xxi). This scholarship, as well, joins the vital archiving of women's writing that, as Patricia Coughlan notes, "attests to the aesthetic excellence of women's current writing and the importance of its collective contribution to the development of Irish literature" (195). We also hope that this book points to the renewed collective feminist organizing and protesting in the post-Tiger period—most notably with Movement of Asylum Seekers in Ireland (MASI), Waking the Feminists, and Repeal the Eighth—and that it functions in dialogue with these important social and cultural movements.

Notes

1 In a piece in *The Guardian* in 2015, Michael Taft queries the statistics of the Irish recovery, making the point that

> Irish headline growth rates are highly suspect given the impact of foreign multinationals. The Irish Fiscal Advisory Council recently estimated that half of Ireland's strong GDP growth in 2014 was a statistical fiction, while Ireland's Central Bank said a substantial proportion of growth was due to our low-tax financial services centre, which scarcely touches the domestic economy.

2 In a rousing piece, Fintan O'Toole argues that Irish artists must go on strike to protest the level of cuts that were put in place starting in 2008:

> Artists and cultural institutions have been under prolonged attack since the beginning of the crisis in 2008. Most national cultural institutions have taken cuts of around 40 per cent to their annual budgets, leaving some of them on the brink of collapse. Under the current Government, funding for arts, culture and film has fallen from €92.3 million in 2011 to €75.9 million in 2014.

3 Jordan further reports about the "current renaissance" which, according to Enright, has been "'brewing for years.'" Enright elaborates:

> The glorious old-fashioned thing that you can't get a job, you might as well write, has always applied in Ireland…It has something to do with the agility of the small presses and their ability to pick up talent and run with it. Things in the UK feel increasingly corporate – everybody there has amalgamated. (Jordan)

Jordan adds that

> [w]hile the wave of Irish novelists who rose to prominence in the early 90s - Enright, Roddy Doyle, Colm Tóibín, Sebastian Barry - tended to be published from London, the current dynamism of Ireland's publishing scene means that new authors are being picked up there first.

4 See Sara Ahmed's *Willful Subjects* for a comprehensive analysis of feminist willfulness.
5 As Margaret Kelleher notes, "a historical perspective shows how swiftly women's writing may disappear from view" (92), as well as providing a landscape of its populated presences. In "Engendering the Postmodern Canon: The Field Day Anthology of Irish Writing, Volumes IV &V: Women's Writing and Traditions," a reflective piece on her editing of the section "Women and Writing: 1700-1960," Gerardine Meaney remarks that "[m]ost of the groundwork for Volumes IV and V […] was laid prior to the 1990s. It was for precisely this reason that the 1991 version of the anthology could be challenged (19)." Thus, the presence of Irish women's writing—retrieved through vital feminist scholarship of the previous decades—made the gendered absences of the first three volumes of Field Day all the more apparent. However, as Meaney goes on to note, the reasons for the elision of women's writing are ultimately about value and worth:

> The re-evaluation of and recovery of women's work and history was not, however, regarded as part of the serious and central work of defining and redefining Ireland in the 1970s and 1980s. The contested nature of national and political identity in the period often produced self-enclosed binary oppositions, closed to the questioning of national identities, literary canons and historical priorities which an analysis the role of gender in their construction would have necessitated. (19)

6 In a paper given at a symposium in support of Waking the Feminists in February 2016 at Fordham University, Clair Wills raised crucial points about women's writing in Ireland, cycles of forgetting, and the Field Day project.
7 It must be stressed that Rich's "lesbian continuum" has been both lauded and critiqued. While in the 1980s and 1990s it was challenged for being either too all-encompassing or too narrow, more recently it has been revisited for its trans possibilities (see Cole and Cate).
8 This has resonances with Anne Mulhall and Alice Felman's article "Towing the Line: Migrant Women Writers and the Space of Irish Writing," which provides an important analysis of migrant women's writing in Ireland. Mulhall and Felman note: "we can think of the literary tradition and the literary, critical, and scholarly coteries that are 'in line' with it as another kind of material and imaginary space that extends some bodies while curtailing others" (212). Also of crucial relevance here is Moynagh Sullivan's salient point that women writers are ultimately elided from the canon because woman (as woman-as-Ireland) functions as an "object" that serves the "function of grounding Irishness" (250).
9 We are thinking here of Nuala Ní Dhomhnaill's now canonical essay about a (non)tradition of Irish women's poetry in "What Foremothers?" as well as Eavan Boland's interrogation of her marginality within dominant poetic traditions in *Object Lessons: The Life of the Woman and the Poet In Our Time*.
10 At the beginning of her writing career, Okorie won the *Metro Éireann Writing Award* for the short story "Gathering Thoughts," judged by Irish writer Roddy Doyle. From there, her work has been featured in the following collections: *Alms on the Highway: New Writing from the Oscar Wilde Centre Trinity College Dublin*, *Dublin: Ten Journeys, One Destination*, and *Trinity's Postgraduate Arts and Humanities Magazine*. See Sara Martín-Ruiz's overview for a fuller account of Okorie's growing body of work.

11 Sara Martín-Ruiz's important research agenda focuses on immigrant women writers, and we want to thank her for connecting us with Melatu Uche Okorie so that her short story might be featured in this special issue.

12 Direct Provision is the system that undergirds Ireland's deportation regime, and it is designed to hold people in perpetuity while their asylum applications are adjudicated. See Martín-Ruiz's account of the Direct Provision system in her preface to the interview with Melatu Uche Okorie in this special issue.

13 All short stories referenced in this section are featured in Gleeson's aforementioned collections.

14 The theoretical dimensions of precarity were the recent topic of a roundtable discussion among Lauren Berlant, Judith Butler, Bojana Cvejić, Isabell Lorey, Jasbir Puar, and Ana Vujanovic. Puar, the editor of the virtual roundtable, acknowledges our collective debt to Judith Butler's 2004 formative work on precarity, *Precarious Lives: The Power of Mourning and Violence*. Covering the unfolding of the term precarity over time and space, the panel debates the multiplicity of its meanings across various registers.

15 *Mainstream* was staged and produced by part of Project 50, Project Arts Centre, and Fishamble: The New Play Company in November 2016.

16 See Moynagh Sullivan for a perceptive and illuminating analysis of class and gender in Higgins's work (2011).

17 In April 2017, Rosaleen McDonagh was elected to Aosdána. She is the first member of the Travelling community to be inducted into this highly esteemed affiliation of creative artists. Travellers are "members of a historically nomadic minority community" and they have "existed on the margins of Irish society for perhaps centuries" (Burke 2). Crucially, after decades of activism, Travellers were finally formally recognized as an ethnicity category by the Irish State in March 2017. However, anthropologists have considered the community as an ethnic group for at least the past half-century. See, for example, Sharon Gmelch's groundbreaking *Nan: The Life of an Irish Travelling Woman* and the more recent *Irish Travellers: The Unsettled Life* by Sharon and George Gmelch. For a comprehensive, incisive literary and cultural account of representations of Travellers, see Mary Burke's *'Tinkers': Synge and the Cultural History of the Irish Traveller*. In addition, Robbie McVeigh's work provides insightful analysis on the politics and mechanisms of discrimination against Travellers in both Northern Ireland and the Republic. The organization Pavee Point (where McDonagh worked for many years), "a partnership of Travellers, Roma and members of the majority population working together to address the needs of Travellers and Roma as minority ethnic groups who experience exclusion, marginalisation and discrimination" (www.pavee point.ie), was integral to the Traveller community receiving ethnic category status.

18 Dan Griffin reports in the *Irish Times* that according to the 2015 Central Statistics Office's survey on income and living conditions, while the gap between the top and average incomes has narrowed, "more than one in 12 people in Ireland are still living in consistent poverty." See Kathleen Lynch, Sarah Cantillon, and Margaret Crean's chapter on "Inequality" in *Austerity and Recovery in Ireland Europe's Poster Child and the Great Recession* for a multi-disciplinary, social scientist view on who bore the brunt of the costs of austerity and the recession.

19 Kathy Davis describes intersectionality as "the interaction of gender, race and other categories of difference in individual lives, social practices, institutional arrangements, and cultural ideologies and the outcomes of these interactions in terms of power" (Davis, 2008, 68). Kimberlé Crenshaw first coined the term in 1989 in a discussion about black women's employment (1989), and race is a key focus of its theoretical articulation. Recent essays by Maria Carbin and Sara Edenheim (2013) and Gail Lewis (2013) establish important critiques and concerns about the elision of race in discussions of intersectionality in European feminist theory.

20 Higgins delegitimizes the status of the Tiger period through a deliberate refusal of capitalization, relegating the proper noun to its common form, evidenced in the lowercase "tiger."

21 Mary Burke's *Tinkers* includes a chapter on "Irish Writing after Traveller Politicization," where she conducts an interview with McDonagh before turning to an analysis of *The Baby Doll Project* as a "writing back" to centuries of Irish representations of the Traveller community.

22 See Kaite O'Reilly's 2013 interview with McDonagh.

23 A more expansive analysis of the play would have to account for Eoin's triple marginalizations: he is gay, he has a disability, and he is part of the Traveller community. McDonagh mobilizes Eoin's complex positionality to comment on the intersectional problematics of the same-sex

marriage referendum, which passed in 2015. Eoin bitingly characterizes the celebration for the referendum as a "great big settled party," adding, "[i]f they can recognize homophobia, why can't they recognize racism" (18).

24 Eleanor has an undiagnosable condition that forces her to negotiate between someone who has a disability and someone who does not. When Eoin presses her, Eleanor responds: "It's not important. Labels and conditions. I don't identify" (16). This is a phrase she repeats in a conversation with Jack, "I don't identify. What's so terrible about that?" (26). Finally, after her debate with Mary-Anne, Eleanor later admits:

> Mary-Anne and Eoin and to some extent Jack — they celebrate their lives, their bodies, and their identity. No big spectacle. Mary-Anne threw my life up in the air in a matter of minutes. Being betrayed by a younger woman. They gave me three different versions of events. Mary-Anne was right — two disabled women. This virus of abuse has to stop somewhere. (47)

25 There is a dearth of research on the institutionalization of children of the Traveller community throughout twentieth-century Ireland. Derralossary House remains operational as a "mainstream residential service" for Traveller children, while Trudder House's History has been effaced in the new economy: it now serves as a site for weddings. See http://tfcare.org/index.php/derralossary-house/ and http://www.trudder-lodge.com/.

26 Initially raised by local historian Catherine Corless's findings about 796 missing infants' and young children's bodies at the former Mother and Baby Home in Tuam, County Galway, the 2017 initial inquiry results raised more questions than answers, and the inquiry continues at the time of this writing.

27 In 2018, this short story was published by Skein Press as part of a collection of short stories entitled *This Hostel Life,* the collection was then published by Virago Press in 2019.

28 For purposes of clarification, Anne Mulhall, in her essay, cites a conference paper given by Nedeljkovic in June of 2014 at the American Conference for Irish Studies. The title of this paper was "Asylum Archive: the (im)possibility of cultural diversity in Ireland."

29 The honey also evokes biblical connotations of the "Promised Land" of "milk and honey," obviously significant in the context of asylum-seeking individuals and the nation-state. For a fascinating and important discussion of the "Promised Land," Exodus, and late nineteenth- and early twentieth-century Irish literature, see Abby Bender's 2015 *Israelites in Erin.*

30 See Ronit Lentin's 2016 article for a reading of these protests in the context of the Irish state and society's disavowal of the plight of people seeking asylum, a long-standing viewpoint of "manag[ing] not to know," just as "Irish state and society managed to ignore workhouses, mental health asylums, 'mother and baby homes,' Magdalene laundries and industrial schools" (21).

Works Cited

Ahmed, Sara. *Living a Feminist Life*. Durham: Duke UP, 2017. Kindle edition.

_____. *Willful Subjects*. Durham: Duke UP, 2014.

Bender, Abby. *Israelites in Erin: Exodus, Revolution, and the Irish Revival*. Syracuse: Syracuse UP, 2015.

Bhattacharyya, Gargi. *Crisis, Austerity, and Everyday Life: Living in a Time of Diminishing Expectations*. London: Palgrave Macmillan, 2015.

Boland, Eavan. *Object Lessons: The Life of the Woman and the Poet in Our Time*. New York: Norton, 1996.

Brah, Avtar, Ioana Szeman, and Irene Gedalof. "Introduction: Feminism and the Politics of Austerity." *Feminist Review* 109 (2015): 1–7.

Braidotti, Rosi. *Nomadic Subjects: Embodiment and Sexual Difference in Contemporary Feminist Theory*. New York: Columbia UP, 2011.

Burke, Mary. *'Tinkers': Synge and the Cultural History of the Irish Traveller*. Oxford: Oxford UP, 2009.

Butler, Judith. *Precarious Lives: The Power of Mourning and Violence*. London: Verso, 2004.

Caldwell, Lucy. "SOMAT." *The Long Gaze Back.* Ed. Sinéad Gleeson. Dublin: New Island Books, 2016. 150–156. Print.

Carbin, Maria, and Sara Edenheim. "The Intersectional Turn in Feminist Theory: A Dream of a Common Language?" *European Journal of Women's Studies* 20.3 (2013): 233–48.

Cole, C.L. and Shannon L.C. Cate. "Compulsory Gender and Transgender Existence: Adrienne Rich's Queer Possibility." *WSQ: Women's Studies Quarterly* 36.3&4 (2008): 279–87.

Coughlan, Patricia. "Irish Literature and Feminism in Postmodernity." *Hungarian Journal of English and American Studies* 10.1–2 (2004): 175–95.

Crenshaw, Kimberlé. "Demarginalizing the Intersection of Race and Sex: A Black Feminist Critique of Antidiscrimination Doctrine, Feminist Theory and Antiracist Politics." *University of Chicago Legal Forum* 140 (1989): 139–67.

Davis, Kathy. "Intersectionality as Buzzword: A Sociology of Science Perspective on What Makes a Feminist Theory Successful." *Feminist Theory* 9.1 (2008): 67–85.

"Derralossary House." *Traveller Families Care*, Web. 9 Mar. 2017. http://tfcare.org/index.php/derralossary-house/.

Gmelch, Sharon. *Nan: The Life of an Irish Travelling Woman.* Prospect Heights: Waveland Press, 1986.

_____. and George Gmelch. *Irish Travellers: The Unsettled Life.* Bloomington: Indiana UP, 2014.

Griffin, Dan. "Disposable Incomes Rise but 8.7% Remain in 'Consistent Poverty.'" *The Irish Times*, 1 Feb. 2017. n. pag. Web. 11 Mar. 2017. www.irishtimes.com/news/ireland/irishnews/disposable-incomes-rise-but-8-7-remain-in consistent-poverty-1.2959247.

Higgins, Rita Ann. *Ireland Is Changing Mother.* Northumberland: Bloodaxe Books Ltd., 2011.

Holohan, Carole. "In Plain Sight: Responding to the Ferns, Ryan, Murphy and Cloyne Reports." *Amnesty International Ireland*, Sep. 2011, 1–436. Web. 2 Feb. 2017. http://www.atlanticphilanthropies.org/app/uploads/2016/04/report_in_plain_sight.pdf.

Jordan, Justine. "A New Irish Literary Boom: The Post-crash Stars of Fiction." *The Guardian*, 16 Oct. 2015. n. pag. Web. 20 Nov. 2016. https://www.theguardian.com/books/2015/oct/17/new-irish-literary-boom-post-crash stars-fiction.

Kelleher, Margaret. "'The Field Day Anthology' and Irish Women's Literary Studies." *The Irish Review* 30 (2003): 82–94.

Kennedy, Sinéad. "A Perfect Storm: Crisis, Capitalism and Democracy." *Ireland under Austerity: Neoliberal Crisis, Neoliberal Solutions.* Eds. Colin Coulter and Angela Nagle. Manchester: Manchester UP, 2015. 86–109. Print.

Lentin, Ronit. "Asylum Seekers, Ireland, and the Return of the Repressed." *Irish Studies Review* 24.1 (2016): 21–34. Print.

Lewis, Gail. "Unsafe Travel: Experiencing Intersectionality and Feminist Displacements." *Signs* 38.4 (2013): 869–92.

Lynch, Kathleen, Sarah Cantillon, and Margaret Crean. "Inequality." *Austerity and Recovery in Ireland Europe's Poster Child and the Great Recession.* ***Eds. William K. Roche, Philip J. O'Connell, and Andrea Prothero. Oxford: Oxford UP, 2017. 252–271. Print.

McDonagh, Rosaleen. *Mainstream.* London: Bloomsbury Methuen Drama, 2016. Kindle edition.

McVeigh, Robbie. "The 'Final Solution': Reformism, Ethnicity Denial and the Politics of Anti-Travellerism in Ireland." *Social Policy and Society* 7.1 (2008): 91–102.

Meaney, Gerardine. "Engendering the Postmodern Canon: The Field Day Anthology of Irish Writing, Volumes IV &V: Women's Writing and Traditions." *Opening the Field: Irish Women, Texts and Contexts.* Eds. Patricia Boyle Haberstroh and Christine St. Peter. Cork: Cork UP, 2007.

_____. *Gender, Ireland, and Cultural Change: Race, Sex, and Nation.* New York: Routledge, 2010.

Mulhall, Anne. "Dead Time: Queer Temporalities and the Deportation Regime." *Social Text Online*, 10 July 2014. n. pag. Web. 1 Mar. 2017. https://socialtextjournal.org/periscope_article/dead-time-queer-temporalities-and-the-deportation-regime/.

_____. "Structural Adjustments: Literature of Protest and the Politics of Criticism in Neo-liberal Ireland." IASIL 2016 Conference, the International Association for the Study of Irish Literature, 28 July 2016, University College Cork, Cork, Ireland. Plenary Session.

_____. and Gavan Titley. "'Direct Provision' Is a Holding Pen Where People Are Kept for Efficient Deportation." *TheJournal.ie*, 15 Oct. 2014. n. pag. Web. 28 Feb. 2017. http://www.thejournal.ie/ readme/direct-provision-centres-ireland-1725662-Oct2014/.

_____. and Alice Felman. "Towing the Line: Migrant Women Writers and the Space of Irish Writing." *Éire-Ireland* 47.1&2 (Spring/Summer 2012): 201–20.

Nedeljković, Vukašin. "Asylum Archive: The (Im)possibility of Cultural Diversity in Ireland." Conference paper. "Critical Ecologies." ACIS (American Conference of Irish Studies). University College Dublin. 12 June 2014.

_____. "Asylum Archive." http://www.asylumarchive.com/.

_____. *Asylum Archive*. Dublin, Create National Development Agency for Collaborative Arts and Arts Council of Ireland, 2018.

Negra, Diane. "Adjusting Men and Abiding Mammies: Gendering the Recession in Ireland." *The Irish Review* 46 (2013): 23–34.

_____. and Yvonne Tasker, "Introduction: Gender and Recessionary Culture." *Gendering the Recession: Media and Culture in an Age of Austerity*. Durham; London: Duke UP, 2014. 1–30.

Ní Dhomhnaill, Nuala. "What Foremothers?" *The Poetry Ireland Review* 36 (Autumn 1992): 18–31.

O'Reilly, Kaite. "20 Questions…. Rosaleen McDonagh." *Kaite O'Reilly*, 17 Sep. 2013. Web. 2 Feb. 2017. https://kaiteoreilly.wordpress.com/2013/09/17/20-questions-rosaleen mcdonagh/.

O'Toole, Fintan. "Culture Shock: Why it's Time for Irish Artists to Go on Strike." *The Irish Times*, 3 Jan. 2015. n. pag. Web. 26 Nov. 2016. http://www.irishtimes.com/culture/culture- shock-why-it-s-time-for-irish-artists-to-go-on-strike-1.2053120.

Pavee Point. Pavee Point Traveller and Roma Centre. Web. 14 Mar. 2017. http://www.paveepoint.ie/.

Puar, Jasbir, ed. "Precarity Talk: A Virtual Roundtable with Lauren Berlant, Judith Butler, Bojana Cvejić, Isabell Lorey, Jasbir Puar, and Ana Vujanović." *The Drama Review* 56.4 (2012): 163–77.

Rich, Adrienne. "Compulsory Heterosexuality and Lesbian Existence." *Journal of Women's History*, 15.3 (2003): 11–48.

Sullivan, Moynagh. "Feminism, Postmodernism and the Subjects of Irish and Women's Studies." *New Voices in Irish Criticism*. Ed. P.J. Mathews. Dublin: Four Courts Press. 243–51.

_____. Moynagh. "Looking at Being Somebody: Class and Gender in the Poetry of Rita Ann Higgins." *Irish University Review* 41.2 (2011): 112–33.

Taft, Michael. "Ireland Is No Model for GREECE." *The Guardian*, 10 Jul. 2015. n. pag. Web. 1 Dec. 2016. https://www.theguardian.com/world/economicsblog/2015/jul/10/ireland-no model-greece-troika-austerity.

Trudder Lodge. *Trudder Lodge*, 2014. Web. 13 Mar. 2017. http://www.trudder-lodge.com/.

Claire Kilroy: An Overview and an Interview (with a 2020 Addendum)

Mary Burke

An Overview

In many ways, the interview that follows this preface is a post-Celtic Tiger follow-up to one published in the *Irish Literary Supplement* that I conducted with Claire Kilroy in 2006 at the very zenith of that boom, and in which the novelist expressed unease at the direction taken by Irish society (Burke, 2007). Kilroy's work is attentive to the nature of identity in a globalized Ireland in which rootlessness is necessitated by the job market. In her novels, Kilroy troubles middle-class normative values by foregrounding alienated protagonists who live without steady income, accommodation, or relationships. In addition, identities are likely to be false, doubled, or unstable, characters are amoral, nationless, and historyless or in possession of entirely fabricated accents, histories, or nationalities. Stylistically, this suggests a postmodern refusal both of literary conventions and of the notion of coherent, stable identity, but thematically it may be read as a comment on the fragmented nature of life in the postnationalist Ireland of Kilroy's adult life. Although the former is in many ways the aspect of Kilroy's *oeuvre* that makes her one of the most distinctive literary voices of her generation, the latter constitutes the concern of this overview, a response to the overall themes of this *LIT* Special Issue. This leitmotif also emerges in the initial portion of the appended interview, but it should be noted that although Kilroy had seen an early draft of the overview in preparation for our conversation, my survey does not necessarily follow the interview's foci, especially towards the conversation's close, when the author frankly discusses how motherhood has impacted her creativity. This is perhaps in part because, as Kilroy noted, she had just submitted her first non-fiction piece, "F for Phone," prior to the interview, whose searing topic was the physical, emotional, mental, and neurological fallout of childbirth and motherhood (2015).[1] Moreover, by the end of the conversation Kilroy and I had quite spontaneously agreed to include the metanarrative about the obstacles to conducting the interview due to the constraints imposed by childcare needs (further explication below). Thus, in order to preserve a sense both of the interview's ultimately freeform nature and the fractured manner in which it had to be planned and effected, I have resisted the urge to edit the overview so that it is in greater lock-step with that conversation or *vice versa*. In many ways, the overview speaks to the public face of the working mother, striving to conform to the norms of her profession. The ruptures (of various sorts) of the interview, by contrast, are a more honest representation of the behind-the-scenes compromises, interruptions, distractions, and restarts that presenting that façade entails. Like the overview then, the interview ultimately reflects this issue's concerns regarding the invisible or unappreciated negotiations often required of women and mothers in our contemporary globalized world.

In Claire Kilroy's second novel *Tenderwire* (2006), written when the flush Irish ignored just how it was that the economy was being flooded with too-easy credit, an unearthed photograph of a crooked Irish *Taoiseach* [Prime Minister] implicates Eva's wealthy father in various kinds of corruption. Six years later, *The Devil I Know* (2012) examines the manner in which unscrupulous political and construction interests colluded in the overheating of the Irish economy by 2008. Kilroy noted in our 2006 conversation that the bleakness of growing up in recessionary 1980s Ireland "had an enormous impact on me because, being young, I had no conception of it being temporary" (Burke, 23). Her third novel, *All Names Have Been Changed* (2010), was set in 1980s Dublin during that recession and its accompanying heroin plague. The choice of theme was provocative, since she started writing it during a boom in which the Irish were invited to celebrate the newly globalized capital, to participate in an "easy, globally-digestible" "Irishness" business (Ging, "Screening the Green" 186), and altogether to forget *that kind* of Dublin, even as deaths from overdose, which had been well documented in the 1980s, continued in inner-city working-class enclaves. Such lives and deaths no longer garnered much attention in the later period since they did not gel with the mainstream media narrative of cosmopolitan Dublin, whose supposed addiction culture of Champagne and cocaine was depicted with sneaking admiration as one that spoke to the Irish capital's worldly and expensive tastes.[2] *All Names Have Been Changed*, with its perverse return to the pre-boom capital, was written at the height of the consumerist frenzy that all were assumed to wish to celebrate and document. The setting suggests an inevitable trajectory that the boom-time mania of the novel's period of creation will end in a return to the earlier recession it depicts. Moreover, the setting is likewise a refusal to engage with the self-congratulatory celebrations of Irish achievement and purchasing power that were commonplace in present-tense novels of Dublin created during the Celtic Tiger; it is significant that *All Names Have Been Changed* was the first of Kilroy's novel since her 2003 debut, *All Summer*, that did not boast a present-tense or near present-tense setting. As a sequence, the novels eerily predict the repetitions of bust-and-boom free market capitalism in the

Ireland of the author's lifetime, and the photograph referred to in boom-era *Tenderwire* hints at the endemic corruption that becomes the main theme of her most recent, post-crash novel, *The Devil I Know*.

I should stress that this is not to suggest that one can reduce Kilroy's playful and self-reflexive novels to little more than a mirror up to Celtic Tiger Ireland and the recessions the book-end it, since they are profoundly argumentative works of the imagination that simultaneously incorporate and transcend mundane questions of social documentary. Nevertheless, the manner in which Kilroy's undeniably postmodern and experimental works also function as a record of a very particular period in recent Irish social history merits as much attention as her stylistic achievements. It may not be an overstatement to suggest that when future instructors on Irish literature courses seek out a representative *oeuvre* of the Celtic Tiger period, they will turn to the work of Claire Kilroy.

"Any impression of autonomy was an illusion," muses the troubled Eva in *Tenderwire* (238). Diane Negra and Yvonne Tasker note that the "market mind-set" of the boom "coincided with an intensification of polarized gender norming" that led to a "postfeminist" emphasis on women's consumption and their "choice" to retreat from public roles (1).[3] And yet, throughout the period, and though the very category of "Celtic Tiger fiction" was disputed,[4] the boom was coolly appraised by Kilroy and other Irish women writers such as Marina Carr, Emma Donoghue and Anne Enright, even as the era's defining image was of the frivolous woman laden down with Brown Thomas bags.[5] In particular, Kilroy's work increasingly shares the "cynicism" regarding Dublin's unthinkingly celebrated "materialistic cosmopolitanism" of Donoghue's *Landing* (Casey 67). It's worth noting that the Celtic Tiger era's fetishization of female excess deflected attention from the macho politicians, builders, and developers hustling the economy away; a disordered male capacity for dangerous risk taking[6] was irresponsibly parlayed into the national economic strategy. *The Devil I Know* is attentive to the role that gender played in the boom's madness, appearing to skewer what Cormac O'Brien has identified as the Celtic Tiger "Corporate Warrior," a "culturally imagined paradigm of aspirational Irish manhood" (133). Moreover, the flatly characterized Edel, whom we see only through the clouded prism of protagonist Tristram's desire, seems to be the idle trophy wife of retrograde Celtic Tiger fantasy. In both *Tenderwire* and Kilroy's debut novel of three years earlier, *All Summer*, a disoriented woman obsesses over a beautiful but possibly inauthentic object. With the benefit of hindsight, it seems significant that Kilroy's first two novels were produced at the zenith of a boom during which certain deliberately hard-to-find designer shoes and handbags became outright fetish objects. Of course, as with the $600,000 violin of hair-raisingly obscure provenance that Eva in *Tenderwire* goes to enormous risk to acquire, for those who couldn't afford designer bags or rarefied objects and sought to acquire one through a back channel, desire was accompanied by the anxiety of inauthenticity. Kilroy's novels critique the manner in which women were sold the fantasy that the right acquisition (be it a Birkin bag, a valuable painting, or a purported Stradivarius) would ensure happiness. Moreover, as a novelist who has dedicated most of her working life to writing the kind of literary fiction that enjoys critical acclaim but does not necessarily provide huge remuneration, Kilroy's work can also been seen to critique the manner in which aesthetic works are obliged to become commodities with fluctuating price tags.

It is no coincidence that the phenomenon of the "chick lit" novel, with its celebration of consumerism and free-market "girl power" feminism, took off in Ireland with the boom. (It is too tempting *not* to note that one of Irish popular fiction's biggest successes in the period was Cecelia Ahern, daughter of Bertie Ahern, an Irish *Taoiseach* popularly blamed for the economic collapse!) One might fall into the trap of denigrating a genre associated with women writers and readers by stating the Irish iteration of "chick lit" fetishized individuality at the expense of the common good and impoverished creative writing in Ireland. Although the manner in which women's fiction appears to be considered less "serious" and less worthy of major awards has finally begun to receive sustained attention,[7] nevertheless, it is unarguable that Ireland had been a culture in which, prior to the boom, the mainstream media had generally lauded writers for their artistic achievements rather than their huge sales or advances. Likewise, during the Celtic Tiger, Louis LeBrocquy paintings of Yeats and Joyce were used in government-sponsored adverts enticing multinationals to Ireland in the international financial press. Of course, the majority of creative artists live on next-to-nothing, a situation that goes from bad to worse during a recession,[8] and Kilroy noted in our 2006 interview that a middle-class writer of serious bent must abandon the values of her class: "You have to forget about stability, and home building, and security, and approval, and remaining within the fold, because those safety nets are no longer an option. Nobody was impressed when I announced that I was leaving my job to do this instead" (23). Although he has left a trail of financial destruction in his wake, Tristram seems to think of himself as a victim by the close of The Devil I Know; during the recession, a narrative emerged of Irish masculinity in crisis due to high male unemployment rates caused by the crash of the overheated Irish construction industry.[9] However, post-boom government austerity cuts to welfare and the budgets actually impacted women more, since women are more likely to be living in poverty, to be raising children alone, or, in the case of working mothers, are more likely to be employed in a public sector that endured deep pay cuts across the board (Duvvury and Finn 63–64).[10] Equality (like funding for the arts), was presented as a luxury that cannot be afforded in times of austerity, when the needs of men are prioritized (Negra and Tasker 2).

"It's only - what? - 20 years since the death of communism and socialism was announced, and now the age of the self-regulating free market turns out to have only lasted 20 years. Right now, I think that's The Great Subject," observed theatre director Richard Eyre in 2009 (qtd. in Harris 21). *The Devil I Know* tackles The Great Subject in the specifically Irish context and by deploying the specifically Irish "Big House" genre,[11] a tradition in which Irish women writers have excelled, from Maria Edgeworth's foundational work to the novels of Molly Keane and Jennifer Johnston in our time.[12] The "Big House" was a useful literary trope for probing the political and social apprehensions of earlier periods, and in Kilroy's hands, it continues to be useful in examining particularly twenty-first century anxieties. Gearóid Cronin notes that although it has "undergone a total demise in Irish history," the Big House "has not experienced a parallel demise in Irish literature; rather, it seems to have been given a new lease of life" (Cronin 215). *The Devil I Know* plays an important role in the ongoing development of this primarily female genre, since it may be the only novel that deploys a "Big House" backdrop in order to examine the recent crash. Indeed, it arguably conveys a realistic picture of the Gothic excesses of Celtic Tiger Ireland *precisely because* it is not written in a realistic mode. The glamorization of hard drinking—the most excessive of the period's excesses—is dissected in that novel and also in *All Names Have Been Changed*, in which the drunkenness of the renowned writer Glynn is treated as a literary event by his students. Sinéad Molony suggests that the endemic heroin crisis in inner-city Dublin, also charted in *All Names Have Been Changed*, and the more socially acceptable addiction epidemic of alcoholism in Ireland are rooted in a "neoliberal regime that fetishizes consumption, choice, and agency..." (183). It is striking that rates of alcohol consumption went through the roof during the boom, particularly for women, which suggests that marketing plays a role too. Tristram's alcoholism in *The Devil I Know*, Eva's dependences in *Tenderwire*, and the heroin epidemic charted in *All Names Have Been Changed* all depict the role gender norms and the imperative to consume play in addiction in contemporary Ireland.

Of course, Kilroy's interest in the boom-and-bust cycle of Irish economic life (and Irish livers) probes the deeper, underlying implications of the enormous social, cultural, and spiritual changes of recent decades. After the late 1950s, Ireland slowly transformed from a predominantly agricultural and religious society to a place subject to the forces of global economics and secularism. Even by the period of Kilroy's birth in the early 1970s, Ireland remained a hair-raising place for women in many ways: in 1970, Irish women required a husband's signature in order to open a bank account, were not actively called to jury service, and earned 54.9 percent of men's wages. For those more familiar with Anglo-American feminism, the unconsciously Catholic inflections of feminist concerns in the Ireland of the period can be jolting. For instance, there was no mention of lesbian rights or any insistence on the legalization of abortion or divorce in *Chains or Change*, the foundational 1971 manifesto of the Irish Women's Liberation Movement (IWLM), Ireland's first radical feminist group. *Chains or Change* foregrounded basic demands such as the removal of the marriage bar (the rule that obliged Irish women to resign government posts upon marriage), equal rights in law, equal pay, and the legalization of various forms of contraception. Indeed, the manifesto called for the "rehabilitat[ion] of the unmarried mother"! (Stopper 3; 28; 69–78). Despite massive change in terms of most of these issues, in certain ways free market capitalism and consumerism have now co-opted the language of feminism for their own ends. Moreover, there is enough memory left of this very recent past for *The Devil I Know* to be able to invoke the trope of selling one's soul to the devil to indict Irish collusion in the country's manipulation by the global finance system. In throwing away religiosity in Ireland, the Irish arguably invited an equally damaging mindless acceptance of the market into the vacuum. Tristram's belief that the devil still operates in the world is emblematic of the things that the market cannot account for, and suggests Kilroy's interest in the deeper conundrum that although Ireland has at last outgrown religion, it also became disillusioned with consumerism during the crash. Ultimately, Kilroy's most recent novel with its cast of morally vacant and substance-abusing protagonists implies that there is currently a troubling spiritual vacuum at the center of Irish life that no shopping spree at Brown Thomas can assuage.

An Interview: Dublin, September 4, 2015

Note on the conducting of the interview: In the vast majority of author interviews, one gets no sense of the arrangements and planning needed to get the interviewee or interviewer in a particular place at a particular time. In Kilroy's case, this was an intensely difficult appointment to arrange as she is the mother of a toddler and currently tries to fit her writing into the hours that her son is in preschool, so that everything else she needs to do must occur either in his company or at home while he naps. Kilroy is an author profoundly interested in the manner in which gender norms shape contemporary Ireland, so to that end (and in light of this journal issue's overall theme and the contents of the interview below), we agreed by the interview's close that I would include the behind-the-scenes nuts and bolts of both arranging and conducting the exchange in a manner that does not hide how motherhood impacts a woman's professional life. (These moments are in italics.) I am the mother of a school-aged child, and when I interviewed Kilroy in Dublin, I was staying with family members. In the hope of keeping Kilroy's son occupied while I interviewed her, I arranged for my nephew to come around to play with Claire's son as they were of similar age, and hoped that my somewhat older daughter would be distracted from the fact I was absent from the playroom by the presence of the two younger children. (I hasten to add that there were four other adults present: my husband, my sister-in-law, and my parents-in-law!) Arranging for my nephew to be in the house at a particular time in turn necessitated a great deal of arranging with my sister-in-law, who had to draw up a schedule of my nephew's varied day-care hours and nap schedule during the week in which I was in Ireland and could meet Claire, and run that list alongside a similar document from Claire regarding her son's Montessori hours and nap schedule so that we could find a time when he would not be napping that also suited both mothers and the other toddler. This sounds comically complicated—and it is—but it is also a somber reality with which primary care parents (generally mothers) can identify. In the interests of much-needed transparency regarding this issue, therefore, I'd like to draw attention to the labor of the many who facilitated the interview: my parents-in law, Mary and Noel, for taking care of the children as they played; my husband, Maurice, for entertaining them and bringing in the tea and scones Mary had made; my sister-in-law, Maria, for going to the trouble of ensuring that her son would be available to distract Claire's son. It really does take a village to care for a child, but on most days in our society, that task is left to one villager alone. Most of all, I thank Claire herself, of course, for her graciousness and generosity in allowing me to interview her yet again, and for her profoundly courageous frankness in what follows.

MB: **Taken as a whole, your novels delineate the bust-and-boom cycles of the Ireland of your lifetime. Did you foresee that unfolding because, as a writer, you didn't fully participate in the boom, or is it a vision that has gradually revealed itself to you?**

CK: Very few people saw the whole picture because it was such a powerful ideology.

I've compared Ireland during the boom to *Invasion of the Body Snatchers*, in which everyone around you is on message. Being unsalaried, I wasn't on message anymore, but I felt that maybe they were right. It was creepy, shocking, and weird. My peer group got hoovered up into great jobs and all the trappings that went with that, while I decided to be a writer. It was quite stark to see my path diverge so radically from everyone else's path. And then I remember realizing that my friends felt sorry for me. I'd say "no" to group dinners because, as a writer, I had no money. To feel myself being pitied: that's when I started feeling deeply alienated. *All Summer* was not influenced by the

Celtic Tiger that I can think of, but *Tenderwire* is, because by the time I finished *All Summer* in 2001, my rent doubled and I was given two weeks' notice to quit when I couldn't afford Celtic Tiger-level rent, and I had to move back in with my parents, so I wanted to write about the feeling of losing a home. That's what *Tenderwire* is about: Eva tries to come home and realizes that it's gone. It's *Tír na nÓg* [the Land of Eternal Youth of Celtic tradition]: you come back years later and it's not home anymore. The original opening of *Tenderwire* was about losing your home, but I dumped it. It got set in New York instead of Ireland, but that feeling of losing a home is what started me. I had no home anymore because the cost of living was squeezing out the likes of artists and writers and the streets started looking different and that *really* influenced *All Names Have Been Changed*, which came next. That was an archaeological novel: "This is what you destroyed." Dublin became like a British high street, full of all these weird—well, weird to me—trendy bars and places that I had no interest in but that suddenly predominated.

MB: That 1980s recessionary kind of Dublin is what got taken away?

CK: Yes, we were ashamed of it, ashamed of ourselves. Irish women started to have orange [fake-tanned] skin and yellow hair. We were trying to not look Irish! It was all such a revolt against what we had been!

MB: Dublin was one of the most expensive cities in the world in which to live during the boom, so did it become easier to survive economically and artistically in the recent recession?

CK: I moved house five times between 2011 and 2015—that is, after the crash—because the apartments we rented were subsequently repossessed by banks and sold by liquidators. It was life imitating art: I'd just published a book about reckless borrowing and reckless building! That said, there really has been a huge U-turn, a sort of dignity restored to artists. During the mania, say 2006-2007, in particular, you had to be earning a lot of money and had to be part of this group think. And if you were a writer, unless you were successful in a commercial genre, you were at odds with this. Unless you were coining it, you weren't invited to the party at which we apparently "all partied."[13] However, the wheels had come off by the Farmleigh Conference:[14] I remember turning on the radio to hear Neil Jordan say that the banks have failed us, the Church has failed us, the state has failed us, but the arts have never failed us. "Imagine Ireland" [a state-funded arts program] was conceived of at that point, and I was sent to America to do readings; the writer's stock was suddenly up. We were no longer to be pitied for being broke. There weren't many significant literary debuts during the boom, other than Kevin Barry, but since the collapse, there has been enormous activity and the big prizes and advances have returned to Irish literary fiction. It's happening because in recent years it was acceptable to not be in "gainful" employment, so people had permission to write again. I have a nine-to-five writing ethic, but there is also a lot of aimlessness.

MB: So, you have a driven aimlessness?

CK: (*Laughing*) Yes I have. You need that aimless period. And people have had time to do that again in recent years. They didn't get hoovered up into some well-paid industry.

MB: So, you are very explicitly tying the trajectories of creativity and economics?

CK: Yes. All the people saddled with Celtic Tiger-era enormous mortgages have been taken out of creative circulation because they can't afford to write. I know people who made a choice to opt out, but those who opted in cannot reverse that decision because they are in such negative equity.

MB: So, there's a lost generation, absent voices?

CK: Yes, a sterilized generation. It's noticeable that there aren't many major Irish literary writers born in the 1970s.

MB: And *The Devil I Know* was born out of the worst moment of the crash?

CK: Yes, we were well on our knees. Suicide was everywhere and it was a very frightening time. I really wanted to write about the fear in *The Devil I Know* because no other country had yet experienced it as we had; it's not really understood outside of Ireland. The identity of Mr. Deauville fell into place in 2010 during the big snow [of November 26-27, 2010] when…

Ten minutes into the interview: "Mommy, mommy," comes the strident voice of my daughter from the other side of the closed door. "Mommy, I NEED you!" She marches in with a box of raisins for me to open. I ask her to share with Claire's son and her cousin, and to ask her father when she needs help with anything for the next hour or so. "Mommy is working," I tell her. She looks at me doubtfully.

CK: …that snowstorm was the buildup to the bailout [on November 28, 2010]. The government was denying that IMF, EU and ECB—the Troika—was coming, that we were about to lose our sovereignty, while the foreign press was saying that it was about to take over.

There were all these horror stories circulating about what was going to happen. It was rumored that when the IMF went into Lithuania it closed down hospitals. This panic and fear led to people taking money out of ATMs, and some poor old bachelor farmer was found with €70,000 strapped to his body when hospitalized; nobody trusted the banks. I heard of people who bought tinned peaches in case food ran out. And then the snowstorm came—and Ireland doesn't suffer from snowstorms—and the government persisted in saying, nobody is coming to take over our finances, but on the ground I could hear people asking, Will there be petrol? Will the schools stay open? Will they shut the hospitals? Will the weakest start to die? I remember feeling this shivery thrill that we were being invaded. Christ, they're coming! It's a siege! Before that, the IMF was for developing countries, to my mind. The foreign press was claiming that the IMF officials are boarding the planes, while the Irish government kept denying it. I remember looking up at the sky, stupidly, waiting for the planes to come into view! Strangely enough, I ended up doing a reading at Villanova with Paul Murray and Kevin Barry just two days after the bailout, and we wondered...

17 minutes into the interview: Claire's phone rings at this point. I tell her to take it, but she demurs and jokes, "it's probably just my husband, asking, 'What do I feed the child?', even though I have the child!"

CK: ... and we wondered, are they going to close the airport? Can we get back into our country?

MB: **It's striking that you have just used the word "invasion" to describe both the crash and the boom!**

CK: Yes, they were equally alienating. In the case of the crash, it *felt* like punishment. We had messed with the Powers, with the free market. And all the talk at the time of selling government bonds and worrying if "the market" would like it, and what would "the market" do, and I began to wonder, *who* is "the market"? Is it a kind of Wizard of Oz figure? And that's where Mr. Deauville [in *The Devil I Know*] comes from. He is "the market," the sinister anonymous power that controls our lives. We yielded to temptation. We were punished.

MB: **You also keep using the vocabulary of religion to talk and write about the crash...**

CK: ...yes, I was schooled in that language, and even if I don't believe it—and I don't—it is a pertinent vocabulary. The punishment that came was so dark. A kid I went to school with killed himself. He bought in

Priory Hall, so he had huge negative equity but no home for his family.[15] This narrative that "we all partied." No, we didn't. We were having bullets shot at our feet, so we *had to* party. The pressure to get on the property ladder was immense. I remember bringing Cava to a party, and the hostess sneered because it wasn't Champagne. It was a systematic forgetting of who we were and a forgetting that there was a time when the Irish could not afford champagne. A *very long time!* (*laughs*). And I get it: we were so starved of the sweet shop that as soon as we were let in, we went bananas. That said, there's a point at which, once you've gorged, you should walk away from the trough. And that didn't happen. The mythmakers had already taken over, saying, "We have balls, we deserve this."[16]

MB: **That language is a reminder that the Celtic Tiger was a retrograde step because it was generally men making the big money, and their success seemed to reinforce gender binaries. I'm thinking of the *Devil I Know* characters of Edel the trophy wife or Svetlana, a barmaid whose male boss feels entitled to offer her body to moneyed male associates.**

CK: Edel was this fantasy being perpetuated by the Sunday newspaper social diaries. These fat old developers with young blonde wives with giant handbags, orange skin, and the shoes with the red soles [Louboutins]: all the signifiers. Edel was *that*. And all these beautiful Eastern European girls showed up in Ireland in the boom and those types of men…(*pauses*)…Things were being monetized that shouldn't be monetized. Svetlana's situation was observed, rather than being invented. A lot of things in that book were observed. I wanted to answer back. We've been so voiceless for so long, that once it was exposed…

MB: **…who exactly was "voiceless"?**

CK: I felt voiceless. I felt disenfranchised because I didn't have a Celtic Tiger salary, and I lost my home, and I was of no value to [Irish] society. I lost my city: it was cardboarded over with a different city.

MB: **But you've said that you feel that you've regained Dublin again in recent years; does Dublin need a degree of penury *to be* Dublin?**

CK: (*Laughs*) Well, Dublin needs a degree of reality, of humor, to be Dublin. Humor was absent during the boom. We were all trying to keep up with each other and to show how well we were doing, and when it all went tits up, it became *okay* to…

29 minutes into the interview: We are interrupted by a call from a Dublin friend who wants to arrange a playdate between my daughter and her son on one of the small handful of days left in our trip to Ireland. She is a single working mother and we have been trying to connect in order to carve out time in her complicated schedule, so I feel obliged to speak with her briefly.

MB: *Finnegans Wake* **is overtly present in** *The Devil I Know,* **but Stoker's** *Dracula* **and Wilde's** *The Picture of Dorian Gray* **are also subtly present. What is it about the contemporary moment in Ireland that means that the Gothic mode is suddenly useful again? In particular, can we turn to your use of the often allied "Big House" genre? What factored into that choice? Does Tristram's castle stand in for the Irish state?**

CK: I used the Big House trope to show how much we'd lost. Tristram loses his castle and his family name: he is the last in a line of earls. Hickey [the builder] was the narrator originally, but it occurred to me that Hickey was too stupid to feel remorse and he had nothing to lose. He had no Big House, no heritage. We gambled away our sovereignty, our inheritance. I invoked Joyce in *The Devil I Know* for the same reason. He is the Ireland I clung to during the boom. He is of totemic importance to me in terms of where I came from. For me, Ireland is great writers, not great property developers or great shoppers. Joyce is my tribe, the striker on my football team (*laughs*), and my heritage. The close of the book is set in 2016, and here we are in [September] 2015 and it feels like we are beginning to run our country again, but when I wrote that book [in 2011], it did not feel like we were. That said, so many of my generation are still in negative equity. My husband is—on a house he bought then—and now we both shoulder that debt. The whole thing feels like a swindle. And it was. I remember the feeling of writing that Hickey line, "what fucker has my money?" Where is the money? (*Laughs*) Somebody has the money! (*Laughs*) I don't have the forensic accounting skills to figure it out, but *somebody* has the money!

MB: **I want to return to your comment that only commercially successful writers got invited to the glitzy parties of the boom. Was part of that selling off of heritage a selling off of the literary heritage that Joyce epitomizes for you?**

CK: The literary scene did change. Crime fiction and commercial women's fiction did really well. I think Banville's turn to crime fiction was a financial decision. Literary fiction regularly got dressed down for not explicitly addressing the Celtic Tiger, and more than anyone, I wanted to say something about this, but the boom was a disorientating flux and I didn't know *what it was*. The novel form is so long-term that I couldn't figure out how to address it, couldn't see a narrative arc, so I ended up writing about the 1980s. Our big literary novelists almost all wrote historical fiction in response.

MB: **I can see the theme of recent Irish economic history in some of your novels in terms of the characters' acquisitiveness and the fact that they cover the exact 25-year period of the recent boom-and-bust cycles.**

CK: How strange the change from minor to major to minor again. I'm not old, but I've seen this twice. As a kid, I was really affected by the 1980s depression in Ireland because dad was an architect. We had our visas for Australia. We were going to emigrate. I didn't want to. I *really love* living in Ireland, and that love informs my work. I was raised for export, taught German in school for the express purpose of living there. I worked in BMW in Munich after my Leaving [high school final exams], and after that I went to New York. And then something weird happened by the time I finished college [in the mid-1990s]: I got a job in Ireland, because the Irish film industry started to take off and I worked on *Ballykissangel* [a BBC TV show depicting an idealized rural Ireland]. It had never been on the cards, so it felt like a "Get Out of Jail" that I didn't have to emigrate. I'm a real home bird. I really like this place, and that fed the anguish I felt seeing it being dismantled in front of me during the boom and being replaced by somewhere fake. A fake bling Ireland. *Ballykissangel* was a fake rural Ireland, but what we constructed was a fake metropolitan Ireland.

MB: **For you, then, the authentic Dublin is the more insular Dublin of Joyce and Beckett?**

CK: For me, "real" Dublin had fun and collegiality. The newer Dublin had too much boasting, shaping up, dissembling, and shouting. It was all very anti-art. The Celtic Tiger was intrinsically anti-art because it tried to monetize everything. And these people weren't going to read anyway, because they didn't have time. It wasn't that kind of society anymore. Regarding the acquisitiveness of the characters in my first three novels: they are going after a painting, a violin and a writer. They are in search of authenticity, of the transformative power of art. As was I, I suppose. Art is the magical tingly property that makes everything alluring.

MB: What struck me, looking in from the US—I'd left Ireland mid-boom —was the rise of chick lit during the Celtic Tiger. We'd never really had that genre in Ireland.

CK: I don't know much about chick lit, but I'll say this much. There were successful novelists in the genre who were really well placed socially to write about the Celtic Tiger from the inside who chose instead to write adult fairytales. Maybe it was a retreat from sordid reality.

55 minutes into the interview: We hear one of the children rummaging quietly outside the door for a few minutes and decide to wait it out. It eventually ceases.

MB: A male reviewer of a 1962 Sylvia Plath radioplay about pregnancy, birth, and miscarriage complained that its three women characters "all sounded depressed." [17] **Recent generations of women have been raised on the legend of how differently Plath and Ted Hughes were affected by parenthood. I suppose I am asking you how motherhood has shaped your writing (and if I am being honest, I don't think that is a question I would ask of a male novelist!). Even if a male partner is good at sharing the heavy lifting, the bulk of what sociologists call the "worry work"[18] keeps mothers in a state of what neuroscientist Frances Jensen has termed "dementia of the preoccupied,"[19] so it seems inevitable that motherhood will impact one's inner life.**

CK: The way motherhood has impacted me is that I delivered *The Devil I Know* in January 2012, got pregnant in February 2012, and I haven't written a piece of fiction since. I can't find my way back to fiction because of the demands, the constant distractions.

75 minutes into the interview: There is a knock at the door. It's my husband with a query regarding something Claire's son wishes to eat and the offer of tea and scones, which arrive soon after.

MB: Getting back to this issue of what "worry work" does to creativity: have you observed that the way parenthood disrupts the writing process for mothers is not so true for male writers who happen to be fathers?

CK: Put bluntly, my male peers who have recently become parents are still writing. I amn't. I felt so decimated by motherhood because I didn't have a workplace, and I didn't have a moment to myself. You can't even go to the toilet when you need to. Plus, my imagination isn't what it used to be, never mind my singlemindedness, my selfishness. Anne Enright—who is the person I go to for advice—assured me that creativity comes back. She says it's still there, just different. Have faith. Anne is the literary mother figure to all of us. She's compassionate, empathetic, knowledgeable, intelligent, and insightful. She's got all the gifts, which she uses for the good. (*Pauses*) I worry…(*pauses*). I worry about my child and I worry that my brain has been affected beyond repair. It's so…(*pauses*), what is it when it all branches out and fritters away and scatters and…? (*pauses and laughs*) God! I used to have the word I needed on the tip of my tongue and now its, "what's that word with two syllables, it rhymes with x?" My life has turned into charades!

MB: **Can you see this getting better and maybe one day leading to the Great Irish Novel on Motherhood?**

CK: I have no faith that this will come good. I would *hope* that it would. I'm a different person, reprogrammed on every level by motherhood. The last time I went back to *Ulysses*, it was to the scene in which Bloom thinks of his dead son, Rudy. I missed that when I read *Ulysses* in college, totally missed that Leopold, who is younger than I am now, is mourning his dead son. This didn't register in college because I was more interested in Stephen Daedalus then. Joyce is the river you can never step into twice. I used to resent this reprogramming deeply, now I'm seeing that I've gained more than I've lost. If you'd told me before I'd had a child what it would do to me, I'd have refused to do it, but, now, as a mother, if you told me I had to murder fifty people for my child I'd say, "line 'em up!" There's nothing I wouldn't do for him, but that's at the cost of my writing. That faculty—when something happens in my head and I can get it onto paper—is precious to me, and I'm scared of losing it. My son has started junior Montessori school recently, so I hope to find my way back. I owe it to him, because I'd be a shit mother if I ever said, "because of you my writing life is over." I can't be that woman. I can't do that to him. And here's the question for mothers: should we be hush-hush about how unable to function motherhood makes us? If I walked into my solicitor's [lawyer's] office and saw she was pregnant, I'd immediately think, "I need to get a new solicitor." But that undermines women, so should we shut up about how little we can function, or should we instead be humane to those women who are taking bullets for society by having a child? Obviously, it's the latter. Women cover it up to protect their jobs. They have to pretend that they are just as together as before, even though they are now double-jobbing and their brainpower is diluted. As a society, we need to allow for a few years of a new mother not being on the top of her game. But we don't. Women are so heroic. They just suck it up and take all the punches. I've just written a non-fiction piece ["F for Phone"] for Kevin Barry and Olivia Smith about feeling suicidal last year after having my child. Part of me goes, "Jesus! Don't publish that!" But women are going through this silently all the time. I wasn't depressed. A perinatal psychiatrist told me that I was simply respond-ing logically to my altered situation. My son was born in December, and I had a reading in Paris in February, and he screamed when I came back. So did I. So did my husband. I'd had a lovely time in Paris, and it was the thought of coming back to everyday motherhood that made me suicidal.

MB: And yet, do you find that people think that motherhood, like writing at home, is not "real" work?

CK: It's shocking to me that I used to think that motherhood was copping out, that if you were educated you should be in the workforce. I still get depressed when I see women walking buggies [strollers]. Even though *I am* the woman walking the buggy! Anytime I see a man walking a buggy or picking his kid up, I feel a detonation of "woo hoo!" in my head.

MB: Because it's not valued when a woman does it, so a man visibly parenting somehow validates that role?

CK: I haven't untangled all of these feelings yet. I know I will write about it all because I'm both very angry and full of this new love. I don't have the drive I used to have, and that scares me. Part of me thinks, "this is stupid" when I'm in a playground (*laughs*). I know it's important, but it's so mindless (*laughs*). And stressful. Incredibly stressful. That's why I get a burst of joy when I see a man parenting because I think, "now he'll realize how stressful it is and appreciate how hard it is."

MB: So, you will try to write about motherhood?

CK: I'm going to write about the anguish of motherhood. None of my novels have successful relationships. There are things I have been unable to capture. But then I wasn't in a real relationship until I met my husband in 2009. I'd like to write a relationship, but then I'd also simply like to write about what it's like to go for a really nice walk (*laughs*). John Kelly [the Irish novelist and broadcaster] says that people who don't write don't understand that writers need to write like other people need to exercise. So, I'm not getting to the gym at the moment, and I don't feel well! Everything is unrecorded. I used to respond to everything. Now, I don't listen to the news, I don't know what's going on, I don't know who I am. I need to start recording again.

MB: You have just described a component of your creative process very clearly here: in order to write about contemporary Ireland, you pay a lot of attention to current events.

CK: Yes. I have a dog in the race. I live here. But I can't tune in anymore because I'm on baby-detail. For instance, the whole [Irish legislature-run] Banking Inquiry is going on right now, and *The Devil I Know* closes with a fictional banking inquiry going on in 2016, but I can only hear snippets of the real inquiry in between distractions.

MB: You have just finished your first stint teaching creative writing when you held the Heimbold Chair of Irish Studies at Villanova University in 2015. How was that experience?

CK: It was enriching to teach these bright young Americans, and on a purely practical level, Villanova was the way back to writing again. It gave me the tools to not be a full-time mother. Before marriage, I lived alone and had space. But after the baby, my desk was in the bedroom under a load of baby stuff. Thanks to the Villanova money, we bought a house and now I have a study, and Villanova paid for childcare. I couldn't ask my husband, "darling, could you fund me to sit in a room and practice my driven aimlessness?" (*laughs*). However, once the driven aimlessness is on the clock, it's no longer aimless. It's panic…

Two hours into the interview: We look up at the slowly opening door. My daughter's little hand and then her face appear. We negotiate with her for a few minutes as Claire needs to leave soon due to her son's schedule, so we are running out of time. We've just got my daughter to agree to give me a few more minutes when Maria pops in and whispers to Claire, "I think it's a poo." Claire goes off to attend to her son's diaper, and my daughter takes the opportunity to install herself in the vacated seat, and proceeds to eat my scone. The interview is, it seems, over.

Postscript

I had not read Kilroy's still unpublished "F for Phone" when our interview was conducted or when working on earlier drafts of this overview. Now that "F for Phone" has been published, it seems to me that the profound effect that motherhood has had on Kilroy's creativity and sense of the world may well cause her future fiction to travel in surprising new directions. As someone who has read and taught the author's work from the earliest days of her career, I was disarmed by the raw directness and emotional depth of "F for Phone," which is a departure from the detached postmodernism of her novels to date (notwithstanding that the non-fiction personal essay is an entirely new genre for the author). It will be interesting to see how this new turn manifests itself in Kilroy's next novel, for, despite the doubts voiced in the interview, there *will be* a next novel, as evidenced by the fact that "F for Phone" may possibly be her best writing to date. Its opening discussion of the writer's block caused by birth and motherhood provokes a wry smile by the time one has finished the beautifully-written piece. Rather than blocking her creativity, Kilroy's recent experiences seem to have, after a hiatus, unleashed new depths in her writing.

Notes

1. "F for Phone" is also available online at < http://winterpapers.com/vol1/selected-content/f-for-phone?page=f-for-phone >.
2. An interesting case in point was journalist Justine Delaney-Wilson's *The High Society*, a Celtic Tiger-era *exposé* in which an unnamed Irish government minister allegedly admits to being a regular cocaine user. Doubts were cast doubt over the veracity of the book, but its topic speaks to a public appetite for tales of the expensive addictions of the Irish elite.
3. Debbie Ging notes that "Within this new rhetoric, freedom is understood less as the legacy of second-wave feminism and increasingly as something given to us by an open, liberal market [...]." ("New Gender Formations" 53). Angela McRobbie provides a succinct definition of "post-feminism": [It is a vocabulary that] "positively draws on and invokes feminism as that which can be taken into account, to suggest that equality is achieved [...]" (12).
4. See Ingman (xiii; 237–58); Cahill (13–14).
5. This gendered representation continues in the post-Tiger period. Diane Negra notes that a "predominant interpretation of events characterizes the recession as a national moral reckoning where a 'soft' feminine consumer culture is now appropriately in retreat. New rhetorics of manliness have sometimes seemed to be creeping into Irish popular culture in tandem with the shift toward economic uncertainty" ("Adjusting Men" 45).
6. See Meier-Pesti and Penz. Michael Lewis's analysis of the economic collapse in Ireland is amusingly alert to the role gender and heterosexual Irish male entitlement played in events: "Ireland's financial disaster shared some things with Iceland's. It was created by the sort of men who ignore their wives' suggestions that maybe they should stop and ask for directions, for instance. But while Icelandic males used foreign money to conquer foreign places— [...] the Irish male [...] decided what they really wanted to do with it was to buy Ireland. *From one another.* [...] when I arrived in early November 2010, Irish politics had a frozen-in-time quality to it. In Iceland, the business-friendly conservative party had been quickly tossed out of power, and the women booted the alpha males out of the banks and government. (Iceland's new prime minister is a lesbian.) [...] Ireland was the first European country to watch its entire banking system fail, and yet its business-friendly conservative party, Fianna Fáil [...], would remain in office into 2011. [...] Morgan Kelly, a professor of economics [...] saw house prices rising madly and heard young men in Irish finance to whom he had recently taught economics try to explain why the boom didn't trouble them. [...] the two men who sold the Irish people on the notion that they, the people, were responsible not merely for their own disastrous financial decisions but also for the ones made by their banks [were] Prime Minister Brian Cowen and Finance Minister Brian

Lenihan. [...] Across Europe just now men who thought their title was 'minister of finance' have woken up to the idea that their job is actually government bond salesman" (174).

7. For instance, in an August 2015 Jezebel.com article, a woman author claimed that the same manuscript was much better received by potential agents when sent under a male *nom de plume*. http://jezebel.com/homme-de-plume-what-i-learned-sending-my-novel-out-und-1720637627

8. A 2015 Authors Guild Member Survey revealed that full-time authors reported a 30% drop in income since 2009. https://www.authorsguild.org/industry-advocacy/the-wages-of-writing/

9. In Ireland, "a large proportion of men (one in five) were employed in the construction sector prior to the recession" (Duvvury and Finn 61).

10. For a related discussion of how the financial crisis and its aftermath impacted women in the United Kingdom, see Pearson and Elson.

11. The "Big House" is an Irish usage for the mansions (or sometimes more modest manor houses) of the dethroned Anglo-Protestant elite of pre-Independence Ireland and is also the name of an Irish literary genre in which such dwellings play a central role.

12. Of course, there have been notable exceptions such as John Banville.

13. In 2010, then Minister for Finance, the late Brian Lenihan, notoriously defended the charge made on current affairs program *Prime Time* (on national broadcaster *RTE*) that the state had been correct in bailing out seemingly reckless Irish bankers because "we [the Irish] all partied." Footage of the relevant segment of the interview is available at https://www.youtube.com/watch?v=YK7w6fXoYxo. Accessed 29 January, 2016.

14. The biennial Global Irish Economic Forum, modeled on Switzerland's World Economic Forum, was first held in 2009 in Dublin's Farmleigh House, an official state residence, and was given widespread coverage at the time because of the concurrent implosion of the Irish economy.

15. Priory Hall was an apartment complex built in Dublin in 2007, at the very height of the housing bubble, whose residents were forced to flee when its dangerously shoddy construction was discovered in 2013. At that point, the complex became an emblem of the lack of oversight and corruption of the Celtic Tiger era's housing boom.

16. These words echo the self-serving speech in the barbecue scene in *The Devil I Know*: "Behind us, McGee was proclaiming that they deserved everything the Celtic Tiger had brought them because they had *balls*" (218). In turn, this braggadocio ultimately follows the thrust of the widely-reported speech made at the *Irish Times* Property Advertising Awards in September 2005 by Sean FitzPatrick, then chairman of Anglo Irish Bank, which played a major role in the Irish credit bubble and its dramatic bursting: "'We had ideas, and we had balls. We would put in whatever hours and whatever miles it required to take those ideas and turn them into business successes'" (qtd. in Lynch 182). For details of FitzPatrick's rise and fall, see Lynch, 175–82.

17. Burns Singer. Rev. of *Three Women*. *The Listener*. 30 August 1962, 330. *Three Women*, Plath's only play, was commissioned for the BBC Third Programme and broadcast on August 19, 1962. In 1971, it was published in *Winter Trees*, the posthumous collection of Plath's poems. My thanks to Sarah Berry of UConn for drawing my attention to the play and its reviewer.

18. Even when heterosexual couples ostensibly share household and child-rearing tasks, argues social psychologist Francine Deutsch, "one of the last things to go is women keeping track of the kind of nonroutine details of taking care of children—when they have to go to the doctor, when they need a permission slip for school, paying attention at that level..." Francine Deutsch, quoted in "Mom: The Designated Worrier" *The*

New York Times http://www.nytimes.com/2015/05/10/opinion/sunday/judith-shulevitz
-mom-the-designated-worrier.html. Accessed 29 January, 2016. For a related analysis,
see Susan Maushart, *Wifework* (New York: Bloomsbury, 2001).

19. Jensen coined the phrase during a January 2015 interview with NPR's Terry Gross to
describe how multi-tasking and constant interruption prevents the consolidation of
memories. Frances Jensen, "Dementia of the Preoccupied" *Psychology Today* https://
www.psychologytoday.com/blog/the-teenage-brain/201502/dementia-the-preoccupied.
Accessed 7 June, 2016.

Works Cited

Burke, Mary. "Kilroy is Here: An Interview with Claire Kilroy." *Irish Literary Supplement.* Fall
(2007): 22–25. Print.

Cahill, Susan. *Irish Literature in the Celtic Tiger Years* 1990-2008: *Gender, Bodies, Memory.*
London; New York: Continuum, 2011. Print.

Casey, Moira E. "'If Love's a Country': Transnationalism and the Celtic Tiger in Emma
Donoghue's *Landing.* " *New Hibernia Review/Iris Éireannach Nua* 15.2 (2011): 64–79.
Print.

Cronin, Gearóid. "John Banville and the Subversion of the Big House Novel." *The Big House
in Ireland: Reality and Representation.* Ed. Jacqueline Genet. Dingle, Co. Kerry, Ireland:
Brandon/Mount Eagle, 1991. 215–230. Print.

Delaney-Wilson, Justine. *The High Life: Drugs and the Irish Middle Class.* Dublin: Gill and
Macmillan, 2007. Print.

Duvvury, Nata and Caroline Finn. "'Man-covery': Recession, Labour Market, and Gender
Relations in Ireland." *Gender, Sexuality & Feminism* 1.2 (2014). Print.

Ging, Debbie. "New Gender Formations in Post-Celtic-Tiger Ireland." *Transforming Ireland:
Challenges, Critiques, Resources.* Eds. Debbie Ging, Michael Cronin and Peader Kirby
Manchester: Manchester University Press, 2009. 52–70. Print.

——. "Screening the Green." *Reinventing Ireland: Culture, Society and the Global Economy.*
Eds. Luke Gibbons et al. London: Pluto, 2002. 177–95. Print.

Harris, John. "And Now for the Good News: The West End's Struggling, the Art Market's
Faltering… But Might the Slump be a Boon for Culture?" *Guardian* (London), Oct 21,
2008, 21. Print.

Ingman, Heather. *Irish Women's Fiction: From Edgeworth to Enright.* Dublin: Irish Academic
Press, 2013. Print.

Lynch, David J. J. *When the Luck of the Irish Ran Out: The World's Most Resilient Country
andIts Struggle to Rise Again.* New York: St. Martin's Press, 2010. Print.

Kilroy, Claire. *All Names Have Been Changed.* London: Faber, 2009. Print.

——. *All Summer.* London: Faber and Faber, 2003. Print.

——. "F for Phone." *Winter Pages.* Eds. Kevin Barry and Olivia Smith. Sligo, Ireland: Curlew,
2015. 185–89. Print.

——. *The Devil I Know.* London: Faber & Faber, 2012. Print.

——. *Tenderwire.* London: Faber & Faber, 2007. Print.

Lewis, Michael. "When Irish Eyes Are Crying." *Vanity Fair* 53:3 (2011): 174. Print.

McRobbie, Angela. *The Aftermath of Feminism: Gender, Culture and Social Change.* London:
Sage, 2012. Print.

Meier-Pesti, Katia and Elfriede Penz. "Sex or Gender? Expanding the Sex-based View by
Introducing Masculinity and Femininity as Predictors of Financial Risk Taking." *Journal of
Economic Psychology* 29:2 (2008): 180–196. Print.

Molony, Sinéad. "House and Home: Structuring Absences in Post-Celtic Tiger Documentary." *Gendering the Recession: Media and Culture in an Age of Austerity*. Eds. Diane Negra and Yvonne Tasker. Durham; London: Duke UP, 2014: 181–202. Print.

Negra, Diane. "Adjusting Men and Abiding Mammies: Gendering the Recession in Ireland." *Irish Review* 46 (2014): 23–34. Print.

Negra, Diane and Yvonne Tasker, "Introduction: Gender and Recessionary Culture." *Gendering the Recession: Media and Culture in an Age of Austerity*. Durham; London: Duke UP, 2014. 1–30. Print.

O'Brien, Cormac. "Sons of the Tiger: Performing Neoliberalism, Post-Feminism, and Masculinity in 'Crisis' in Contemporary Irish Theatre." *Masculinity and Irish Popular Culture: Tiger's Tales*. Eds. Conn Holohan and Tony Tracy. London: Palgrave Macmillan, 2014. 126–141. Print.

Pearson, Ruth and Diane Elson, "Transcending the Impact of the Financial Crisis in the United Kingdom." *Feminist Review* 109: 1 (2015): 8–30. Print.

Stopper, Anne. *Mondays at Gaj's: The Story of the Irish Women's Liberation Movement*. Dublin: Liffey Press, 2006. Print.

2020 Addendum

I checked in with Kilroy by email at the close of 2019 and again in January 2020 regarding possible updates to this interview. In the years since, she has continued to work on the novel about motherhood, which has been titled *Darling* and which she summarizes as follows:

> *Darling* is an address by a mother to her sleeping child explaining all the things that went wrong, and why they went wrong, and how hopeful she is that they won't go wrong for her child if motherhood is understood a little better. Her child is a boy. It's totally different from my other work. It's episodic, no plot, written on an emotional plane, one [of] the main characters has no dialogue because he's an infant so it's an interior monologue, or rant, rather. It's about loss of the self and the rebuilding of a new self.[1]

Kilroy has published two excerpts from the novel-in-progress, "After the Fight" (2016), which appeared in *Winter Papers 2*, and "From *Darling*" (2018), which was published in *Reading the Future: New Writing from Ireland*. She has also recently published a non-fiction piece on motherhood and writing called "Locked Out of My Head" (online 2018; print 2019). I should expand briefly on the non-fiction "F for Fone" as, thematically, it is the experiential and artistic ground zero from which Kilroy's subsequent work has emerged. It describes her birth experience, the natural pain of which was hugely amplified by the wholly manmade dysfunction of the Irish health system:

> I spent two nights in the Victorian workhouse that is the semi-private antenatal ward. Girls paced the corridors at all hours, blind to everything but their pain. There were queues outside the toilet. Labouring women queuing for the toilet – it wasn't good, it wasn't what we'd hoped for. We would have liked a little privacy. We'd have liked a little soap too. ("F for Phone")

Kilroy evokes a torture facility in describing the horror of the other women with whom she labored whenever a screaming mother-to-be was wheeled toward the Great Unknown behind the birthing ward doors. The language of the warzone is used to convey the paranoia and defenselessness of grown women made to endure often unnecessary humiliations and from whom necessary information and pain relief were withheld, not to mention the cruelty of "new-born babies fresh out of the womb whose mothers are temporarily incapacitated" being "placed under fluorescent strip lighting and left to listen to each other's screams." To extend the war metaphor, Kilroy's subsequent work seems to chart the PTSD caused, in part, by the manner in which the birth process is handled in the gravely mismanaged, overburdened, and seemingly structurally misogynistic Irish health system, an often-needless trauma that leaves the psychologically and physically damaged new mother ill-equipped for all the demands that begin right after the birth.

In "After the Fight," the narrator mother recalls a visit to West Cork tourist mecca Skibbereen with her young son and husband. Her monologue suggests that she is emerging from a post-natal shrinking of her world that affected her marriage, her productivity, and her confidence: "I used to have a mind," the narrator tells her son, "then I had you." Emerging from a shop with the young child, she is—in a moment that recalls the work of both Kate Chopin and Virginia Woolf[2]—"confronted with the sky":

> I gaped at it and thought gosh, look at that. It was a big picturebook sky, blue with pillowy white clouds. I hope you'll never quite understand what I'm going to say next, honey, but I had been looking down for so long – I had been staring at floors, at corners, at my empty hands for so long – that when I did encounter the sky in that manner on that occasion, it came […] as a revelation of sorts. It is amazing, darling, what you acclimatise to over time, what becomes your reality. The sky had been there all along […] but I had been huddled over my despair for such a protracted period that I had adapted to it. (98)

Gazing at herself with the eyes of the public realm, the narrator imagines that motherhood and marriage have caused a complex inner self to be replaced with a outward pre-assembled type: "That morning, I had sat at the hotel dressing table to put on the pearls, the pastel cotton shirt, the good mother uniform, and I had stared at myself, wondering: who is this person, this *wife*?" (98)掠 Most strikingly, "After the Fight" suggests that a profound awareness of the manner in which death invariably shadows love has entered Kilroy's writing since giving birth. Telling her son about falling in love with his father, the narrator remembers:

> The first time we met, your father levelled that gaze at me and, although I had never laid eyes on him before, I recognised him. […] the look on his face, when he came upon me, said: Oh, its *you*. Because he recognised me too. And within a few days I knew […] that I would be holding his face when he died […]. In our first look, I saw our last look. One of us will be left behind. (97–98)

The 2018 excerpt from the novel-in-progress that appeared in *Reading the Future: New Writing from Ireland* is a mesmerizing slice of what can only be called post-natal Gothic in the fine tradition of Charlotte Perkins Gilman's

"The Yellow Wallpaper" (1892): distressed and bleeding, the new mother narrator lies on a forest floor in the company of what she, in a kind of cataleptic
rejection of anthropocentrism, names only as "other wild animals":

> I grew calm as I abided there with the other wild animals and after a time the for-
> est absorbed me into it. Birdsong, squabbles on branches, the drone of insects—
> the volume crept back up. Woodpigeons reembarked on their conversations.
> They were probably talking about me. ("From *Darling*," 344)

The narrator's darting inner monologue reveals the dementia of the overtired
and hormonally disrupted new mother:

> Green is my favourite colour, I thought, gazing up at the leaves. I hadn't had
> time to think in so long. My world had become too chaotic. A balance, the great
> balance I hadn't known had been looming over me all those years, had abruptly
> tipped. I was sliding off. Plus I had forgotten to drop the black bags to the cloth-
> ing bank. (344)掠

After moving on, she stumbles on a hatchling fetus with "[d]isproportion-
ately large head, tiny body...and...skin...thin as clingfilm," (346) and the
excerpt's gradual dismantling of all barriers between woman and female animals culminates in an unsettling encounter between mother and equally distressed mother bird. In a subsequent January 2020 email, Kilroy confirmed
my assumption that the character is a very new mother with a detail that
suggests the degree to which her recent fiction and non-fiction writing are
thematically entwined:

> There is a connection with F for Fone and the forest excerpt. The forest excerpt
> indeed depicts a (very new) mother abandoning her baby, then hiding in a forest
> to kill herself. I mentioned in F for Fone that I felt suicidal, or thought I did. I
> thought I was depressed and that my child would do better without me. He was
> 2 and a half months old. The forest episode has its origin in that wild episode.[3]

Further into the same email Kilroy refers to an article I had just published
on lisheens, quasi-secret unconsecrated burial sites for stillborn and premature
babies located in liminal rural places that were once common on Ireland's
western seaboard due to a Catholic Church interdiction on the burial of the
unbaptized in consecrated ground. In light of what Kilroy then goes on to detail, it is worth noting that the lisheen (or killeen) custom generated folklore of
encounters with the ghosts of unbaptized infants in isolated places[4]:

> I had not heard of lisheens, as such, but as an aside, in the forest extract, the
> next thing that happens to the narrator is that she hears a baby crying. It is too
> far away to be her baby, or any living baby, so she reckons she is standing on an
> unmarked grave. "Desperate things happened to infants in the past, desperate
> secrets were buried by desperate women. And desperate girls."[5]

This extraordinary aside and the quotation from *Darling* suggest that in an emotionally heightened postnatal state, a contemporary Irish woman may uncannily tap into folk memories of the clandestine history of traumatic births and their aftermaths in Ireland, even when not consciously aware of that history. (It may be argued that *Darling*'s unmarked grave scene draws on a conscious awareness of the events that led to the Kerry Babies Trial, but that occurrence too, as my article argues, may be understood as a metropolitan criminalization of rural Ireland's poorly documented lisheen custom.)

Kilroy's most recently published non-fiction meditation on birth and motherhood, "Locked Out of My Head," first published online in 2018, reiterates the toll she sees it as having taken on her ability to think and work without constant interruption:

> When I had a baby, [...] [s]uch was the clamour, the level of constant panicky demands, I could no longer think. I barely had time to speak in full sentences, let alone write them. [...] I had to give up writing when I became a mother because childcare is so expensive in Ireland.[6]

Nevertheless, she expresses hope in the piece regarding the fact that her growing son's school day will soon be longer, though her scrupulous computation of exactly how much time his new routine will buy her ("Next year will be better for my writing life as the school day will go up to five hours and forty minutes, 183 days a year") is at once comical and depressing.

In the first email regarding this update in November 2019, Kilroy noted that although she was making progress with *Darling*,

> I had hoped for a 2021 publication but it'll probably be 2022. That's a whole decade after *The Devil* [*I Know*]. Jesus. In my defence, the Irish school day is so short it [has been] difficult to get a run at things.

Still, as Kilroy had predicted in "Locked Out of My Head," the pressure on her time has eased: "[My son] is in first class now which means he's in till 2.30—the extra hour has made a big difference."[7] Kilroy went on to convey the further good news that in August 2019 she was named as one of the recipients of the inaugural Markievicz Award in support of the creation of a final draft of *Darling*.[8] This new Arts Council/Ministry for Culture, Heritage and the Gaeltacht bursary for artists commemorates the centenary of the appointment of Constance Markievicz, Irish revolutionary and the first woman elected to the Westminster Parliament, and it is intended to support artists creating works centered on Irish women's lives in any period of the last 100 years. When I asked Kilroy how she intended to use what she termed her "Markievicz money," she tellingly replied, "I am employing a [child] minder [for after-school care]." For all the seeming progress Irish women have made, it turns out that the systemic issues that held women back in Markievicz's day remain in place more than a century later. A further upbeat note is that at time of final editing of this update (March 2020), Kilroy has just been invited by Abby Bender of Sacred Heart University to speak on her most recent publications at the October 2020 Mid-Atlantic and New England American Conference for Irish Studies, a joint regional meeting of the most prominent annual conference in the Irish Studies field. This invitation may well indicate a growing awareness of the role Kilroy's newest writing is playing in bringing Irish Studies attention to her recent theme of the structural impediments that make motherhood and work difficult to reconcile; Irish historiography and literary studies increasingly tell us that women have been elided, but do not always give sufficient attention to the systemic impediments that produce that silence and invisibility.

As predicted by "F for Fone," the psychic wound of motherhood has indeed allowed Kilroy's creative writing to plumb new depths. She may not produce at the same clip as before, but what she is producing is visceral in its emotional frankness, a directness achieved through a poetic exactness of language. Despite Kilroy's doubts regarding her ability to recapture the creativity of her pre-baby days, the excerpts that have appeared from *Darling* duplicate the precision with which her highly structured previous novels convey what she terms her favored theme of emotional chaos ("Locked out of my Head"). The joltingly immediate excerpts audit the heavy psychic, physical, emotional, financial, and time costs that childbirth, the post-natal period, and motherhood continue to extract from women in the absence of any meaningful recognition in public life of all that the private realm of maternity demands. ("Who mothered the mothers?" one of Kilroy's narrators poignantly asks ("From *Darling*")). If the excerpts are anything to go by, *Darling* will be Kilroy's best novel yet. Indeed, what Kilroy mourns as a regrettable delay in finishing *Darling* will, ultimately, testify to the truth of its theme of the personal and professional hiatus that motherhood—as currently constituted in late capitalist Ireland—forces upon women. *Darling* promises to be a very important novel. It will be well worth the wait.

Notes

1 Personal email from Claire Kilroy, 27 November 2019.
2 The representation of a woman gaining insight into the tremendous mental and physical strain she has been under when she grasps the immensity of the sky also occurs in Kate Chopin's short story "The Story of an Hour" (1894) and in Virginia Woolf's essay "On Being Ill" (1926). My thanks to Abby Bender for drawing my attention to these interesting parallels to Kilroy.
3 Personal email from Kilroy, 7 January 2020.
4 See Anne O'Connor, *Child Murderess and Dead Child Traditions* (Helsinki: Suomalainen Tiedeakatemia, 1991) 76, 78, 79.
5 Personal email from Kilroy, 7 January 2020.
6 I quote here from the initial November 2018 online publication of "Locked out of My Head."
7 Personal email from Kilroy, 27 November 2019.
8 See the 2019 Markievicz Award press release at https://www.chg.gov.ie/announcement-of-markievicz-awards-2019/

Works Cited

Mary Burke, "Tuam Babies and Kerry Babies: Clandestine Pregnancies and Child Burial Sites in Tom Murphy's Drama and Mary Leland's *The Killeen*." *Irish University Review* 49.2 (2019): 245–61.

Kilroy, Claire. "After the Fight." *Winter Papers 2*. Eds. Kevin Barry and Olivia Smith. Sligo: Curlew Editions, 2016. 97–102. Print.

_____. "From *Darling*." *Reading the Future: New Writing from Ireland*. Ed. Alan Hayes. Dublin; Syracuse: Arlen House, 2018. 344–47. Print.

_____. "F for Phone" http://winterpapers.com/vol1/selectedcontent/f-for-phone?page=f-for-phone. Online.

_____. "Locked out of My Head." https://kaleidoscope.efacis.eu/claire-kilroy/locked-out-my-head and in *The Danger and Glory: Irish Authors on the Art of Writing*. Ed. Hedwig Schwall. Dublin; Syracuse: Arlen House, 2019. 182–84. Online and print.

"no difference between the different kinds of yesterday:" The Neoliberal Present in *The Green Road, The Devil I Know,* and *The Lives of Women*

Mary McGlynn

Midway through *The Green Road* (2015), Anne Enright depicts a "woman chased into a corner by her own house" (168), an uncanny adaptation of a longstanding association of women with domesticity. This reinterpretation is made trenchant by the novel's timing—this moment occurs in late 2005, at the height of the Irish real estate boom, when a house was less a home than it was untapped capital. But after years of exponential gains (notably, an 8% annual growth rate in the 1990s and housing value increases surpassing 400%),[1] the Irish economy imploded in 2008, partly due to the contemporaneous global economic crisis but exacerbated by extensive domestic borrowing and lending in residential and commercial real estate markets. It is thus unsurprising that a post-boom Irish novel would make an antagonist out of real estate. Enright is hardly alone: in explicit confrontation of the excesses shaping the crisis, Claire Kilroy's *The Devil I Know* (2012) traces the deterioration of a castle, Big House, and luxury high rise development in County Dublin. Tana French's 2012 thriller *Broken Harbor* features ghost estate hauntings; Donal Ryan's *The Spinning Heart* (2012) revolves around Pokey Burke and his unfinished estate; and Colum McCann bookends his 2013 novel *TransAtlantic* with scenes in a cottage that acts as money pit. In the aftermath of the bust, even novels set in earlier times or distant locales figure the home in economic terms: Emma Donoghue's *Frog Music* (2014), set in San Francisco in 1876, features a heroine who owns an entire building, only to have it sold out from under her by a con man, and the dark plot Christine Dwyer Hickey's *The Lives of Women* (2015) hinges on anonymity and class tensions in a 1970s American-style housing development in an unnamed Irish suburb.

Of course, women's fiction is frequently concerned with domestic space, an inclination historically criticized both for supposed insularity or lack of political engagement and for a realist mode dismissed as documentary reportage. Curiously, twenty-first-century fiction more generally seems to be moving in both of these directions—towards the apolitical and the realist—in response to a cultural climate of neoliberalism, espousing a neoliberal value system that takes the quantitative dimension of economics as a truthful, definitive measure of society mindset and privileges the literal and the present. Jeffrey Williams has incisively defined the "neoliberal novel" in American fiction: it articulates disenchantment with politics, lacks faith in collective action, and finds meaning and solutions in the private realm. Williams tracks a naturalization of the belief that "we can only successfully solve problems through private means and individual action" (95), arguing it leads to a state of affairs in which the "main societal choices" occur not just personally, but "within the economic sphere" (93), rather than collectively and in moral, aesthetic, or political spheres. Williams traces the rise of a "plutocratic imagination" in which an (often politically liberal) oligarchy makes decisions. He contends that the privileging of private over public, individual over group, and economic over political and cultural is so pervasive that even novels critical of their society operate within the neoliberal context.

Likewise, literary critics Eugene O'Brien and Eamon Maher maintain that during the heyday of the Celtic Tiger, there was little sustained cultural counter-narrative to the "close identification between cultural and economic forces" (6); like other nations in the Global North, boom-era Ireland reconfigured its interpretive landscape to privilege a financial viewpoint, "as if economics had now become the new master discipline" (5), with growth, development, and progress as unquestioned virtues. The era's persistent interest in real estate instantiates an outgrowth of neoliberalism's monetization of the domestic, an acquiescence to the reframing of the home as capital.[2] As a place already identified with privacy and the individual, the commodified house offers an ideal means of tracking the conversion of subjects to consumers and the naturalization of the neoliberal belief in the futility of public or collective action.

Much Irish fiction resists the primacy of the economic and registers such commodification as a threat, with recent fiction by women particularly well-placed to scrutinize the elision of home and property. The Irish economic crisis has opened a space for critique as well as unearthed the imbrication of the cultural sphere and a market-oriented mindset. However, I would contend that certain stylistic tendencies in much current Irish fiction seem to function as traces of the neoliberal moment—from the persistent, pervasive use of present tense, to a staccato form of expression evocative of text messages and memes, to a departure from standard grammaticality that calls to mind the inventions and varieties of global Englishes. I read such formations in their Irish context as sites for questions about the extent to which the nation bears blame for its economic crisis. Although many recent novels use such technical means to fault neoliberal ideology for its relentless focus on development, they find themselves formally indebted to its subterranean structural premise, the philosophical framework of neoliberal immediacy which presents the status quo as natural and without alternative. I examine in particular three very different novels—*The Lives of Women, The Green Road*, and *The Devil I Know*—that share both a thematic preoccupation with domestic space and a willingness to play with temporality, both at the grammatical level of tense and in the refusal of linear structure in their novels. It is at this intersection of content and form that we can see Dwyer Hickey, Enright, and Kilroy grapple with the extent to which it is possible to write a novel critiquing neoliberalism without capitulating to that ideology's framework.

We can see evidence of such capitulation—of the sort of literal-minded, quantitative mindset affirmed by neoliberalism—in the ways the Irish press has noted a supposed dearth of novelistic responses to first the boom, and then the crisis (Cahill 7).[3] Such critiques partake of a tradition bemoaning the lack of the Great Irish Novel, all made only through conscious efforts to disregard a wide body of contestants for the title.[4] The current lamentations help to bolster a narrow neoliberal focus on the present, overlooking how fiction about the past still "engages with the time at which it is written" (Cahill 7). More tellingly, they "ignore the output of contemporary Irish women writers... such fiction does not register for these critics" (Cahill 13–14).[5] The three novels I examine in detail here, all by women, show the limits of a cultural framework that is too focused on the immediate and the literal. They thus rebuke the unwillingness in sectors of Ireland's popular press to recognize the output of women or to see how novels treating the past or the domestic make ideological interventions in the present and the political.

The opinions of a few book reviewers aside, the Warwick Research Collective notes that critiques of capitalism via gothic tropes date back to Marx himself (75), citing Stephen Shapiro's insight that "the gothic reemerge[s] in similar moments in the recurring cycles of long-wave capitalist accumulation" (96).[6] Ironically, given the construction boom of 2001–2007, the precarity of the home in Irish novels of the subsequent decade is frequently expressed via neo-gothic motifs of decay.[7] The iteration of the gothic in post-boom novels features crumbling structures, laden with hidden secrets and stocked with repressed, maimed bodies, the half-finished buildings of the boom embodying gothic deterioration. The term "ghost estate" directly evokes the spectral haunting of the gothic, originally present in classical economics via Adam Smith's evocation of an eerie "invisible hand." Faith in this ethereal motor of growth motivated the construction of remote housing estates, though the underlying logic had less to do with classical supply and demand than with magical thinking about unending economic expansion. Much recent Irish fiction—not only the texts I analyze here but novels across generic, stylistic, and ideological spectrums, from Sebastian Barry's *On Canaan's Side* to Tana French's *oeuvre*—wrestles with murky, seemingly unforeseeable or inexplicable economic outcomes through recourse to the irrational, the magical, the uncanny, similar to what WReC insightfully characterizes as an ascendant mode of "irrealism (57)" in contemporary fiction.[8] In the absence of the conventional functioning of cause-and-effect, supernatural solutions equate ghosts and markets as irrational and inexplicable, a capitulation in the public mood that Enright, Dwyer Hickey, and Kilroy all recognize and reconsider via their use of the gothic in their novels.

The ghostly home is juxtaposed with another common thread in recent Irish novels: the globalized non-place. I draw here on Marc Augé's analysis of the excesses characteristic of supermodernity, which undermine a sense of local time and place, giving rise to "a space which cannot be defined as relational, historical, or concerned with identity" (63). All three novels I focus on here—*The Lives of Women*, *The Green Road*, and *The Devil I Know*—depict the mundane and interchangeable materialism of airports, hotels, and global technologies, what Diane Negra calls the "idealized, cosmopolitan mobilities" shaping the Irish experience in the Tiger years ("Adjusting" 235). But the cosmopolitanism that structures each plot, with its seamless migrations and commodified excesses, also puts into relief the persistence of the home and the repressed past it contains.

These three novels measure the pressures upon a society long invested in ideals of nation and home. As Ireland detaches from place-based identification, converting itself rapidly into an exemplar of bourgeois subjectivity, its cultural critics question both its original narratives of cozy homes and the monetized ones replacing it. If "progress is a disaster and backwardness a shame" (Schwarz quoted in WreC 62), then there is an embeddedness in the present moment marked by present-tense narration and the irruption of irreal, gothic elements. The gothic inflections of each novel link nonlinearity—an uncanniness of time—with non-place—an uncanniness of setting. In this exploration of unresolved tensions, all three texts overtly critique the official neoliberal narratives of progress that privilege economics. But neoliberal logic re-insinuates itself via a vernacular, unofficial rhetoric of inevitability, assuming a guise of "always and everywhere" in part through its appropriation of the instantaneous.[9]

In unearthing in these three examples of recent Irish women's writing the confluence of the gothic and non-place, bounded by temporal instability, I move beyond detailing thematic similarities or generic preoccupations and connect literary form to a changing social landscape, one indelibly imprinted by its neoliberal era, and specifically by the 2008 economic crash. Dwyer Hickey alternates between a twenty-first century contemporary and a 1970s past, with verb tenses that equate the two periods. Enright also plays with tense in a novel that parcels time through place. And Kilroy sets her novel in the near future, deploying a narrative present tense to interrogate economic practices of the boom era. The novels register irreconcilable situations via gothic inflections, associating the persistence of the past with haunting and a lack of responsibility with anthropomorphism. All three undermine triumphalist Tiger-era narratives of teleology and progress. All three explore the role of gender in the mindset that created the boom and crash. However, while these novels stage robust critiques of neoliberalism, complicating the complacencies and ongoing sexism of Irish culture, they ultimately remain bounded by its contours. And as we shall see, they all struggle with the tension between the official neoliberal narrative of development and its informal embrace of space-time compression, which necessarily constructs a temporality of presentness, of the ongoing and eternal.

Japanese Knotweed[10]

In playing with tense and time, post boom novelists comment on a long-standing Irish preoccupation with the relationship between tradition and modernity, inflecting it in the contemporary crisis with an economic dimension, particularly within the conflicted space of the house. One technique seen in many Irish novels since the crash is the use of a narrative present tense. Narrative present has a long history (Cervantes, Joyce), but its frequency has been on the rise over the last 60 years in English, with a particular spike in the last decade.[11] Many critics tie the current popularity of the present tense to a contemporary moment of immediacy, what Urry describes as a shift from "clock" time to "instantaneous" time (107). Others link the increase in present-tense writing to the growing publication of fiction by women—William Gass correlates this with a supposed tentativeness in female writers (1987), while others connect it to "the writers' willingness to openly challenge the male-dominated values and conventions" (Miyahara 253).

The most conventional and accepted analyses within narratology argue that relating past events as though they are ongoing helps novels achieve a feeling of immediacy and urgency (Waldron Neumann 66). Since narrative past is the default for most novels, present tense would thus function to heighten emotional intensity, in what Dorrit Cohn terms a "highlighting impact ... expressed in terms of enhanced vividness, dramatic effect, or presentification" (99). Cohn's example of such a use of the "suspension of normal tensual semantics" is *David Copperfield*, a choice which indicates the technique has a solid pedigree in realist fiction.

While *The Lives of Women* does not use present tense entirely, Dwyer Hickey's deployment of it accounts for nearly all of the novel, which alternates present-tense first-person sections about the present with largely present-tense third person sections about the past, moving to future tense for the final few sentences of the narrative. Given the novel's main setting in an unnamed, undefined Irish suburban locale, these manipulations of verb tense offer a key to the novel's views about the questions of linearity and progress that occupy post-boom novels. The title notwithstanding, Dwyer Hickey's book is mostly about the lives of teenagers, in an anonymous ring suburb of an anonymous city (presumably Dublin) in an anonymous nation (presumably Ireland). The local setting remains a mid-century cipher, with vaguely described cul-de-sacs that isolate the estate from outside traffic. By contrast, after the novel's climax, when the narrator and protagonist, Elaine, moves to New York, the novel informs us of what neighborhood and even what street she lives on there. Likewise, we know by name what hotel her mother stays in when she visits Elaine during her years in culinary school in Paris. The lack of specificity in Ireland renders the home a distinct non-place, indistinct and interchangeable.

Augé's non-places tend to be spaces of transition, but he does include the housing estate, "where people do not live together and which is never situated in the centre of anything" (86–87). "The space of non-place creates neither singular identity nor relations; only solitude and similitude," (83) a characterization dovetailed with Elaine's description of her neighborhood as akin to "a ship, a big ship permanently anchored. A different group of passengers in each cabin. … huddle[ing] and whisper[ing] with their own little group, … look[ing] out on the same stagnant ocean" (38). Such a description captures the generic, identical qualities of a non-place, which bleed into a sort of non-time as well when we learn that the suburbanites perform identical chores in unison: "Bins are left out on Tuesday mornings. On Saturdays, cars are given their sponge baths. … On Sundays, lawnmowers rumble" (40). The absence of actors here gives the scene an agentless mechanical momentum, the self-propelled anthropomorphic lawnmowers merging technology and ghosts, as described by a girl confined to her bedroom—a gothic touch that underscores the uncanny dynamism of the trappings of suburbia.

The sense of endless, unchanging repetition is reinforced by the consistent tense throughout the novel. Dwyer Hickey controls the formal structure tightly, alternating chapters entitled "Winter Present" and "Summer Past," each narrative advancing sequentially, month by month, in chapter subtitles. The use of present tense in both eras produces a jarring effect that creates simultaneity between two periods separated by the rise and fall of the Celtic Tiger, belying any sense of teleological progress. And the novel is certainly concerned with questions of development: its plot hinges on a contemporary reopening of a long-suppressed neighborhood secret. We slowly learn that Elaine's friend Agatha, a blind girl with an absent father and distant mother, has become pregnant. The local teens develop an elaborate plan to help Agatha abort the fetus, a plan which goes awry, spurring Agatha to attempt the procedure on her own. She dies and the teens are scattered, Elaine moving to New York with an American mother and daughter who lived briefly in the estate.

Agatha's choice to attempt an abortion on her own supports the hypothesis of an Irish setting, as abortion in Ireland was—and remains—nearly entirely illegal. Using present tense highlights the parallels between the two periods and emphasizes how little Ireland has changed, particularly for women, a challenge to the narratives of progress or rise and fall often proffered about the Celtic Tiger, which is seen to conceal a fundamental stasis. The vague anonymity of the non-place housing estate that could be anywhere makes Agatha's tragedy itself overabundant, an accusation of what happens when supermodernity collides with a failure of modernity.[12]

The Lives of Women ends with Elaine's decision to return to New York, having written her version of events, which may or may not be the novel we've just read. It bleeds at this moment into a ghostly image: "There will still be those nights of waking suddenly to the sound of something scuttling: inside the wall, under the bed, on the far side of the ceiling. Bleats of shadow will inhabit my days. There but not there, caught but not caught, always one scurry beyond my line of vision" (278). The imagery here is of conflation: sound is light, a haunted space is also time, and nights are the same as days, which will themselves, in a final space-time compression, be inhabited. Further, the passage merges present into future tense, ending with a sentence devoid of verbs, and therefore of time or movement. Here we see that the alternating sections of the novel have been working in tandem with the plot's emphasis on lack of progress. Like Agatha's effort to abort her fetus in the novel, like Elaine's own stunted emotional fluency, the perpetual present and verbless future deny development. Elaine, unable after Agatha's death to forge any sort of emotional commitment, ends the novel alone—single and without offspring. Dwyer Hickey effectively critiques neoliberalism's authorized teleological narrative, showing in both the abortive pregnancy and in Elaine's own childless status at the novel's end that conventional goals aren't compulsory or desirable. *The Lives of Women* faults a public discourse that leaves women anonymous and essentialized in discussions about reproductive freedom, suggesting this insistence on silence is a continuous force in Irish culture.

Indeed, the novel itself succumbs to the pressures of silence. While Elaine makes reference to her rejection of the silences that shape the novel, Dwyer Hickey links her condemnation of Agatha's fate to an excoriation of a midcentury middle-class habitus, the non-place of the suburbs depicted as suited to evasion of responsibility. Place is faulted instead of an individual, or even a policy. In thus making a critique of neoliberalism's surface ideology, Dwyer Hickey remains indebted to its structural premises—actors are so embedded in their habitus as to be unable to escape or imagine alternatives —which in turn muffles her message. The explicit emergence in the final paragraph of the gothic (via the ghostly presence that will scurry ahead of Elaine's vision) is a trace of the unworkability of the neoliberal form, a parallel to the elliptical, underexplained storyline. The novel remains silent on several major plot points—who impregnates Agatha, most notably. There are a few faint hints in the novel that suggest that Mr. Shillman, a neighbor with diplomatic ties, is the unnamed figure Elaine sees having sex with Agatha, but the text declines to specify, just as it is never clear why Elaine herself is banished after the botched abortion, or why her father is such an elusive character. The loose ends and unresolved conclusion leave the reader uneasy, uncertain about how to assign agency or blame. In critiquing the official narrative of neoliberal progress, Dwyer Hickey nevertheless reinscribes avoidance, replicating a neoliberal norm in which there is no clear accountability.

"No difference between a man and his ghost..."

Enright's novel about the Madigan family, *The Green Road*, explores ideas about a lack of progress or denial of development via temporal shifts, as well as via recursive narrative sections and recurrent, if subtle, references to ghosts that defy spacetime. *The Green Road* is arranged into two sections that in themselves suggest an implosion of space and time. The first half of the novel is titled merely "LEAVING," a spatial gerund that embodies a paradox of ongoing departure. Each chapter within this section is titled with the name of a Madigan, a place, and a date; the dates advance chronologically. These chapters, structured like short stories, don't actually tell stories about departures from Ardeevin, the family home. A common thread is hard to discern, set as they are on three continents, from 1980 to 2005, with protagonists aged twelve to seventy-six. While each depicts a moment of isolation and loss, the valence of these losses varies. All are about self-knowledge—or more, the failure of each Madigan to achieve self-knowledge. Their collective climax comes in the chapter about Rosaleen, the mother, who feels suddenly and entirely like she is in the "wrong" home. "Rosaleen was living in the wrong house, with the wrong colours on the walls... where could you put yourself if you could not feel at home in your own home?" (165). The uncanny sensation moves Rosaleen to decide to sell her home. The solution to a feeling of wrongness appears then to be financial, and the "leaving" of the title comes to apply to all the Madigans; any idea that Rosaleen stood for what was being left is displaced by her own choice to sell up. Rather, what is being left is the temporal and spatial matrix of home, which we can infer, from the steady reflections on modernization in LEAVING, is representative of residual constructions of the Irish family and mode of living that ill suit the "cosmopolitan mobilities" of the new millennium.

Part two, "COMING HOME 2005," covers a few days in late December 2005, with a brief coda some months later. Enright begins with chapters whose titles are just place names—Toronto, Shannon Airport, Co. Dublin—shifting to more evocative, elusive titles: "The Hungry Grass"; "The Green Road" (a chapter comprising a series of short, unnamed chapters, not just section breaks); "Waking Up"; "The Eyes of the Buddha"; "Paying Attention." Some of these latter headings share the gerund format of the titles of the two parts of the novel, which provides a sense of ongoing activity but also creates a lack of symmetry. This jarring structural choice makes no meaningful distinction between place and time, with the effect of immersing Ireland fully in a global world as well as problematizing notions of linear progression.

Certainly the text from its outset undermines the processes by which humans seek to impose order: in its opening chapter, "Hanna, Ardeevin, Co. Clare 1980," Enright decouples space and time, beginning the novel with the word "Later" (3). Already looking forward, the novel recounts Rosaleen's reaction to an unwelcome announcement from her elder son, Dan, that he intends to study for the priesthood. Taking what Dan calls "the horizontal solution" (13), Rosaleen stays in bed for two weeks. Enright narrates this period—endless for twelve-year-old Hanna—via a recursive narration, in which the first paragraph of the novel is repeated in its entirety at the chapter's conclusion. This circularity sits in tension with the linearity of the horizontal solution and the tight geometry of the chapter, which is organized via two trips to the pharmacy and two trips to Galway, lovely structural parallels that still do not reconcile time into an easy progression. The narrative both relies upon and bridles against structure, as when Hanna feels "her uncle's eyes resting on her, and in them something like pity. Or joy" (6), a non-parallel comparison similar to Hanna's realization later that her mother's ideas were "either true or beside the point" (34). Such grammatically correct constructions remain semantically unresolved, an early hint at the novel's larger message that existing modes of communication are ill-fitted to their purpose. The narrator's efforts at knowledge and explanation are inadequate, as are the characters', not to mention those of the reader, who must also work circularly in trying to assemble a narrative logic.

For instance, we eventually discern that Rosaleen's withdrawal from the family arises as a consequence of her conviction that Dan is becoming a priest because he's gay; her re-emergence comes because she deduces (falsely, we learn later) that the existence of a girlfriend means he isn't gay. But there isn't a clear answer, a theme underscored when, amidst Rosaleen's weeping, her husband Pat leaves the dinner table and dessert's apple tart has to be cut differently. Dan immediately cuts it in fifths, rather than sixths with one left for Pat for later: "Five was a whole new angle, as he moved the cake slice through the ghost of a cross and then swung it eighteen degrees to the side. It was a prising open of the relations between them. It was a different story, altogether. As though these might be any number of Madigans and, out in the wide world, any number of apple tarts" (12). The infinite narratives and infinite possible selves multiply outward and forward throughout the novel, specters of potential stories untold.

LEAVING thus begins with domestic crisis and ends with the choice to sell the house—its temporal advance combined with lack of progress is emblematized by a clock in Rosaleen's chapter. She keeps thinking it is ten o'clock, only to recall, recurrently, that the "clock had been stopped for years, maybe five years" (153). The uncertainty about time intersects with the novel's persistent uncertainty about space. Staring at a wall painted a dusty rose (a color evocative of 80s décor), Rosaleen recalls "Under that was the 1970s terracotta, Tuscan Earth it was called, up on a chair herself, coat after coat of it, to cover the wallpaper beneath, fierce yellow repeats of geometric flowers that kept breaking through" (145–46). She cannot recall what is under the wallpaper but imagines a renovation that would replace the wall with glass. Via this speculative excavation that drills down to uncoverable flowers and ends with a fantasy of transparency, Enright stresses the persistence of the past and the idea of its resolution via spatial clarity.

But the uncanny undertones of the scene, with its irrepressible wallpaper— Charlotte Perkins Gilman offers a gothic intertext—assume an increasingly spatialized and menacing aspect as the evening drags: Rosaleen faces yet another night like so many before, aware of "something wrong with the house... Rosaleen was living in the wrong house, with the wrong colours on the walls...And where could you put yourself: if you could not feel at home in your own home? If the world turned into a series of lines and shapes, with nothing in the pattern to remind you what it was for" (165).[13] The fragmented final sentence sets forth a condition but no main clause, a grammatical incompleteness that indicates the emptiness of form and pattern without a goal. The recognition of the absence of meaning in the home makes the perception of space uncanny, driving Rosaleen to put herself elsewhere. As in "Hanna," "Rosaleen" organizes itself via Rosaleen's physical place in the world, the irruption of the gothic elements disrupting the seamless identification of woman with home, the references to decorating trends in particular serving to underscore how commodified such spaces already are.

Enright times the sale of the home just as the Irish housing market approaches its apogee—in the case of a used house in Ireland (outside Dublin), the average value increased from 1991 to 2007 by 489% (O'Callaghan et al. 125).[14] We witness the excesses of the economic peak in two Christmas Eve scenes—first, Constance's manic grocery shopping, which hits €410 even before she notices in the car park that she has to go back in for Brussels sprouts and ends up also buying butter for brandy butter, honey, foil, "potato salad, coleslaw, smoked salmon, mayonnaise, more tomatoes, litre bottles of fizzy drinks for the kids, kitchen roll, cling film, extra toilet paper, extra bin bags" (231), and fresh flowers, only realizing on her way home that she's forgotten the cornerstone of an Irish dinner, potatoes. Imagining herself "digging some out of a field, …with her hands in the earth, scrabbling for a few spuds," she raises "her head to howl" (232), these latter primitive reactions an index of Ireland's proximity to its terrestrial poverty, implying a heritage disavowed yet near at hand. A similar scene arises when Constance's siblings, Emmet and Hanna, enter the local pub and find all the patrons dyed, "dressed, clipped, groomed" (220); a place that "in their youth, smelt of wet wool and old men was now a gallery of scents, like walking through the perfume department in the Duty Free" (220-221). Enright juxtaposes past and present via the senses, culminating her descriptions with references to the non-places of the modern grocery store, with its array of global produce whatever the season, and an international airport lounge, another sign of a nation cut off from its past.

The story's climax comes at Christmas dinner, when Rosaleen, having previously announced her plan to sell the family home, further declares her intention to move in with Constance. Soon after Constance resists the latter pronouncement, "they heard Rosaleen's little car coughing into life outside and the wheels chewing the gravel" (255). As elsewhere throughout the novel, Rosaleen's possessions are animated, and indeed, when the next chapter shifts to Rosaleen as focalizer, "the car drove itself," stopping at "the edge of things" where [Rosaleen] "got a slightly sarcastic feel off the ditches…like the countryside was laughing at her" (261).[15] What follows this anthropomorphic awakening of the land and objects is a ghostly sequence in which Rosaleen senses the presence of her long-dead husband, Pat. Pat had spoken at length in courting her, but "grew silent with the years" (265). His early stories, steeped in folklore that blurs distinctions between living and dead, culminate with his promise to "worship her with his body, with his entire soul, until the day he died…. And that is the way he saw the land, with no difference between the different kinds of yesterday. No difference between a man and his ghost, between a real heifer and a cow that was waiting for the end of the world. It was all just a way of talking. It was the rise and fall in the telling, a rounding out before the finish" (263).

In this sequence, Enright first brings objects and landscape to life, then reanimates Pat Madigan. The non sequitur on which the passage hinges is the vow of lifelong devotion juxtaposed with a series of denials of difference. The implosion of temporal distinctions calls to mind Claire Bracken and Susan Cahill's insight that Enright "enacts a disruption of linear and chronological time, with past times interrupting and breaking 'open' the narratives" (7). Pat's stories of Ireland's mythic past, told in 1956, shape Rosaleen's interaction with the landscape in 2005, in a novel published in 2015. The four moments embedded within one another here parallel Enright's complex temporal shifts throughout the novel, in which each episode is set within multiple past moments, forming a novel of past progressives, of events that are temporally complete and yet psychologically ongoing—there is no differ-ence between the different kinds of yesterday. In this, Enright testifies yet again to the power of history to speak within present events; in choosing to set her story of Rosaleen's serendipitously canny real estate deal in 2005, Enright reminds readers that the economic highs of 2005 contained multiple yesterdays—of the previous decade's growth as well as the stagnation of the decades prior, not to mention the deep yesterday of the deprivations of hunger, evoked by Rosaleen's encampment overnight in the "little famine house" (278), a space suffused with ghostly domesticity and heavy with history. But by 2015, 2005 is itself another yesterday, one that cannot be ignored or downplayed by those emerging from the recession. Ireland cannot absolve itself from the materialism of the Boom, nor treat the dismal after-math as disconnected from what came before. At the same time, the variety of yesterdays here contests neoliberal notions of teleology, a cautionary warning for a nation eager to move past its recent recession—if there is no difference among the different kinds of yesterday, then no narrative of progress can downplay or obscure those moments that challenge fantasies of an upward trajectory.

As the frantic search for Rosaleen escalates, Enright stages a series of historically fraught images but inflects their traditional resonances with a further flattening of time. First, Rosaleen sees "a satellite moving through a delicacy of stars above her, and it was as though she could sense the earth's turning" (280), an image of modernity amid circularity that lulls her to sleep. She wakes to a "huge noise like a plane taking off in her ear. The plane reversed, and then it went forward again. Reversed. There was a cow on the other side of the wall, breathing, tearing a few mouthfuls of midnight grass" (280). Not only does the scene conflate a cow with a plane, the rural with the modern, the animal with the mechanical—it also characterizes its movement as an alternation back and forth, akin to the rotation of the satellite and earth. Progress is an illusion caused by the world spinning, by looking too narrowly at a moment in time—long-wave economic cycles cannot be seen in the granular analysis of a neoliberal present.

Much as time becomes broadened by Rosaleen's night in the famine cottage, place does as well. Once she is discovered, while they await the gurney that will carry Rosaleen to the ambulance, Dan, her favorite child, comforts her with a series of wry remarks. First he mocks displays of affluence by their in-laws: "'real coffee is where the McGraths are at these days'" (288); also "'Bollinger in the boot. I kid you not. *Where will it end*, that's what I say'" (288). These remarks extend the novel's critique of consumption at the same time as they gesture to Ireland's increasingly globalized way of life, using a vernacular of space-time compression. Next, captivated by the way the moon "lifted the landscape to his eyes … the most beautiful road in the world, bar none" (288), Dan makes the curious comment that "'You could be anywhere'" (288). In an odd slippage, the extremely local beauty becomes generalized, just when the text's focalization slides from Dan's reflections on how little his mother has seen of the world into Rosaleen's own conflation of this road with one in Amalfi, where "she had a little glass of limoncello, free at the end of the meal" (288). The collective consciousness of the Madigans thus emerges not as an elemental force of the Irish landscape—although this space has unearthed it—but as a timeless non-place of its own, inflected and shaped by consumption. Memory is not a sanctified national treasure but a construct of commodity exchange.

Enright thereby returns to a well-rehearsed space in the west of Ireland, writing about it free of its well-worn tropes. *Road* disallows an easy reconnection with the land and the past as a solution to the alcoholism, cancer, self-centeredness, and emotional coldness that complicate the Madigans' relationships with their mother. Rather, Rosaleen's night in the crumbling cottage underscores the falsity of attempts to escape the complexities of the family past, and by metonymic extension, the national past. The references to hungry grass and other signs of history are swiftly displaced by space-time compression, itself succeeded by a bidding war and swift sale of the Ardeevin house. While the sale is lucrative, and Rosaleen shares the proceeds with her children, all the novel's interpersonal relationships remain fraught and unresolved. Just as the nation learned it could not borrow its way out of economic crisis, the Madigans discover they cannot spend their way out of family crisis. In setting the novel at the moment when Ardeevin can yield the greatest profits, Enright proclaims how little difference such a windfall makes.

The novel's solution to this dilemma of neoliberalism—the false promises of personal gratification through upward mobility—is tentative, structured in a forward-and-reverse movement akin to that of the plane-cow. In the brief chapters that act as coda, each Madigan has moments of emotional growth staged via visual metaphors: Emmet takes to heart the idea of the Buddha whose eyes are painted last, using a mirror to avoid a direct gaze: he reaches out to the girlfriend he loved in Mali, with the effect that he "listened to his life opening" (298). Similarly, Dan makes amends to someone he hurt with his indifference during the AIDS epidemic in the early 90s, and Hanna, though unable to overcome her alcoholism, has happy moments with her partner and their child. Most indicative of the novel's embrace of incomplete progress is Rosaleen's own concluding chapter. Titled "Paying Attention," it shows her acting with characteristic egocentrism, taking Constance's cancer diagnosis as a personal affront and fleeing Clare. She arrives in Emmet's suburban Dublin home and sits alongside Denholm, his Kenyan lodger, noticing, apparently for the first time, that people with black skin have lighter palms. The novel ends with her apology to Denholm, in a sentence that feels weighted down by symbolism and the looming crisis: "'I have paid too little attention,' she said. 'I think that's the problem. I should have paid more attention to things'" (310). There *was* an alternative, in contrast to prevailing neoliberal convictions.

In contrast to Dwyer Hickey's haunted future, Enright's novel closes with a past participle, a suggestion that there could have been a different path; the gerund in the chapter title may also imagine change, an understanding of difference that makes very tentative steps towards addressing the inequality that brings Denholm to Dublin. Awareness acts as a means of resistance within neoliberalism, though without clear promise of meaningful change.

"Nothing is past. Everything is tense."

Kilroy's novel, more overtly gothic than the two considered thus far, is also more overt in its indictment of Ireland's elite in the country's economic crisis. *Devil* tells its allegorical story via reliance on such gothic tropes as baroque setting, dissipated aristocracy, and supernatural forces: the last in a line of Ascendancy scions, Tristram St. Lawrence returns in 2006 to the crumbling castle where he grew up, entering into real-estate deals of increasingly high stakes with his old schoolmate Hickey, members of Dublin's political-economic elite, and a mysterious figure known as M. Deauville. Published in 2012 but set in 2016, the novel, like Enright's, reflects back through multiple embedded time frames upon the period prior to the economic crash. In Kilroy's case, the final frame is a speculative one as her novel is set in the future, timed to coincide with the centenary of the Easter Rising that Ireland celebrated in April 2016. Structured as what at first appears to be a trial but turns out to be merely a fact-finding hearing, the book reflects and implicates Ireland's own incomplete, ineffectual efforts to come to terms with its spectacular boom and subsequent crash. The shadowy M. Deauville, never seen by anyone except Tristram, reveals himself to be the devil, if he even exists. Deauville initially appears to be Tristram's Alcoholics Anonymous sponsor, with the suggestion that substance abuse is akin to the type of rash investment addiction seen in himself and other characters, who giddily pursue property acquisitions in days-long benders. The implication is that Ireland is tempted into extravagant, imprudent investments by the very forces that ought to serve as stabilizers.

Well beyond the spectral Deauville, the novel is laced with references to the supernatural. A faithful old servant, Larney, converses with Tristram throughout the novel but is actually already dead. Tristram himself is assumed by many of the characters to have died. There's even some hint that he may be already/still dead during the novel's events—he is repeatedly referred to as "uncanny." This term first crops up at the moment that Tristram, whose death was recorded in a Belgian hospital following an overdose, suddenly revives. But its more consistent and continuous appearance comes alongside characterizations of Tristram's status as conduit. By profession he is a translator, a job he explains as requiring him to be "hollow ... a perfect conduit" (6), a comparison that gains force when he notes its parallel to how capital moves through the shell company Deauville creates, (73) such that later in the novel, "Money moved through me as freely as languages" (231). The interchangeability of the two systems of signs—money and language—indicates the imaginative, alchemical dimension of finance, as well as construing translators and finance as non-places. Tristram repeats several times that uncanny is a term used by others, an unnamed "they," about him. "That was the word [they] used" (6, 73, 231). The indefinite pronoun itself acts as both a conduit and empty signifier, opening space for Tristram to be constructed by others.

In this way, the uncanny becomes the intertextual; Tristram exists as a combination of acts of imagination by others. His full name is Tristram Amory St. Lawrence, a name with historical and fictional antecedents: Armoricus Tristam, a conquering Norman who adopted the name St. Lawrence in honor of the feast day of the Norman victory, built Howth Castle in the twelfth century, where the fictional Tristram lives. As the novel overtly references with its opening page, which reproduces the first two sentences of *Finnegans Wake*, James Joyce equated Howth with his protagonist, HCE, converting the original Armoricus Tristam to "Sir Tristram, violer d'amores" (Kilroy vii). Joyce's heavily intertextual novel of course gestures towards *Tristram Shandy*, itself also an extensive reflection on the circularity of time and paradoxes of narration. Furthermore, Kilroy bestows the middle name Amory, also the first name of F. Scott Fitzgerald's protagonist in *This Side of Paradise*. Amory Blaine, like Tristram, is a wealthy, self-destructive mama's boy. Kilroy's contribution to the character is his pedigree as thirteenth earl of Howth (historically, the title is extinct). In using a defunct earldom, Kilroy creates an occult genealogy for her tale of greed and excess. Goethe's *Faust* offers another clear intertext for Kilroy, given the novel's ongoing references to property speculation as alchemy. *Devil* projects a vision of the contemporary economy as magically generating wealth.[16] The accumulated intertexts, from Sterne to Goethe to Joyce, work to resist the relentless pressure of the present, providing history and grounding in opposition to neoliberalism's present of non-places and empty conduits.

Devil's domestic topography functions as a history of the plutocracy in Ireland, spanning an ancient castle housing titled aristocrats, a Big House now devoid of its Anglo-Irish gentry, and a sprawling modern suburban ranch home. Such varied domestic spaces seem for much of the novel to be peripheral to the plot, however, which focuses on investment properties: tracts to be developed into more homes, hotels, flats, skyscrapers. The new construction featured in *Devil* is sleek, modern, and anodyne, part of the push to reconceive Dublin within global metropolitan supermodernity. When Tristram and Hickey go to secure financing for a hotel they seek to build, they travel to a district peppered with skyscrapers all "built of the same jade glass," entering a boardroom that "occupied the penthouse suite of one of the glass towers. A panorama of cranes spanning the horizon was engaged in a courtly dance" (138). An architectural model of the proposed hotel project is set out for display: "The skyscraper hotel closely resembled the building we had assembled in, which in turn resembled the building next to it, and the building next to it again, and so on throughout the docklands and across to the opposite bank of the Liffey. Those dollar-green towers were a contagion that had ripped through Dublin" (139). The initial description of the skyscrapers references jade, cranes, and courtly dancing, a decidedly Orientalist undertone evoking the Asian Tiger antecedents of the Celtic Tiger, an image supplanted by the sequential accumulation of buildings now compared to spreading disease and to dollars, the elegant dance replaced by a violent gash. This latter image of the skyscraper as defacement, associated with Americanness and a blotting out of local culture, brings the image in line with the non-place of the boardroom, where later on, Tristram, Hickey, and their investors will go on a multi-day, multi-continental acquisition binge, buying—in a conflation of space and time—properties they will never see, places that are money, not locations.

Throughout the novel, past, present, and future dissolve into one another, not just in Tristram's indeterminate vitality, but also in Kilroy's shifts of verb tense. "I don't know why I'm talking about all of this in past tense. Nothing is past. Everything is tense" (33).[17] Tristram's pun highlights the fundamental unease that accompanies a sense of unfixed time, but it also suggests the paradoxes that underlie the act of narration itself. As another mode of invention, like alchemy or real estate speculation, fiction is laced through with its own illogicality. Later, in his testimony offered on the ominously titled "Final day of evidence 24 MARCH 2016" (337), Tristram notes that "nothing can conclude matters for me" (353). On the one hand, the word "final" incontrovertibly implies an end, while Tristram's remark invokes the endless, inescapable recurrence hinted at by his name.

Indeed, the novel's mode is not eternity but circularity: Binswanger notes that *Faust* predicts financial boom-and-bust economic cycles; Kilroy's reader is also able to foresee Tristram's downfall. But for all of our anticipation and insight, the novel ends without resolution on the legal and financial front—its closure comes from the enforced suicide of the protagonist at the requisition of the devil. Although foretold, this suicide is not within the novel—the future events themselves have speculative outcomes in the even further future. In this flattening of temporal difference, Kilroy moves gradually into present tense via a series of declarative sentences that seem to pressure the narrative to leave past tense narration aside: "Deauville had come to collect. A debt must be settled. That is the nature of a debt. The Devil linked my arm and we began the descent. I closed my eyes but my eyes would not close. They would not close. I tried and tried. I'll keep trying. I must keep trying. I can only keep trying. I am afraid of what I will see." (361). The doxa here about how debts function—itself a neoliberal analysis of macroeconomics that stands in contrast to the Keynsian model that prevailed throughout much of the twentieth century—is conveyed in brief, syntactically straightforward sentences as though to emphasize its austere truth. Such an oversimplification stands in contrast to the recognitions earlier in the novel, via intertextual references, of the intersectional complications of global finance and national history. The unworkability of the narrative of an easy exit from debt via austerity is revealed in the text's move through such simple sentences into a Beckettian language that links Tristram's journey to the persistence and repetitions of the past. The novel oscillates in its close between a critique of neoliberalism via a strategic intertextuality and a surrender to the pressures exerted by the endless present.

The novel falls somewhat short of its target in its adoption of the AA movement's rhetoric of powerlessness to characterize the addictive properties of speculation, which gives the events leading up to the crash a feeling of inevitability. Also troubling is Tristram's belated realization that he has been blind to his beloved Edel's treachery. Edel, Hickey's wife and Tristram's lover, is revealed to have been the acquisitive mastermind who stripped Tristram's family home of its artefacts. While Edel's acquisitive eye—she steals a valuable chandelier from Tristram's Big House ruin—breaks the association of women with an uncommodified domesticity, her cliché role as temptress, like the very role of the devil, absolves Tristram of some responsibility for his downfall. Both choices suggest a neoliberal narrative of inescapability.

Nevertheless, the novel's overt critique of property speculators, corrupt ministers, and feckless bankers, as well as of the toothless fact-finding enquiry that structures the narrative, is mirrored by a critique of the Irish public itself. Recurrent efforts to expose truth or indict wrongdoing meet with no change, progress, or even outrage; Tristram's efforts to shed light have no effect on the Easter Rising Centenary getting underway at the novel's close. The Irish public is implicated via its absence, a ghostly populace who appears only to engage in frantic bidding wars to inhabit the non-place flats Hickey constructs. Like Enright's narrative, *Devil* reveals the futility of insight without meaningful break-through or change. The judge overseeing the hearing is never heard to speak, and the format in which Tristram merely offers testimony acts as a recording of history as though it is unchangeable. The postdated setting in particular underscores the way in which the critique of neoliberalism is in tension with the novel's narrative mode: we are made to think there is no alternative, even about time that has not yet passed.

Conclusion: T.I.N.A.?

Felix Martin's "unauthorized biography" *Money* defines its subject as a "social technology" (27). In contending that we can best understand the nature of money via examination of "episodes of acute monetary disorder in modern times" (22), he offers the case study of the closure of Irish banks during a six-month strike in 1970. Amazingly, in what was at that point one of the 30 wealthiest economies in the world, a personalized system of credits and debts, transacted largely through pubs and a few un-unionized banks, substituted for the institutionalized banking system. Martin's moral is about the importance of creditworthiness, which in Ireland in 1970, was established and confirmed very locally, over a pint of stout. My interest is in the fact that the story is largely unremembered, disregarded because it did not conform to the dominant story of the Irish economy's meteoric rise. Martin emphasizes the size and robustness of the Irish economy in 1970, a contradiction of myths of origin casting Ireland as a stagnant backwater. The incident suggests as well that frantic efforts to "save the banks" in the United States and Europe in 2008 relied on false assumptions of their centrality and necessity. While society functioned for 6 months in 1970 without banks, one lesson of 2008 is that it was the banks that could not function without society.

As much as this anecdote repudiates the hagiographies of free-flowing capital and affirms the value of the local and the collective, the context of its reception shows how successful the narratives of growth and globalization have been. That banks need a social safety net accentuates a glaring weakness in neoliberal ideology: the self-actualized individual, operating free of institutional support or constraint, is an utter fabrication. Each novel here reveals the poverty of this model of individualism. Similarly, they reject the idea of discrete moments in time, refusing to accept any narrative of linear time that locates the boom and recession as a distinct moment in Irish history, asserting instead an ongoingness. All three place the home at the center of their analyses of the relationship of past to present, particularly in relation to notions of development and change, critiquing the Tiger for promising progress but failing to provide change. The materiality of the home is in tension with its intangible monetary value, and the imaginary and intangible have the ability to destroy the real.

As we have seen, what distinguishes a novel in neoliberalism from a neoliberal novel—at least in Ireland, post-boom—is the degree to which it offers resistance to the present. While all three novels under consideration push back against official narratives of progress and teleology, all three also dip to varying degrees into a form I here call the Neoliberal Present, a paradoxical position of resistance to the naturalization of Williams' "plutocratic imagination" that nevertheless finds itself indebted to a mode of narration that stresses intractability and inevitability.

To be fair, none of the novels above is complicit in depicting an Irish neoliberal present as inescapable; nevertheless, the reconfigured home and recourse to individual agency structure each resolution. *The Lives of Women* pointedly critiques the combination of Irish traditionalism with the mechanized, uncontrollable social climate, but it also suggests there are no responses except death, capitulation, or escape. Elaine does not attempt to change her father or her estate, instead "choosing" to leave, the novel's persistent present tense underscoring the limitations Dwyer Hickey presents and accedes to. *The Devil I Know* also offers a clear indictment of the mix of Ireland's longstanding social inequality with the unfettered flow of capital throughout a world viewed through the lenses of investment and profit. In turning her tale into a medieval morality play, however, and rendering the story via testimony in present and future tense of a powerless witness, Kilroy's novel ultimately accepts the things it cannot change. Even Enright's novel, with its more tensually complex "should have," which is able to link its critiques of the Irish past and the Celtic Tiger present to the possibility of new ways of seeing, expresses pessimism about an exit from its condition. Enright's recognition of how little people change suggests a limited escape from the compulsion to repeat, but the idea of the many possible Madigans, the eyes of the Buddha, the final understanding of humanity and racial difference within Ireland itself—this coincidence of small changes gestures towards localized resistances, assertions of individual humanity instead of individual responsibility.

Despite the anxieties about meaningful intervention, current fiction by women affirms the central role of Irish fiction in not just representing the crisis but in shaping cultural ideas about home and time. If previous constructions of these concepts in Ireland helped to fuel the boom, the cautionary notes about non-place in each novel, as well as the assertion of the need to "pay attention" suggest how to read and talk about time and inequality.

Notes

1. Coulter and Nagle, 5.
2. See Buchanan, "Home of the Tiger," for analysis of this dynamic during the Celtic Tiger.
3. Cahill names John Banville, Fintan O'Toole, and, especially, Julian Gough as embodying this line of thought. Jason Buchanan tracks responses to the crisis in a pair of excellent articles, noting "Along with [Anne] Haverty and [Donal] Ryan, Claire Kilroy, Gavin Corbett, Anne Enright, Barry McCrea, John Kelly, Deidre Madden, Colin Barrett, Declan Burke, Hugo Hamilton, Catherine Brophy, John Mulligan, and Conor McPherson have all written about the effects of the Celtic Tiger" (Article Draft).
4. Joe Cleary, David Lloyd, and most recently, Seamus O'Malley all examine theories as to why there is no Irish *Middlemarch* in the nineteenth century. See Lloyd's discussion of the "crisis of representation" (6) and Cleary's suggestion that "There has been a distinct

tendency … to identify realism with Englishness, and to identify the Irish novelist tradition …as inherently 'fantastic' or 'anti-realist'" (49).

5. Fiction about Tiger era being written by women was also dismissed as consumerist chick lit, part of the larger project to fault women for excessive consumption—see Bracken on a "caricature of middle-class Irish womanhood… as materialistic, self-absorbed and shallow" (170).

6. WReC is a collaborative group of scholars based at the University of Warwick and particularly focused on theorizations of a world literary system.

7. In a further irony, Ireland now faces a housing shortage.

8. At a time when economics becomes the basis of culture and yet is presented as too complicated for most people to understand, popular cultural narratives feature heavily fictionalized, magical escapes for individuals whilst the overall system remains in place, as I have written about recent British novels and films (McGlynn).

9. I draw the term "instantaneous" from John Urry (2000: 105). He links this idea to "timeless time" (105) and (2007: 121) "desynchronization" in his characterization of the contemporary lived experience of time.

10. In 2010, "amazingly, an actual majority of novels on the Booker longlist were written in the present tense. It is everywhere in the English novel, like Japanese knotweed" (Hensher).

11. 2010 seems to be when everyone noticed all the present tense novels: see, for instance, http://www.theguardian.com/books/booksblog/2010/sep/14/present-tense-narration. A scan of recent Irish novels shows an uptick of present tense—it comprises the baseline narration of *Winterland* and *Frog Music*; it ends *Red Sky In Morning*, by Paul Lynch, and recurs frequently in McCann's *Transatlantic*, Joseph O'Connor's *Ghost Light*, and French's *The Secret Place*. It might be argued that the dominance of present tense reflects the cultural preponderance of the instantaneous.

12. Dwyer Hickey hereby represents the sort of "uneven development" that the WReC argues is constitutive of "a situation in which capitalist forms and relations exist alongside 'archaic forms of economic life' and pre-existing social and class relations" (11).

13. It is possible, of course, that the fragment merely restates the question in the previous sentence, though its lack of question mark suggests Enright seeks to do more. The fragment registers an intertextual resonance with Bloom's musing in the "Hades" episode of Joyce's *Ulysses*: "If we were suddenly all somebody else," a reflection which acknowledges the relativity of individual subjectivity, suggesting, as does Enright, the illusion of individuality by paralleling the subject to a sentence fragment that has only a subject.

14. As a point of comparison, the change in US home prices in the same period was about 116%.

15. Claire Bracken notes that cars also function as organisms in both *What Are You Like?* and *The Gathering*. Certainly Enright's fascination with the uncanny precedes the economic crisis, repeatedly signaling a discomfort with objects.

16. Hans Christoph Binswanger notes about *Faust*, "It is not vital to alchemy's aim, in the sense of increasing wealth, that lead be actually transmuted into gold. It will suffice if a substance of no value is transmuted into one of value: paper, for example, into money… if a genuine value creation is possible … not bound by any limits and is therefore, in this sense, sorcery or magic" (9). *Faust* Volume two is particularly interested in massive development; see Marshall Berman's *All That is Solid Melts into Air*.

17. Another intertextual echo here, of Faulkner's oft-quoted "The past is never dead. It's not even the past" *(Requiem for a Nun).*

Works Cited

Augé, Marc. *Non-Places: An Introductions to Supermodernity*. New York: Verso, 2008. Print.

Binswanger, Hans Christoph. *Money and Magic: A Critique of the Modern Economy in the Light of Goethe's Faust*. Chicago: U of Chicago P, 1994. Print.

Bracken, Claire. "Postfeminism and the Celtic Tiger: Deirdre O'Kane's Television Roles." *Viewpoints: Theoretical Perspectives on Irish Visual Texts*. Eds. Claire Bracken and Emma Radley. Cork: Cork University Press, 2013. 157–71. Print.

Buchanan, Jason. "Gentrification as Famine." Article draft.

——. "The Home of the Tiger: Economic Speculation and the Ethics of Habitation." *Studi irlandesi: A Journal of Irish Studies*. No. 3(2013): 137–56. Print.

Cahill, Susan. *Irish Literature in the Celtic Tiger Years 1990-2008: Gender, Bodies, Memory*. London: Continuum, 2011. Print.

Cleary, Joseph. *Outrageous Fortune: Capital and Culture in Modern Ireland*. Derry: Field Day, 2006. Print.

Cohn, Dorrit. *The Distinction of Fiction*. Baltimore: John Hopkins UP, 1999. Print.

Coulter, Colin, and Angela Nagle. *Ireland under austerity: neoliberal crisis, neoliberal solutions*. Manchester: Manchester UP, 2015. Print.

Dwyer Hickey, Christine. *The Lives of Women*. London: Atlantic, 2015. Print.

Enright, Anne. *The Green Road*. New York: Norton, 2015. Print.

French, Tana. *Broken Harbor*. Dublin: Hachette, 2012. Print.

——. *The Secret Place*. New York: Viking, 2014. Print.

Gass, William. "A Failing Grade for the Present Tense." *The New York Times*. Books: October 11, 1987. Print.

Hensher, Phillip. "The Booker judges should take a stand against the modish present tense." *The Telegraph*. 9 September 2010. http://www.telegraph.co.uk/culture/books/7991553/Opinion-Philip-Hensher.html Accessed 25 April 2016.

Lloyd, David. *Anomalous States: Irish Writing and the Post-Colonial Moment*. Durham: Duke UP, 1993. Print.

Lynch, Paul. *Red Sky Morning*. New York: Back Bay, 2014. Print.

Martin, Felix. *Money*. New York: Vintage, 2013. Print.

McCann, Colum. *TransAtlantic*. New York: Random House, 2013. Print.

McGlynn, Mary. "Representations of Collectivism and the Thatcher Years." *Twentieth-Century Literature* 62.3 (September 2016): 309–36. Print.

Negra, Diane. "Adjusting Men and Abiding Mammies: Gendering the Recession in Ireland." *Irish Review* 46 (2013). 23–34. Print.

O'Malley, Seamus. "Populism, the Land League, and United Ireland: George Moore's *Drama in Muslin*. " Presentation to the Columbia University Seminar for Irish Studies, 2 December 2016.

Urry, John. *Mobilities*. Cambridge: Polity, 2007. Print.

——. *Sociology Beyond Societies*. London: Routledge, 2000. Print.

Waldron Neumann, Anne. "Time of History? Present Tense and the Occasion of Narration in J. M. Coetzee's *Waiting for the Barbarians*. " *The Journal of Narrative Technique*, Vol. 20, No. 1 (Winter, 1990): 65–86. Print.

Williams, Jeffrey. "The Plutocratic Imagination (On Contemporary American Fiction)." *Dissent* (Winter 2013): 93–97. Print.

Warwick Research Collective (WReC). *Combined and Uneven Development: Towards a New Theory of World-Literature*. Liverpool: Liverpool UP, 2015. Print.

Transformative Tales for Recessionary Times: Emma Donoghue's *Room* and Marian Keyes' *The Brightest Star in the Sky*

Margaret O'Neill

Introduction: Recessionary Times

Emma Donoghue's *Room* and Marian Keyes' *The Brightest Star in the Sky* represent two bestselling works of fiction in post-Celtic Tiger Ireland. They were published in light of the dramatic social and economic change of the previous twenty years, which saw Ireland become one of the wealthiest countries in the world, followed by economic crisis and one of the most severe austerity policies in Europe. In the 1990s, the economic boom known as the Celtic Tiger saw rapid economic growth and high levels of employment. This arose out of neoliberal ideology, an economic model that centralizes the free market and individual responsibility over State intervention and public services. Under these principles, foreign investment and property speculation, exacerbated by reckless lending and a lack of government oversight, fuelled the boom. In the context of global economic recession, the collapse of the property bubble and the bailout of the banking sector by the Irish State in 2008 caused a crisis in public finances. The resulting negative equity, mortgage arrears, rising unemployment and cutbacks in public services, intensified by stringent austerity measures, saw a devastating effect on Irish society, especially its most vulnerable members.[1] Published in the height of the recession, Donoghue's *Room* and Keyes' *Brightest Star* provide insight into the immediate aftermath of the bailout, the early years of austerity, and its effects on a society still absorbing the shock of the downturn.

Room, a text that echoes the stringent measures of Ireland's austerity policy and holds cultural resonance within the global context of recession, illustrates the violence inflicted by neoliberal systems of economic and social repression. The tale is one of five-year-old Jack, the narrator, and his mother "Ma." Imprisoned by the sexual predator Old Nick in an 11-by-11-foot backyard shed known to Jack as "Room," the family is completely dependent on their cruel captor for survival. Actually born in Room, Jack has never been outside. When he turns five, Ma begins to explain the world to him, which he cannot comprehend until after his "Great Escape." As with so much of Jack's reality, Ma describes their escape plan by referencing the world of TV—in this case, the World War II prisoner of war epic, *The Great Escape*. Within Room, Ma creates a magical world through games and storybooks, which, though shaped out of terrible necessity, provides a warm and loving home for Jack. In the outside world, paradoxically, neoliberal governance seeks to mould Ma and Jack through biopolitical control, seen, for example, in the lurid reaction of the media to Jack's "different" body, as well as in dominant discourses of gender asserted through materialist culture. Moving from one home to another, Jack's disorientation, and the unsettling effect he has on observers can be described in light of Sara Ahmed's queer phenomenology, as a "migrant orientation." That is, "the lived experience of facing at least two directions: toward a home that has been lost, and to a place that is not yet home" (2006b, 10). As *Room* demonstrates, Jack's queer orientation—gazing at what is behind him as he moves into the future, resisting social pressure to look forward and not back—opens the possibility of discovering other life paths beyond the biopolitical recreation of the neoliberal subject. In an outside world endorsing austereness and "hard" feelings, different or "soft" emotions such as the love and terror Jack associates with Room hold the potential to leave a new mark on the world and inform generative social and ethical possibilities.

Brightest Star tells the stories of the lives and loves of couples and singletons living in flats in an old Georgian house in Dublin. Although not imprisoned in a physical sense, the characters, especially the couple Maeve and Matt, are trapped in a number of ways.[2] Maeve and Matt live in negative equity due to the economic downturn. Taking anti-depressants to get through the day, they have stopped engaging with life, family, and intimacy in their relationship with each other. The reader eventually learns that an ex-boyfriend has raped Maeve and the Director of Public Prosecutions has failed to bring charges. Maeve and Matt deal with their unprocessed trauma and their horror over her ex-boyfriend's ability to rape Maeve and suffer no consequences by self-medicating, which allows them to attempt to minimize feeling emotions like sadness and despair. Similar to *Room*, therefore, the space of this Georgian house is subject to economic and social controls. As these controls are realised through norms of self-investment and hegemonic speech acts, *Brightest Star* shows how subjects come to embody the contradictions of neoliberalism. For example, characters are drawn to the plethora of market choices—such as the paraphernalia seemingly "required" to rear babies—positioned as a mode of self-expression in a materialist culture that, in actuality, is totalizing and homogenizing. Intertwining a dark fairytale narrative, *Brightest Star* further emphasizes the sinister side of neoliberal pathways, implying, in an allusion to *Snow White*, for example, that the "juicy red apple" is not all that it seems (543). In this magical realm,

Brightest Star draws attention to a neoliberal culture that seeks to hide the very emotions that it produces, and the text reactively subverts daily life, lending support to a new moral economy. Ultimately, Maeve and Matt are exhorted to leave their "bad feelings" in the past and look ahead, investing their hopes for the future in the figure of a child who embodies the promise of happiness. However, as Ahmed argues, "it is the very assumption that good feelings are open and bad feelings are closed that allows historical forms of injustice to disappear" (2010, 50). Indeed, a return to the subjects "who refuse to let go of suffering" might offer "an alternative model of the social good" (Ahmed, 2010, 50). In this light, this essay argues that while *Brightest Star* compellingly attends to the social and economic injustices imposed on subjects under neoliberalism and appeals for a more equal society, these critiques are ultimately subsumed into a heteronormative fantasy that preserves straight lines of direction on a neoliberal life course.

Together, *Room* and *Brightest Star* provide an important site to explore the popular imaginings of the post-Celtic Tiger recession. By interspersing its readings rather than focus on the two novels separately, this study creates a dialogue between the texts, thereby expanding our understanding of contemporary women's writing as it responds to and explores the post-Celtic Tiger years. This is especially pertinent given that popular fiction, an understudied scholarly area of Irish fiction, has been prominent in representing dominant narratives of femininity and masculinity and the excesses of the Celtic Tiger era.[3] Novelist, playwright and literary historian Donoghue is a critically acclaimed, Man Booker Prize shortlisted author, while novelist, short story, and non-fiction writer Keyes is one of Ireland's most successful writers of popular fiction. It is productive to consider these texts alongside one another not only in light of their shared preoccupations but also in view of their comparative international success. An international bestseller on its publication in 2010, *Room* has sold well over two million copies, in 35 languages.[4] Widely acclaimed, it won numerous honours and awards and, in 2015, was adapted to a successful film shortlisted for four Academy Awards, with Brie Larson winning Best Actress for her role as Ma. To date, Keyes' novels have all been bestsellers around the world, selling over 30 million copies, in 33 languages.[5] *Brightest Star*, Keyes' 2009 novel, has been adapted into 11 languages, forthcoming in four more.[6] Comparative to *Room*, then, a rough estimate puts *Brightest Star* at two million copies sold.

This essay reads these works side-by-side to consider their insights into the national, gendered subject under the politics of austerity and to illuminate the ways in which characters re-shape these constructions to undercut the social and political forces that seek to control and exploit them. Central to these readings, this article foregrounds the usefulness of a queer methodology in the process of uncovering a compelling alternative to the political imaginary of the neoliberal State. It is notable that these texts illustrate the power of resistance in everyday life: for example, in opposition to consumerism in *Room*, every object has a purpose, and in local activism in *Brightest Star*, wherein Maeve and Matt take part in a public rally protesting the low conviction rate for rapists. In these moments of defiance, characters stand together in relationship and in solidarity with others. In this way, the texts resist the championing of individualism under neoliberalism. Foregrounding the potential for transformation through emotion, uncovered in the realm of the imaginary and in the face of injustice and exclusion, together these novels challenge the discourses that situate the body as a site of control. In connection with this experimentation, both *Room* and *Brightest Star* represent the figure of the child as mode of negotiating the past in the present and envisioning the future. A queer phenomenological perspective shows that each text draws attention to different directionality, with *Room* emphasising a refusal to align to cultural expectations. As close readings of these narratives bear out, neoliberalism operates to exclude difference and commercialize stereotypes under the guise of individual freedom. The normalizing operations of neoliberal ideology, as they direct subjects on a life course, therefore require a sustained heteronormative critique. Such an approach provides for recognising alternative social forms and new pathways that might otherwise be hidden from view.

Language and the Violence of Neoliberalism

In their exploration of language, *Room* and *Brightest Star* represent the discourses of neoliberalism in the public sphere as lurid and unfeeling. Cultural critics Michael Cronin, Debbie Ging, and Peadar Kirby, in their introduction to *Transforming Ireland: Challenges, Critiques, Resources*, refer to the managerial Newspeak of Irish life. A term drawn from George Orwell's *Nineteen Eighty-Four*, Newspeak is a controlled language devised to meet the needs of the totalitarian state Oceania. In neoliberalism, the corporate language of business and economics is applied indiscriminately across the public sector. For example, it is employed in health, education and the arts, where patients and students are "consumers," facilities are "world-class" and every board has a "strategic plan" (Cronin, Kirby and Ging, 4–5). The language and perceptions of the elite and powerful thus become a universal structuring language for all. In *Brightest Star*, the reductive nature of media language can be observed in the whitewashing of gardener-turn-TV-personality Fionn's gift with gardening and herbal healing. His foster mother Jemima, quoting from the pitch, states that the new TV show will provide "'An entire support system for our twenty-first-century lifestyle.' ... 'Our lives are moving ever faster, but we have a need to get back to the land. The buzzwords are *Fresh! Organic! Grow your own!*'" (70). This language markets the show as a promise of self-definition through ethical choices in a homogenizing market, whereas in actuality the show is ascribing and universalizing a lifestyle. Testifying to the force of neoliberal ideology, Fionn is swept up in the celebrity culture of the show. His magical gift of healing is commodified and then erased in a totalizing corporate and media world.

Connectedly, emotion is also harnessed and used for profit in the charged atmosphere of the neoliberal workplace. For example, it is evident in the hegemonic, masculine language and behavior of the sales industry. The text illustrates such public worlds and connections as empty; similar to Fionn's TV show, they contain only fabricated feelings. Matt, a young salesperson pressured to live up to this hegemonic ideal, "burst into the room where the men were waiting and launched into growly, good-humored noises. 'Yah-haaahh! How's it going?' … He was grabbing shoulders and giving them friendly shakes and doing gentle shoving and pushing. That was the way Matt did business. Mates, yes, everyone was mates… . Discussing hangovers. Discussing cars. Discussing sport" (208–9). In this display of hypermasculinity, emotional self-control is harnessed as a sign of tough impermeability as opposed to more affective forms of communication, which would open Matt up to signs of weakness in this environment. This aggressive approach to judgements in business testifies to a cultural hierarchy described by Ahmed wherein emotion is perceived to be "soft," yet, "*Hardness is not the absence of emotion, but a different emotional orientation towards others*" (2004, 4, Ahmed's italics). Ahmed's theory here provides for recognizing the dominant discourses of the public realm as failing to acknowledge feeling. *Brightest Star* criticizes this ethos, revealing the emptiness of success in business for Matt as he struggles in his personal life; a struggle starkly depicted in his depression and attempted suicide. Thus, the text draws attention to the violence inflicted on lives scripted by the narratives of hegemonic masculinity intertwined with the neoliberal economic model and the calculated exploitation of emotion to produce dividends.[7]

In *Room*, Jack's unique blend of personal and cultural meanings gestures to the alternatives that lie outside the austere, "hard" language of neoliberal society. Jack's capacity for co-autonomy in relationship, deriving from the extended mother-child bond in Room, means that he is not yet determined by the symbolic system of the outside world. Moynagh Sullivan, in a TedX Talk on *Room*, discusses the importance of feeling and connection and emphasizes that stories of transformation are central. As Sullivan describes, in his relationship with Ma and through story and play, Jack develops and learns to shape himself to new and strange landscapes.[8] Following Sullivan's illumination of the power of affect in Room, it may be argued that through Jack, "soft" emotions such as empathy, trust, and joy in the nearness of the other, fostered in the realm of the imaginary, can inform moral decisions, and produce different, more affective, ways of relating than those of the austere world outside.

The linguistic violence of the outer world is captured when the media simplifies and sells the story of Jack and Ma's imprisonment, adding grotesque details: "'bachelor loner converted the garden shed into an impregnable twenty-first-century dungeon. The despot's victims have an eerie pallor and appear to be in a borderline catatonic state after the long nightmare of their incarceration'" (205). The language of academia is similarly detached, cold in its framing of Jack's story:

> 'We're all Jack, in a sense,' says another man sitting at the big table. 'Obviously,' says another one. Are they called Jack too, are they some of the million? 'The inner child, trapped in our personal Room one oh one,' says another of the men, nodding. I don't think I was ever in that room. 'But then perversely, on release, finding ourselves alone in a crowd …' 'Reeling from the sensory overload of modernity,' says the first one. '*Post*-modernity.' There's a woman too. 'But surely, at a symbolic level, Jack's the child sacrifice,' she says, 'cemented into the foundations to placate the spirits.' Huh? (366–67)

Jack's interruptions, his framing of the media and intellectual accounts of his imprisonment with a child's questions, serve to disrupt any attempts to critique, rationalize, or sensationalize his story. As Cronin, Ging and Kirby state, "beleaguered minorities, articulating the distress of the economic and social majority of the planet, have the potential to destabilise the placid certainties of Newspeak" (6). As a child and through his unique perspective on the world developed in Room with Ma, Jack is an outsider to discourses of power and his outlook holds the potential to shape a new reality. Discussing *Room*, Donoghue states, "We need to engage heart and brain together, I suppose; all intellect, and you sound cold and snide, but all sentiment leads you into the manipulative vulgarities of the kind of TV interview I satirize in Room" (104). In light of Jack's evaluation of "outside," informed by a different framework of emotions and articulated in simple vocabulary not yet imbued with neoliberal assumptions, it can be said that he brings heart to a society that values cold logic, thereby presenting alternative pathways to hegemonic patterns of thought and action in a neoliberal world.

Gender and the Politics of Austerity

Room and *Brightest Star* both interrogate a heteronormative culture that upholds neoliberalism and economic austerity through an unpacking of prevalent cultural tropes of masculinity and femininity in the recession. In *Room*, Old Nick is laid off and struggling to provide for Ma and Jack. There is a certain irony, as Donoghue notes, in that his sexual fantasy has become a daily chore:[9]

'You have no idea about the world of today. I mean, where do you think the money's going to keep coming from?' … 'Six months I've been laid off, and have you had to worry your pretty little head?' … 'Are you looking for another job?' They stare at each other. 'Are you in debt?' she asks. 'How're you going to—?' 'Shut your mouth.' (89)

That Old Nick has to provide for Ma and Jack under the threat of foreclosure is the underlying terror that propels Jack's "Great Escape." As Ma explains to Jack, the bank owns the house and if Old Nick stops paying the mortgage, the bank will repossess it. The implication of potential foreclosure, Ma knows, is that Old Nick would never let anybody find them. In a version of *Jack and the Beanstalk*, Jack thinks of himself as Jack the Giant Killer who will save his Ma before the giant grinds their bones to make his bread. In this manner, Old Nick, despite his efforts, fails to conform to a dominant cultural trope of successful masculinity. Although Old Nick is in little danger of being overtaken by five-year-old Jack, his prowess is coming under question. However, there is little marked sympathy, in this text, for the idea of "masculinity in crises" recently proposed in the face of economic and social change.[10] Instead, Old Nick's insecurities appear small and the power he enjoys is diminished in the context of a text that foregrounds the narrative of Ma and Jack's imprisonment.

Brightest Star also unravels popular cultural tropes of masculinity as it satirizes them. A powerful, hegemonic male, Conall "Slasher" Hathaway swoops in to take over and streamline failing companies, mainly through cutting jobs (33). Conall's business acumen is shown to reflect his sexual prowess. For example, in a verbal game, his girlfriend Kate questions him on which world financial leaders he would beat in a fight until, "He covered her mouth with his and, after a moment, she ceased her questioning. She would never know who would beat who in a fight, the head of the International Monetary Fund or Conall, but suddenly it no longer seemed important" (29). A workaholic, Conall lives his love life with the cold calculations that inform his job: assess, acknowledge, adapt and move forward (355). He is the epitome of a culture of austerity that normalizes the optimisation of profit, regardless of the social consequences.

Jeannine Woods demonstrates that economic and political decision-making interacts with cultural conceptualisations of masculinity:

With the rise of the Celtic Tiger and its championing of a neoliberal economic model and agenda, Irish masculinity became increasingly defined by the acquisition and display of affluence; though still bound up with aggressive risk-taking and bravado, such energies were to be channelled into the pursuit of wealth and the accumulation of consumer goods, through which identity is constructed and affirmed. (29)

As *Brightest Star* and *Room* both illustrate, in the post-boom years performances of masculinity remain aggressive and competitive while configurations of the feminine revert to a passive position, dependent on men for their survival.[11] In *Room*, Ma is dependent on Old Nick for her continued existence, while in *Brightest Star*, Conall's girlfriend Kate is reliant on him for her job (he falls for her when he descends on her workplace). Both texts present an irony-inflicted critique of these gender constructions, mocking them while simultaneously recognizing the precarious and limiting ways in which they shape men and women's subjectivities.

On the other side of the elevation of hegemonic masculinity, then, women, children and single parent families are figured as particularly hard-hit by the economic downturn. Evocative of *Room*, in *Brightest Star* a mother and son are shown living in a one-bed flat. Gardener Fionn, in his mid-thirties in the "now" of the novel, is 12 when he arrives in Pokey with his mother Angeline in the early 1980s, one of Ireland's bleakest economic periods. Like Jack, he is mistaken for a girl "Because of his tousled, shoulder-length blond locks and his pretty, pouty face" (153). The small family are immediately met with suspicion; rumor is that Angeline is on the run from the law. She cannot hold onto a job and it is said that she is lazy: "*A lazy drunken Dubliner. Who wears too much make-up. And gives our men the glad-eye. And has a fake daughter, don't forget the fake daughter... . Drugs*, someone else whispered, behind their hands, *and no father for the ladyboy*" (153, Keyes' italics). Speaking to a culture of self-serving interests and nepotism, echoes of a larger market-system, no one offers to help the family because they have not lived in the town for more than four generations. However, when Angeline dies from emphysema it is clear that she was genuine after all. Speaking to the precariousness of vulnerable populations in times of economic downturn, Angeline had "been seeking fresh air to mend her poor damaged lungs when what she'd really needed was medication. But because she was a fragile, impractical type, who was desperate for positive outcomes, without any understanding of how to make them happen, she hadn't asked for help" (153–54). In the story of this family, Keyes is commenting on the so-called community of these towns—the word "pokey" is a slang term for jail. Without roots in the town, Angeline is in a sense convicted without trial and thereafter left to suffer. Only a recent outsider herself in Pokey, Jemima, intervenes into the situation to save and foster Fionn.

In depicting past events, Keyes is commenting on wider social issues, across generations, in addition to the contemporary post-Celtic Tiger period. Turning to the contemporary moment, in comparison, Lydia, a young taxi driver, is struggling to care for her mother, Ellen, a widow in the early stages of Alzheimer's disease. In this case, Lydia, a local, experiences an opposite problem to Angeline: the local doctor refuses to send her for an MRI scan because "There's not a bit wrong with her. I've known this woman all my life" (288). Adding further insult to his infuriating paternalism, he states to Lydia: "You heard your mother. I've a waiting room out there full of real sick people so don't be wasting my time" (289). In the struggle between Lydia and the doctor, his refusal to refer her mother becomes a point of principal. In these vignettes, Keyes insinuates the punitive economics of the State as cyclical and entwined with a deceptive morality tale whereby a controlling paternal government is held as the saviour of an irresponsible population. In this sleight of hand, as Keyes demonstrates, vulnerable populations, including single mothers and widows, seemingly cannot win.

Both *Room* and *Brightest Star* represent a different morality tale to that of austerity. They speak to an Irish society in which every citizen is paying for the banking bailout, but some more so than others, as they demonstrate structures of inequality and the intersections of gender and class. In another example of those who do not have the means to replicate the consumerist lifestyle that characterizes the market-driven world, Kate, in *Brightest Star*, sets out to get baby essentials for her "short-of-funds single mother" friend and is overwhelmed by "the sheer volume of baby paraphernalia" that bulges from the shelves (280). One Family, an organisation supporting one-parent families in Ireland, draws on the European Union Statistics on Income and Living Conditions to note, "those living in lone parent households continue to experience the highest rates of deprivation with almost 60% of individuals from these households experiencing one or more forms of deprivation."[12] It also shows that over 85% of these families are headed by a mother (Census 2011) and families already experiencing poverty before the crises were hardest hit (EU SILC). Old Nick, Ma's captor and abuser, tells her: "I don't think you appreciate how good you've got it here … Plenty girls would thank their lucky stars for a setup like this, safe as houses. Specially with the kid (86)." Old Nick's comment is indicative of a neoliberal social attitude towards low-income families, suggesting that inequality is a choice and support is an unwarranted luxury (86).

The legacy of the economic boom is apparent, then, in the considerable inequalities articulated in these texts. In *Room*, Ma's and Jack's frugality is portrayed in stark contrast to the materialism and waste of the outside world. Less is shown to be more, however, as the vast emptiness of cultural life on the outside provides an impoverished comparison to the rich imaginary world of their creation inside Room. This is epitomized in the choice of Jack's aunt and uncle to take him to the mall instead of the museum and the commercialized existence that he observes there. The mall is the epitome of excess: "extra bright and ginormous" (303). To Jack, it is like a TV universe. Speaking to the polarization of gender in this culture, his Uncle Paul would prefer to buy Jack a bag "that's not pink," such as Spiderman (304). Though the mall initially fascinates Jack, after his short-lived excitement wears off, he expresses a desire, "to be in bed with Ma in the dark and her all soft and no invisible music and red-faced wide persons going by and girls laughing with their arms knotted together and bits of them showing through their clothes" (308). This testifies to the artificiality of the calculated allure of the outside world as opposed to the emotions such as love and connection affected by the intimacies of the personal. The intersubjective realm of Room provides a space wherein Jack and Ma can experience emotional safety in connection with each other. Such security is not supported by the oppositional formulations of the outside world, in particular due to the polarization of gender, wherein difference is asserted over sameness. In the mall scene, gender-specific toys, obesity, and raunch culture abound. In Room, in contrast to the mall, a piece of thread has a hundred uses and baby socks are puppets in later years. Strikingly, however, in the recent economic downturn Ma's thrift has become fashionable, to the extent that her lawyer advises: "I'd imagine you've a lot to teach the world. The whole living-on-less thing, it couldn't be more zeitgeisty" (250). In addition, then, to foregrounding the one-parent family, such allusions to the stringent measures of Ireland's austerity policy further place Room within the specifics of the Irish recession, while the novel also carries cultural resonance within the global economic context.

It is ironic that Ma is encouraged to package and sell her resourcefulness given that her position outside of a culture of commodification was responsible for this frugality. The trope of the resourceful female is a reoccurring one in the popular culture of the recession. As Negra and Tasker comment, "as in previous periods of economic uncertainty, a surge in traditionalist discourses of gender and labor is … evident in nostalgic evocations of, for example, maternal (but also fashionable) thrift" (Negra and Tasker 6). While postfeminist ideology denies the reality of gender inequality, it encourages neoliberal, individualized solutions to economic inequality and traditional performances of masculinity and femininity. Room is thus critiquing this, as the suggestion that Ma's resourcefulness can be a trend seems ridiculous given the life and death nature of her frugal existence in Room. This further emphasizes the critique of austerity models that Room depicts, also seen in the blend of heart and mind offered by Jack as an alternative to the very austereness of austerity. Foregrounding the experiences of the vulnerable and the marginalized, in particular one parent families, women and children, Room and Brightest Star illustrate the limits of the discourse of austerity as a political response to the economic crises and demonstrate the suffering that such policies inflict on those who are most at risk, and least to blame for the economic crises.

Transformative Tales

The horror inspired by daily life under political austerity, along with the fantastic imaginings within the texts, lends an aspect of the Neo-Gothic to Room and Brightest Star. Gothic horror, as a popular Victorian genre often used to subvert the purity of domestic ideology, draws attention to how this imposes limitations on women's freedoms and on non-normative sexualities. With the return to the domestic ideal in the Great Recession, wherein under neoliberalism women's and men's roles are strategically redefined under the false premise that equality has been achieved, it is possible to identify reworkings of Victorian domestic gothic as a mode of articulating the experience of financial crisis and entrapment in the home. In the gothic horror that they invoke, and tangentially in their intertextual references to Victorian fairytale, *Room* and to an extent *Brightest Star* may be read as such. In *Room*, horror is inspired in the form of Old Nick, whose name is a familiar name for the devil: He rapes Ma every night while the child Jack is in the wardrobe. Jack does not believe Old Nick or the world outside Room to be real in the way that he and Ma are real. He considers that on the other side of the door to Room, Old Nick evolves eerily with the stars, spaceships, planets and aliens (59). In *Brightest Star*, horror is humorously depicted in the form of the Grim Reaper, "the old buzz-wrecker himself" (585). This devilish figure, however, only carries away those who have made their peace with death, such as Jemima, or the likes of manipulative, violent Dave, a rapist. When Maeve says to Matt, "We're not in Little Red Riding Hood" (399), this further speaks to the Gothicized nature of the text, as it moves beyond the postfeminist fairy tale of equality in contemporary Irish society, into a darker world. In this manner, these texts draw attention to the gendered division of labor and the violence inflicted by unequal power relations in recession era homes and society more widely.

Both *Room* and *Brightest Star* are prefaced with poems deriving from myth and fairytale, at the outset foregrounding imaginary realms and illustrating the important role that emotion will play in the texts. *Room* begins with an epigraph from the poem the "Danaë's Lament" by the Greek poet Simonides. The poem is about a child Perseus, the legendary Greek hero who slayed monsters, and his mother Danaë, who are both trapped in a chest by order of her father and set afloat on the sea. Reminiscent of *Room*, the child's mother is troubled as he dreams "in the joyless wood," unaware that he is enclosed (3). *Brightest Star* leads with "Little Red Riding Hood," by Christina Reihill. As Little Red Riding Hood follows "a smiling lie" into the wood, "No one saw /The wolf in hood" who would attack her (15; 19–20). This recalls the story of Maeve's attack by the seemingly innocuous Dave, whom no one would believe to be a rapist. Both poems symbolize a desire to protect the child as fantasy gives way to reality, and gesture to the fear that accompanies this movement from the relative safety of the mother and child realm to the dangers of the external world. The central emotions, besides fear, are expressive of love. By opening out fantastical spaces from which to negotiate the historical repetitions of oppression and violence, then, *Room* and *Brightest Star* illustrate the potential to in turn reshape these forces by circulating different emotions back to them, in this case, the love which accompanies fear of entry into the symbolic world.

In both *Room* and *Brightest Star*, therefore, the discourse of austerity is challenged through otherworldly spaces. Surpassing the gothic imaginings of the texts, these realms foreground connection, shared meaning, and empathy as a force for change in social and cultural life. Centrally, a powerful, otherworldly presence makes itself known at the outset of both narratives. In *Brightest Star*, the story is witnessed by a mysterious spirit, not omniscient but with the capacity to unravel past events and read the inner workings of the minds of those living in the flats of the Georgian house. The spirit describes, "I've been flying over the streets and houses of Dublin and now, finally, I'm here. I enter through the roof. Via a skylight I slide into a living room" (1). As the story progresses, it is revealed that the spirit is a soul waiting to be born. The soul has the power to choose its own parents but, at the same time, it is dependent on free choice in their coming together. The origins of the spirit are elaborated in a text within the text—a tale "The Man Who Knew Everything" from a collection *Celtic Myths*. The King of the Fairies grants a wish; the spirit can choose to be born into a new life but will lose the ability to know everything. Ultimately, the spirit chooses life. His heart leads him to a humble, good couple who love each other so deeply that their souls have become as one. Though they have endured much sorrow, the soul knows that he can make them happy:

> When Killian's spirit had become housed within his new mother, the king of the fairies tapped Killian on the head. 'With this touch, I retrieve your knowledge and gift you with innocence in order that you may be born again.' Killian began to tingle and spark. Like an incoming tide washing away traces on the sand, he disappeared little by little, clearing the way for his soul to be rewritten by a brand-new person. (295)

When the spirit-child is sent to them, the couples' hearts are restored to happiness and love; it is a symbol for a new beginning. In the outer world in *Brightest Star*, the spirit finds a home in Maeve and Matt. In this, the realist and fairytale narrative intertwine, foregrounding the vitality of life over traditional forms of knowledge to elicit hope and empathy.

In establishing a fixed point of identity in the figure of the child, however, *Brightest Star* enacts a troubling configuration. Lee Edelman describes how the figure of the child encapsulates heteronormative ideology, as this symbol binds past, present and future together by appealing to an investment in the reproduction of the social order: "The Child," as he states, "marks the fetishistic fixation of heteronormativity: an erotically charged investment in the rigid sameness of identity that is central to the compulsory narrative of reproductive futurism" (21). Reproductive futurism attempts to reduce the meaning of sexuality to reproduction, illustrated in the trope of the child that is used to inspire hope. To take another side, according to Edelman, is to be outside of politics. He states, "queerness exposes the obliquity of our relation to what we experience in and as social reality, alerting us to the fantasies structurally necessary in order to sustain it" (6–7). In *Brightest Star*, Keyes compellingly illustrates the violence of political austerity and neoliberal discourses on the body and demonstrates, in the imaginary realm, the potential for emotion to inspire alternative models of subjectivity and a more just society. For example, when the Grim Reaper causes David to die by a lump of ice from the sky hurtling directly onto his head, an event that Matt had fantasized about, Maeve and Matt's "faces are luminous with some strange emotion—that isn't shock" but potentially relief (598). This example, albeit extreme, asserts that the world will be a better place when the modes of subjectivity that endorse rape culture—fostered under a society that normalizes hegemonic masculinity, "hard" feelings that assert aggression over nurturance, and the polarization of gender—are obliterated. In privileging the figure of the eternal child, however, Keyes' narrative ultimately preserves normative family and romantic value systems in a "turn toward the objects given to us by heterosexual culture" (Ahmed, 2006a, 554), unwittingly continuing the straight direction(s) of the neo-liberal project.

Rejecting reproductive futurism, *Room* presents a central contrast to *Brightest Star* in how it represents the figure of the child. While the story of another, spiritual realm and of a passage from one world to another through birth provides an imaginative backdrop to both texts, *Room* refuses the heteronormative social order by queering the space of the family home. In *Room*, Ma invents a strikingly similar story to that in *Brightest Star* to explain existence and birth to Jack: "'Nah, the numbers didn't start till you zoomed down.' 'Through Skylight. You were all sad till I happened in your tummy'" (3). Ma draws upon the story of Mary and Baby Jesus to explain life to Jack. Importantly, however, the father is absent from this narrative, which complicates dominant understandings of the family in social life. Jack understands Ma's story through the print *Great Masterpieces of Western Art No. 3: The Virgin and Child with St. Anne and St. John the Baptist*. This is his favorite image in *Room*, through which he imagines family and birth:

> I wriggle around on her lap now to look at my favorite painting of Baby Jesus playing with John the Baptist that's his friend and big cousin at the same time. Mary's there too, she's cuddled in her Ma's lap that's Baby Jesus's Grandma, like Dora's *abuela*. ... What started Baby Jesus growing in Mary's tummy was an angel zoomed down, like a ghost but a really cool one with feathers. Mary was all surprised, she said, 'How can this be?" and then, 'OK let it be.' (22–23)

In this drawing, the Virgin Mary is seated on the lap of her mother, St Anne, while holding the Infant Jesus. A child St John the Baptist looks on. Anne appears to be of one age with Mary, almost of one body. They smile, their gaze directed at one another, a gaze repeated in the children. According to Freud, Leonardo da Vinci gave Christ two mothers, the Virgin Mary and Saint Anne, who are representations, respectively, of Leonardo's birth mother and his stepmother (1910 in Dyson, trans., 2014). In this context, it is also significant that as Ma and Jack understand it, Jack's being a boy or a girl is incidental and secondary to his existence. Of her previous stillborn child, Ma states:

> 'You know I used to say, when you came the first time, on Bed, you were a girl?' … 'The *her* part of her, that went straight back up to Heaven.' 'She got recycled?' Ma nearly smiles. 'I like to think that's what happened.' … 'Maybe it really was you, and a year later you tried again and came back down as a boy.' (255–56)

In these imaginings, *Room* queers the family space. Ahmed describes how bodies are orientated toward the objects around them. This directionality helps to shape our perception towards others and the world. Ahmed states that "The starting point for orientation is the point from which the world unfolds: the here of the body and the where of its dwelling" (2006a, 545). From this point, we find our bearings, and the world that we are born into takes us in a certain direction. In *Room*, however, the world of the familiar is also strange. For Jack, his background is inextricable from the imaginary and, in his understanding, there is no before or outside of *Room*. When there is no natural standpoint inspired by memory and familiarity, this gives rise to a queer phenomenology. Extending this, it is notable that Ahmed describes how, as we arrange the furniture in a certain way, repetition invites us to inhabit the world along inherited lines. The work—our social inheritance—that goes into the arrangement of furniture disappears to become part of the background. In contrast to this erasure, "A queer furnishing might be about making what is in the background, what is behind us, more available as 'things' to do 'things' with" (2006b, 168). Foregrounding and animating objects through Jack's imaginary, *Room* succeeds in queering the furniture. Furthermore, "queer objects support proximity between those who are supposed to live on parallel lines, *as points that should not meet*" (2006b, 169, Ahmed's italics). Crossing from the imaginary world to the real and in connection destabilizing lines of inheritance, *Room* queers objects and relationships to create the possibility of new social forms. As Ahmed emphasizes, such forms are not free from the norms of capitalism and are not transcendent, but their persistence maintains hope in continuing to trouble the values that define the normative ideal (2004, 165).

Conclusion: New Directions

A photographic exhibition marking people's lives, yet not capturing their images, took place at the Galway Arts Centre in March 2015. It was entitled

"Asylum Archive: Mapping Images," an exhibition by Dublin based artist and researcher Vukasin Nedeljkovic. Featuring objects rather than human subjects, traces of human presence haunt the photographs, as they tell of the system of Direct Provision in Ireland. The architecture, landscape, and objects featured—discarded toys, burst balloons, empty child's swings—speak to the uncertainty and invisibility of life within these centres. In the midst of this, the exhibition also featured expressions of creativity such as images of prayer flags made by children and a lone, homemade cardboard clock. Opposing the precariousness of life in direct provision, absence in Nedeljkovic's work represents an act of defiance. As Charlotte McIvor, of NUI Galway, states: "By haunting rather than inhabiting, the asylum seekers *not* pictured in these frames refuse to perform from familiar repertoires of the bureaucratic performance of refugeeness."[13]

A similar haunting effect is experienced in the final scene of *Room*. Gazing into the room of their confinement, Ma and Jack take in the objects, alien now, that once comprised their world: "Rocker's here and Table and Sink and Bath and Cabinet but no plates and cutlery on top, and Dresser and TV and Bunny with the purple bow on him, and Shelf but nothing on her, and our chairs folded up but they're all different. Nothing says anything to me" (399). Just as with Nedeljkovic's photographs, these discarded objects tell of Ma's and Jack's lives. Traces of their presence are also seen in Jack's birthday markings on the wall, tracks worn into the floor, and remnants of the fingerprinting powder used to verify their existence once they had escaped from their captor. This powder also speaks to a culture of bio-political governance outside *Room* that compels Jack and Ma to re-orientate themselves to expected models of existence in a neoliberal world. In *Room*, as in Nedeljkovic's exhibition, acts of resistance seen in creativity illuminate for the reader or viewer the violence that is imposed when life is concealed and suppressed. These moments of creative insight and the emotions that fuel them speak to a structure of social power relations that inflicts violence on bodies and communities who are other to the ideal national subject; in these examples, the immigrant community in Asylum Archive and the non-normative family in *Room*.

More and more, however, austerity has been configured as but one of a number of possible solutions to the financial crisis. As sociologist Kieran Allen points out, it is but an "imaginary solution for a deep economic crisis" (23). This speaks to the foresight of texts such as *Brightest Star* and *Room*. It is possible to read their invocations of fairytale, which traditionally acts as a moral compass, as counters to the tale of austerity. Donoghue and Keyes depict the marginalized and the silenced: immigrants, single parent families, the elderly and the ill who have shouldered the poverty of the recession. Their texts reflect a culture of social exclusion in Ireland, apparent in the aforementioned system of Direct Provision, which provides basic board and accommodation for asylum seekers. Residents are excluded from regular social welfare payments, social housing, employment, and free third-level education, while the State pays private contractors hundreds of millions to run the institutions. Donoghue and Keyes recall such bio-political control of non-normative bodies in their works, which illustrate how the system of political austerity that suggests that inequality is acceptable in recession times exerts violence on the State's most vulnerable residents.

The child Jack, in particular, illustrates the problem faced by bodies considered non-normative in neo-liberal culture. Having taken shape in *Room*, his body is queer in and to the outside world. As Ahmed delineates, the emotions attributed to bodies shape their ability to act in the world. For example, if that attribution is fear, and nearness is construed as a threat, such bodies are contained, as in the above example of Direct Provision. However, Jack's disorientation on entering the outside world is an opportunity for learning, as his difference opens up alternative possibilities in contrast to a current political economy founded on objectivity and materiality. This alternative vision is one of nurturance, recognizing the importance of a wide range of emotions to create a society that allows for autonomy, connection, and trust. Such a vision represents a significant contrast to the current economic and political system that privileges traits associated with hegemonic masculinity and neoliberal ideology—those of tough feelings such as dominance, aggression and independence. In *Room*, Ma explains to Jack that Old Nick, who embodies norms of aggressive subjectivity, is unable to feel:

> 'He looks human, but there's nothing inside.' I'm confused. 'Like a robot?' 'Worse.' ... 'You know your heart, Jack?' ... 'No, but your feeling bit, where you're sad or scared or laughing or stuff?' ... 'Well, he hasn't got one.' ... 'A feeling bit,' says Ma.... 'What does he have instead?' She shrugs. 'Just a gap.' Like a crater? But that's a hole where something happened. What happened? (139)

The challenge of social transformation lies in recognizing the hierarchy of emotions inscribed by neoliberal ideology and economic austerity, in which "hardness" is elevated over "softness." As Ahmed illustrates, the former does not illustrate a lack of emotions but a particular orientation towards others. Indeed, Jack recognizes the impossibility of a gap; something must have informed it. The circulation of these hard emotions contributes to shaping both the bodies that assert them and those that are informed by them. Together, *Room* and *Brightest Star* illustrate the importance of recognizing heart and mind, a broad spectrum of emotions, in matters of political decision-making. In the context of global recession, such acknowledgement of the capacity for different emotions to shape bodies in new ways holds far-reaching implications in Ireland and beyond.

The central difference in these texts lies in their representation of the child as an object for the investment of hope for the future. In *Brightest Star*, the child embodies a social promise, that of return on the couples' investment in a preordained life course. This is exemplified in Jemima's advice to Maeve that she and Matt must have a baby. Ultimately, as Jemima asserts: "A baby will reclaim the innocence that was stolen from you both" (557). A child, in this view, will give the couple the will to carry on. The social pressure asserted by Jemima here recalls the impressions that the emotions of others make on the body: "We are pressed into lines, just as lines are the accumulation of such moments of pressure" (Ahmed, 2006b, 17). In this way, the text illustrates how life is directed along inherited lines. As Jemima advises Maeve, she can never go back and should try going forward (558). Maeve and Matt, in the end, represent "the good life," looking ahead and returning the investment society has placed in their imagined future.[14]

In contrast, the child Jack, looking back towards *Room* as a home that he will always remember, represents the queer life. In connection, it is significant that Ahmed does not argue, as Edelman does, that the queer has no future:

> Instead, a queer politics would have hope, not even by having hope in the future ... but because the lines that accumulate through repeated gestures, the lines that gather on skin, already take surprising forms. We have hope because what is behind us is also what allows other ways of gathering in time and space, of making lines that do not reproduce what we follow, but instead create new textures on the ground. (2006a, 570)

Jack's queer orientation, gazing at what is behind him as he moves into the future—specifically, the range of emotions and the queer family space opened up in *Room*—opens the possibility of discovering other life paths. Therefore, it can be argued that a full critique of neoliberalism as a straight line on a life course requires a sustained heteronormative critique.

Writing on feminism and the politics of austerity, Avtar Brah, Ioana Szeman, and Irene Gedalof ask, "what a feminist response to the crisis and its purported solutions might look like, and what feminist alternatives to the austere, neo-liberal state and economic policy are emerging" (1). An example of an alternative to the discourse of austerity as a response to the economic crisis is revealed in *Room* and *Brightest Star*. Their accounts of individuals and families and their emotions and experiences within the structures of economic austerity illustrate how such policies regulate bodies. While *Room* is ultimately more successful in imagining an alternative due to its queer vision, in both of these texts neoliberalism is powerfully critiqued by allowing individuals to transform their personal and family environment through the creation of shared magical worlds that cross with the inherited structures of social and cultural life. These narratives make the familiar strange, and the strange familiar. In so doing, they intervene in the lines and patterns that direct bodies and desires. Opening doorways into fantasy realms, these texts reveal the historical repetitions of oppression and violence in light of a diverse world of emotions and judgments, of aims and identities, as new directions appear on the horizon.

Notes

1. In "Ireland in Crisis 2008-2012: Women, Austerity and Inequality" (2013), Ursula Barry and Pauline Conroy discuss the barriers to employment and cuts to income and social welfare that face women, in particular, in the economic crises. This is due to a patriarchal employment market and social welfare system that positions women in the home and in caring roles without adequately valuing this work. This affects vulnerable populations in particular; for example, single parent families and carers, who are often women. Barry and Conroy also show that children are the most vulnerable to poverty and levels of poverty are particularly high among the older population.

2. As well as Maeve and Matt, the house is also inhabited by two disillusioned Polish men who came to Ireland seeking opportunity and share a flat with a taxi driver named Lydia (Lydia is overworked in seeking to support her mother, who is experiencing the onset of Alzheimer's disease). Jemima (an elderly woman who unbeknownst to the others is dying from cancer) and her adopted son Fionn (an attractive gardener embarking on a new venture as the host of his own television gardening show) also have an apartment in the house, as does Kate (a single PR executive just turned forty). As they struggle to improve their lot against a backdrop of materialism, celebrity and economic downturn, the question for the reader becomes who the mysterious spirit might be, and then, as it is a child-in-waiting, which couple will come together to provide it with the spark of life; a gift that it will return by changing their lives. This article focuses on Maeve and Matt as the couple who experience the most turbulence and who eventually give life to the spirit child.

3. It is significant, at this point, to consider debates surrounding the "Chick Lit" genre. To a large extent, "Chick Lit" is preoccupied with "young to middle aged, predominantly white, middle class women and an emphasis on personal growth in the context of romantic and family relationships and the bonds of friendship and community" (O'Neill, 59). Much of this work is notable for its postfeminist assumptions that equality and freedom of choice has succeeded. However, critics have also read the genre as having the potential to represent difference and alternative voices. For example, Pamela Butler and Jigna Desai, in their analysis of South Asian American "Chick Lit," read it as a cultural site that represents a particular "(trans)national, racialised feminist subject," in resistant spaces opened out through the "contradictions internal to the logics of neoliberalism" (8-9). In a similar vein, Keyes' illustrations of the difficulties of living under neoliberal ideology in *Brightest Star* stand out in refusing to rationalise unequal social relations.

4. www.emmadonoghue.com/books/novels/room-the-novel.html

5. www.mariankeyes.com/marian/biography

6. www.mariankeyes.com/books/the-brightest-star-in-the-sky/facts

7. Critiquing the social insistence of hegemonic masculinity, feminist film theorists such as Kaja Silverman have explored the trope of "masculinity in crises." In *Male Subjectivity at the Margins*, Silverman explores "deviant" masculinities—whose desires are defined as "perverse"—as a challenge to conventional male subjectivity. They call into question sexual difference as well as the ideological beliefs that maintain traditional masculinity.

8. www.tedxfulbrightdublin.ie/speakers/moynagh-sullivan/

9. Donoghue comments on this in "An Extraordinary Act of Motherhood: A Conversation with Emma Donoghue," an interview with Tom Ue (103).

10. Texts asserting that men are in decline socially and economically include, for example, Hanna Rosin's *The End of Men and the Rise of Women* (2012).

11. For further reading, see Diane Negra, "Adjusting Men and Abiding Mammies: Gendering the Recession in Ireland" (2014). Negra describes how the financial crises in Ireland has affected men and women in specifically gendered ways, attending to the foregrounding of potent masculinity and abiding femininity in the popular cultural sphere.

12. www.onefamily.ie/policy-campaigns/facts-figures/

13. Quoted from Asylumarchive.com. For further information see www.galwayartscentre.ie/exhibitions/6-asylum-archive-mapping-absences

14. The term "the good life" as theorised by Lauren Berlant (2011) refers to a relation of "cruel optimism" whereby individuals live their day-to-day life based on the unrealizable hope of fulfilling their desires in the future.

Works Cited

"About Marian." Penguin Books Ltd., www.mariankeyes.com/marian/biography. Accessed 28 April 2016.

Ahmed, Sara. "Happy Objects." *The Affect Theory Reader*. Ed. Melissa Gregg and Gregory J. Seigworth. Durham: Duke UP, 2010. 29–51. Print.

Ahmed, Sara. "Orientations: Toward a Queer Phenomenology." *GLQ: A Journal of Lesbian and Gay Studies*. 12.4 (2006a): 543–74. Print.

Ahmed, Sara. *Queer Phenomenology: Orientations, Objects, Others*. Durham: Duke UP, 2006b. Print.

Ahmed, Sara. *The Cultural Politics of Emotion*. Edinburgh: Edinburgh UP, 2004. Print.

Allen, Kieran, and Brian O'Boyle. *Austerity Ireland: The Failure of Irish Capitalism*. Chicago: Pluto Press, 2013. Print.

Barry, Ursula, and Pauline Conroy. "Ireland in Crisis 2008-2012: Women, Austerity and Inequality." *Women and Austerity: The Economic Crisis and the Future for Gender Equality*. Ed. M. Karamessini and J. Rubery. New York: Routledge, 2013. Print.

Brah, Avtar, Ioana Szeman, and Irene Gedalof. "Introduction: Feminism and the Politics of Austerity." *Feminist Review* 109.1 (2015): 1–7. Print.

Berlant, Lauren. *Cruel Optimism*. Durham: Duke UP, 2011. Print.

Butler, Pamela, and Jigna Desai. "Manolos, Marriage, and Mantras: Chick Lit Criticism and Transnational Feminism." *Meridians: Feminism, Race, Transnationalism* 8.2 (2008): 1–31.Print.

"Census 2011: This is Ireland (Part 1)." Central Statistics Office, http://www.cso.ie/en/census/census2011reports/census2011thisisirelandpart1/. Accessed 17 January 2017.

Cronin, Michael, Peadar Kirby, and Debbie Ging. "Transforming Ireland: Challenges." *Transforming Ireland: Challenges, Critiques and Resources*. Ed. Debbie Ging, Michael Cronin and Peadar Kirby. Manchester: Manchester UP, 2009.1–17. Print.

Donoghue, Emma. *Room*. London: Picador, 2011 (first published in 2010). Print.

Edelman, Lee. *No Future: Queer Theory and the Death Drive*. Durham, Duke UP, 2004. Print.

Freud, Sigmund. Routledge, 2014 (first published in 1910). Print.

Keyes, Marian. *The Brightest Star in the Sky*. New York: Penguin, 2011 (first published by Michael Joseph in 2009). Print.

McIvor, Charlotte. "The Absences of the Asylum Archive: Making Reflective Space." Asylumarchive.com, n.d. Web. 1 June 2016.

Negra, Diane. "Adjusting Men and Abiding Mammies: Gendering the Recession in Ireland." *The Irish Review* 46 (2013): 23–34. Print.

Negra, Diane and Yvonne Tasker, "Introduction: Gender and Recessionary Culture." *Gendering the Recession: Media and Culture in an Age of Austerity*. Durham; London: Duke UP, 2014. 1–30. Print

O'Neill, Margaret. "You Still Can Have It All, But Just in Moderation: Neoliberal Gender and Post-Celtic Tiger 'Recession Lit.'" *Assuming Gender* 5.1 (2015): 59–83. Print.

"Room." *Emma Donoghue*. EmmaDonoghue.com. http://emmadonoghue.com/books/novels/room-the-novel.html. Accessed 28 April 2016.

Rosin, Hanna. *The End of Men and the Rise of Women*. New York: Riverhead Books, 2012. Print.

Silverman, Kaja. *Male Subjectivity at the Margins*. New York: Routledge, 1992. Print.

Sullivan, Moynagh. "Creativity and Play as Social Transformers in Emma Donoghue's Room." *YouTube*, uploaded by Tedx Talks, 18 June 2014, www.youtube.com/watch?v=_rJ05xntAPA.

"The Brightest Star in the Sky – Facts." Penguin Books Ltd., www.mariankeyes.com/books/the-brightest-star-in-the-sky/facts. Accessed 28 April 2016.

Ue, Tom. "An Extraordinary Act of Motherhood: A Conversation with Emma Donoghue." *Journal of Gender Studies*, 21.1 (2012): 101–106. Print.

Woods, Jeannine. "Trans-formations of Gendered Identity in Ireland." *Masculinity and Irish Popular Culture: Tiger's Tales*. Ed. Conn Holohan and Tony Tracy. New York: Palgrave Macmillan, 2014. 27–41. Print.

Queer Possession and the Celtic Tiger: Affect and Economics in Belinda McKeon's *Tender*

Patrick Mullen

"I'm his friend, and it's my job to look after him."

Belinda McKeon's *Tender* (2015) tells the story of Catherine Reilly's obsession with her queer friend James Flynn, who comes out to her during her first year at Trinity College Dublin. Catherine responds to his revelation with a care that over the course of a year develops into aggression, or perhaps, the novel suggests, was a mode of aggression all along. The title of the book figures this slippage in a single word as the term characterizes both the tender affections that Catherine extends towards James and the hurt and injury that result as that attention transforms into jealousy, anger, and attempts to control him. As with other recent novels that trace battered Irish psyches, such as Patrick McCabe's *The Butcher Boy* (1992) and Anne Enright's *The Gathering* (2007), the focus on a singular perspective in McKeon's novel brings into view a broader social history. In some sense, McKeon pitches her analysis between these two texts.[1] We might imagine Catherine and James's story unfolding between the damaged life of a Francie Brady, whose narrative indicts the society of postwar rural Ireland, and the painful family history that a Veronica Hegarty recovers in the suburban oblivion of the Celtic Tiger.[2]

The novel is the second work by McKeon and is structured through free-indirect style that recollects the events of Catherine and James's first year of friendship. The violence of Catherine's obsession ruptures their relationship and provokes a stylistic break: the middle section is offered in a spare and experimental prose-poetic form that attempts to capture the intensities of that violence. The final section returns to a free-indirect representation of an older and wiser Catherine who meets James after more than a decade apart. Catherine's obsession reiterates the closeted forms of violence that permeate her rural Catholic upbringing. This repetition registers ironically given that her embrace of James's sexuality, an embrace that she relentlessly puts on display, at first masks her connections to the old rural and religious Ireland. Indeed Catherine's class ascension through the academic, professional, and social networks of Trinity is emblazoned in this distinction: her old guard parents and their narrow provincialism regard James as "troubled" whereas Catherine, by her own warped calculations, enriched by the generous modernization of the economic boom and the new world laid at her feet, comes, as she sees it at one point, to love him (89).

This essay argues that the novel exposes Ireland's mania to possess—both in affective and economic terms—during the years of the boom. The title inscribes complex affective dynamics and simultaneously denotes economic forms of tender. Possession thus operates as a multivalent term, marking the materialism that accompanied the Celtic Tiger, the sense of sexual self-possession that is the promise of sexual liberalization, and the saturation of everyday life by the market forces of neoliberalism. I contend that what at first seems like an intensely psychological novel, focused on the obsessive mania of a particular character, ultimately offers aesthetic tools for broader social and historical critique. In particular, the novel suggests that *the closet*, that pervasive regulatory figure for gay and lesbian identity, appears during the years of the Celtic Tiger under a new historical guise. *Coming out of the closet* emerges as an important social metaphor for the general sexual liberalization and cosmopolitanism that accompanied the boom of the Tiger years. Stepping out of the closet, as a metaphor, helps to frame the freedom, the glamour, the cosmopolitanism, the material abundance, and the transformations of Irish society. The evacuated, if not dismantled, closet further helps to track the residual contradictions, pain, failures, surveillance and paranoia that reappear during the crash and in the era of austerity. Framing the discourses of sexuality and economics in the Irish context, the closet assumes a novel historical form: the unstable dynamics of the closet suggest how newly commodified forms of dissenting sexual identities became available for exploitation during the years of the Tiger. While Catherine starts as a passionate advocate for coming out, she nonetheless quickly constructs and violently defends re-fabricated closets in order to reproduce her own social and psychic value. Gender plays an important part in these contradictory transformations as the novel explores the dangers that the consumerism of the Celtic Tiger years posed for women. Tracing these risks in the story of Catherine and James, the novel clears a space for a critical historical and political accounting of the connections among sexuality, gender, and economics in Tiger and post-Tiger Ireland.

This essay pursues a model of close reading to approach questions about the potential for collective politics. I maintain that certain modes of formalist engagement yield more than simply knowledge about form. As Lauren Berlant suggests, careful attention to form can help to explain how "aesthetically mediated affective responses exemplify a shared historical sense" (3). I return to Berlant's formulation of *cruel optimism* in the discussion of the closet; for now suffice it to say that the key to my own method of reading is framed in the language of the novel itself—beginning with the title—that tracks the complex relations between affects and economics. Ultimately, the novel suggests that what seems most inscrutably individual in the era of neoliberalism, that intensely affective prism of contemporary interiority, must be reread in relation to economic forces and therefore as the subject of, and subjected to, collective politics. After all, both your sexual orientation, particularly if you're still closeted, and that money in your pocket, particularly if you haven't much of it, are felt as intensely personal and private matters. Yet both of these are also undeniably shaped by complex political, social, and economic forces. The language of the novel is therefore conjugated at the level of the interpersonal, and this essay works to expose the social, political, and historical dimensions that this personal language makes thinkable.

Two Sides of the Same Coin

In its acute analysis of the psychology of youth and romance, the novel reveals that Catherine's delicacy of feeling and the ultimate harm inflicted on both James and herself are two sides of the same coin. Furthermore, the price that both characters pay suggests that the social politics articulated with the Celtic Tiger were not a complete break with Ireland's conservative Catholic past, but rather a restructuring of the politics of surveillance and paranoia that dominated much of Irish society in the twentieth century. While there have been political gains made for progressive sexual politics, there are also refigured repressive powers that must be reckoned with. *Tender* affords an accounting of the queer historical transformations associated with the rise and fall of the Tiger and suggests that Ireland, with its increasingly liberal understandings of sexuality and fetishized relations to neoliberal capitalism, is swimming in historical debt and yet potentially rich in progressive aesthetic resources. The novel offers aesthetic tools that assist in the critical framing of the social transformations of both the boom years and the era of austerity. It does more than recount a gripping story: it traces the development of aesthetic sensibilities that represent the pain and pleasure of the past critically and yet still open themselves to the possibilities of the present. It literally tells the story of Catherine and James's aesthetic training: Catherine goes from being a young poet in college to becoming a successful international art critic, and James grows from an awkward teenager into a famous worldly artist. As readers watch the queer story unfold they are trained to watch for the unexpected. In the shock of what happens by the end of the novel, readers are asked to reconsider language that might have at first seemed innocuous but that in retrospect glimmers with suggestion.

Reviews of the novel underscore the subtlety of its psychological insight, but they have not taken up its representation of recent economic history. A survey of the blurbs from McKeon's website captures this emphasis. From *Booklist*: "A fever dream of friendship, love and obsession that is as emotionally raw as it is artfully crafted." From *Kirkus*: "Exquisite... Captures something essential about vulnerability, love, and longing." From *The Financial Times*: "Thrums with sadness, desire and the dizzying desire to possess."[3] *The dizzying desire to possess* is not an empty metaphor for McKeon's text—it captures not only the psychological qualities but also the economic forces that impel the characters.

To begin with the title: *tender* as a term lays bare complex etymological connections among affect, value, and labor. According to the *OED*, it refers in its nominal form to a kind of worker: "One who tends, or waits upon, another"; "One who attends to, or has charge of, a machine, a business, etc., as *bar-tender* (a barman), *bridge-tender, machine-tender*." It also refers to a form of value in a specific legal sense and in its more general usage: "An offer of money, or the like, in discharge of a debt or liability, *esp.* an offer which thus fulfills the terms of the law and of the liability"; "*gen.* An offer of anything for acceptance." In its adjectival and adverbial forms the term qualifies both bodies and emotions and marks a potential receptivity while also suggesting a kind of after state: "Soft or delicate in texture or consistence; yielding easily to force or pressure; fragile; easily broken, divided, compressed, or injured"; "Frail, thin, fine, slender"; "Of weak or delicate constitution; not strong, hardy, or robust; unable or unaccustomed to endure hardship, fatigue, or the like; delicately reared, effeminate"; "Easy to be injured by tactless treatment; needing cautious or delicate handling." These bodily and emotional states connote a relation to youth: "Having the weakness and delicacy of youth; not strengthened by age or experience; youthful, immature." When describing the receiver of certain actions, the term signals injury whereas when describing the one who acts towards another, the term suggests a certain softness and care: "Characterized by, exhibiting, or expressing delicacy of feeling or susceptibility to the gentle emotions; kind, loving, gentle, mild, affectionate." Finally, *to tender* is also a verb that frames an exchange, or an attempted exchange between parties. It can describe both the giver and the receiver, can register as soft or aggressive: "To present (anything) for approval and acceptance; to offer, proffer"; "To become tender; to be affected with pity; to grow soft, soften"; "To have a tender regard for, to hold dear; to be concerned for or solicitous about; to treat with consideration; to regard, care for, value, esteem"; "To make tender or delicate."

This title presents three layers of potential analysis. First, it suggests a self-reflexive appeal to multiple valences. The title is not *Tender Is the Night*, for instance, which privileges the sentimental meanings of the term. Instead it stands alone and thereby summons all of these associations simultaneously. Thus, the novel opens with a speculative gesture that announces a narrative, invites a theoretical perspective on that narrative, and self-consciously puts into play multiple metaphors. Second, moving from the title to the narrative, the work suggests that these associations are not simply etymological but are also ideological. Here I refer to ideology in the sense that these entangled meanings are embedded in the day-to-day and the characters are not aware of the shifts between the economic and affective. Joseph Valente's definition of ideology in his analysis of Irish manhood is apt: "not a generalized misrecognition of the reality of particular social relations but rather social relations that depend for their consistency, hence their particular reality, on a generalized misrecognition" (25).[4] For *tender* to operate within the narrative structures of the novel, the text must in a sense choose among the term's multiple meanings for the story to proceed, and only in retrospect can the importance of alternative valences be revealed. For the reality effect to obtain it must not proceed along all lines simultaneously but must follow certain lines of meaning even as these lines cannot unravel their connections with alternative knotted associations. Third, while the title asks the reader to solve a riddle—*what tender does the story offer?*—this critical task is merely a starting place for the reading of the text. The clarification of misrecognition—the exposure of ideology—is both necessary and non-exhaustive as a mode of critical reading. The next step is to consider what kinds of thinking these formulations of affect and the economic make possible. Given these layered complexities, this essay proceeds through a mode of close reading that unties the knotted connections between economics and affect and then attaches these readings to a broader historical and political context.

The novel conjugates these affective and economic connotations in its metaphors and language. Catherine's initial impression of James echoes the sense of abundance indicative to the economic rise: "James had given her so much, so many new things to think about" (5). Given all of these *new things*, this new material abundance, it is no surprise that the novel offers a richly associative lexicon that frames emotional and sexual relationships through economic metaphors. Catherine's family trades in what she calls "bargaining chip[s]" and "security clauses" in their domestic transactions (10). Catherine's class status and her own insistence on her rural background makes her friend Amy remark that one would "think you'd crawled to college straight from the famine" (26); "culchie"—a slang term for rural background and lower class status—is a frequent barb among her Trinity peers (122, 140, 153, 190). Class ascension, distinction, antagonism, affection and shame converge in these barbs. When she first meets James she worries, "What account would she give of herself?" (34), a question echoed by her parents as they wonder "what kind of account" her late night rush to James in Leitrim would produce in the eyes of the neighbors (87). As Catherine and James contemplate whether the father of a French family on holiday is flirting with her or not, they debate what's "worth" noticing and what's not a "big deal"

(62). In her study of Ted Hughes's poems to Sylvia Plath, Catherine fixates on Hughes's condescending figuration of Plath's interest in her own writing as a "huge/Mortgage of hope" (188). In a certain sense, it takes the heightened sensitivity of Plath's poetry to bring into focus these largely unmarked usages of economic terms by the characters. While the characters in these examples are largely unaware of the economic valences that permeate their day-to-day speech, Plath's poem marshals an economic metaphor for an emotional state and thereby hints at a heightened awareness about the connections between economics and affect, an awareness that the characters as readers of her poems can potentially discover.

More emphatically marked emotional and economic connotations inform the scene in which James drunkenly laments that his social and sexual isolation are his "own stupid fault" and that he "should have a place of [his] own" (145). Catherine responds with language germane to the domain of intimate feelings and to the legal status of commerce: "I promise you. It'll get better, I promise" (149). *Promise* is a term of economic and affective interest, legal bond on the one hand and individual authenticity on the other. In an argument over Catherine's increasingly intense attempts to control James, her clear-headed friend Zoe argues that she needs to "give James some credit" (196). Catherine, dismissing Zoe's concerns, retorts that, "it's [her] job to look after him" (198). Finally, much to Catherine's surprise, James redistributes the emotional baggage of the novel—to use the pop-psychology cliché—in material terms:

> "Well, I'm sorry," she said again, feeling the need to insist on it.
> He shook his head. "You don't need to tell me that, Catherine. That's your business. The being sorry, I mean. That's part of *your* life. I don't mean anything harsh by that. I don't mean it's worthless or anything, your being sorry, or your apology, or sorrow, or however you'd put it. I just mean, it's yours."
> "Yeah," Catherine said, her voice hollow. She felt she was being fobbed off, somehow; she felt as if, all over again, she was being refused.
> "I have my own things," he said, and he gave a short laugh. "Fuckin' plenty of them" (389).

The language of emotion is never far from the language of economics in the text. Here the initial abundance that James provided returns and both readers and characters are asked to reckon with what kinds of economic and affective accumulation the text has traced. James has gone from needing the proverbial *room of one's own* to having *plenty of his own things*, a formulation that accounts for his artistic and economic success and his sexual and emotional experiences. Readers are left to puzzle over Catherine's story as James asks her to account for *her own things*. While Catherine may have "no questions at all" by the end of the novel, it's another situation for readers, who are asked to consider whether the story is a tale of failed passion for Catherine or passionate economic success for James (398)?

These combinations of emotion and commerce might seem minor, but the casual allocation of labor and social value under late capitalism should not be underestimated. On the contrary, the ease with which unremunerated forms of work can be assigned off-handedly, casually, and conversationally along with the fluid translations between commerce and affect suggest the degree to which neoliberal capitalism has saturated the social sphere.[5] These allocations and translations occur frequently within the domain of the private, the interpersonal, the domestic, and the so-called service economy. These are sectors of the broader political economy that are particularly organized around the exploitation of the marginalized: women, racial minorities, the young, queers, foreigners, the poor, etc. Catherine and James are not aware, and do not become aware, of the mingling of affect and commerce in their use of language in these examples. Working out their problems is simultaneously commercial and emotional as they strive to prove themselves valuable during the boom years. As they learn to account for themselves, money and emotion become interchangeable. In this sense, their relation to the language of economics is ideological: they are utilizing an economic vocabulary without being fully aware of its implications.

The Closet: Theory and History

Through this linguistic intermingling of commerce and affect, the novel places Catherine and James in three historical frames that they themselves would not be entirely able to account for. The first is the Celtic Tiger which was ramping up in the early 1990s and whose narcotic effects were just beginning to be felt. Early in the novel, the demise of the Celtic Tiger is part of the impossible futures of these characters, who cannot imagine the collapse of the housing and financial markets and the austerity reforms that underwrite the production of the novel itself and the narration of the final section "Frieze / (2012)." The second is the Troubles, in particular the Good Friday Agreement of 1998 and the infamous bombing in Omagh, which also took place in 1998. The bombing explodes into the text with little warning, disastrous effects, and painful ironies for the characters. The final frame is the transformation in Irish attitudes towards sexuality as the country legalized homosexuality in 1993 and then legalized same-sex marriage in 2015. As the narrative only follows the characters up until 2012, it allows for an analysis of the initial moment of legalization from a vantage point (of the subsequent endorsement in the marriage referendum) that cannot breach the awareness of the characters.

These historical frames are placed within a recursive structure that frames youth from the retrospective gaze of adulthood. This structure operates on multiple levels in the novel: in the reactions of Catherine's parents to the growing friendship between James and herself, a relationship that they read through the lens of their own youth; in the free-indirect style that collects the story and disseminates it through Catherine's point of view after the events have transpired; finally, in the more mature perspective of the final section that looks back on the events themselves and also on the earlier looking back. Given the centrality of the sex and sexuality in the novel, the third historical frame and, in particular, the discourse of the closet, emerge to frame this retrospective gaze and the connections among economics and affect.

The novel represents these historical developments through the telling of the particular story of James and Catherine, a story that in large part is about coming out of the closet. The novel suggests that *the closet*, that pervasive regulatory trope of gay and lesbian identity, is a powerful figure in Irish culture. While critics have examined how North American sexual politics function in an Irish context, *Tender* offers the reverse dynamic: a reconsideration of North American queer theory and politics from the 1990s through the lens of Celtic Tiger Ireland.[6] The historical moment that *Tender* narrates—the mid 1990s—is the moment in which Eve Kosofsky Sedgwick was thinking about the epistemology of the closet and its various impacts on queer culture, politics, and identities. Sedgwick's vital work helped to establish queer theory as an academic discourse and shaped the politics of queer activism. To unpack how the novel refigures the discourse of the closet, first we must consider Sedgwick's theorization of the closet.

Sedgwick's theory of the closet is what she later describes as a mode of paranoid reading—both a reading of paranoid homophobic social structures and a reading practice that through a kind of contagion itself displays paranoid characteristics of suspicion and knowingness. She presents the closet as a historical definitional figure that regulates the relationships between homosexual and heterosexual orientation. For Sedgwick, this figure offers a classic conundrum for the deconstructive critic: a seemingly equivalent pair of terms (homosexual/heterosexual) are actually in a dynamic and differential relationship so that one term is privileged over the other (heterosexual over the homosexual) and yet the privileged term (heterosexual) relies on the abjected term (homosexual) for its own constitution (9-10). The seeming equivalence thus masks a dynamic instability. The social regulation of this dynamic opens this seemingly formal structural problem to the politics that motivate Sedgwick's antihomophobic interventions. A second powerful dynamic destabilizes the problem of homo/heterosexual definition. She casts this as the contradiction between a minoritizing and a universalizing view: "on the one hand as an issue of active importance primarily for a small, distinct, relatively fixed homosexual minority (what I refer to as a minoritizing view), and seeing it on the other hand as an issue of continuing, determinative importance in the lives of people across the spectrum of sexualities (what I refer to as the universalizing view)" (1). So not only are the terms themselves in an antagonistic struggle, but the importance of that struggle shifts so that at times it appears to affect a select few and at times seems to affect a broad spectrum. Finally, given the conceptual entanglement of "knowledge" and "sex" within Western culture (73), Sedgwick argues that a whole series of structuring pairings that seem at first to have nothing to do with questions of homosexual and heterosexual definition, have been indelibly marked by the crisis of the closet. She includes paired distinctions that one might suspect are connected to the politics of sexual definition such as masculine/feminine as well as distinctions that do not seem marked by these politics, such as majority/minority (72). We should remember that Sedgwick opens her book with this bold gambit: she argues that "an understanding *of virtually any aspect of modern Western culture* must be, not merely incomplete, but damaged in its central substance to the degree that it does not incorporate a critical analysis of modern homo/heterosexual definition" (my emphasis, 1). So, for Sedgwick, even when one thinks that the topic at hand has nothing to do with the discourse of the closet, it most likely does.

In her important essay on paranoid versus reparative reading, Sedgwick describes the mode of critique through which she theorized the closet in her early writings as a practice of paranoid reading. She characterizes this critical mode, and paranoia itself, as *anticipatory, reflexive* and *mimetic*, as a *strong theory* as opposed to *weak theory*, as a theory of *negative affects*, and suggests that it places its faith in *exposure* (130). This list aptly describes part of what gave Sedgwick's early work its force. Her theorization of the closet anticipates closeted dynamics that have yet to be addressed. One could imagine how closeted dynamics proliferate as kinds of reflections of each other, and how the analysis of particular closets might crystallize other closets. The economy and elegance of her formulations concerning homo/heterosexual definition and the dynamics between minoritizing and universalizing views suggest how much might be explained by them. Her work on the closet is an excellent example of powerfully strong theory. Finally, one sees the faith placed in the exposure of these violent contradictions as a way to disrupt, resist, and overcome.

The historical influence of the Catholic Church from the middle of the nineteenth century until its wane during the period of the Celtic Tiger helps to explain why the discourse of the closet as theorized by Sedgwick—as a structure of double binds on definitions of sexuality, as socially pervasive, as politically volatile, as paranoid and vigilant—was especially powerful in Ireland. The structure and force of Catholic confessions, when used in their worst articulations as tools for social and individual subjection, helped to foster an ethos of paranoia and surveillance that permeated Irish society. Scholars examining this period have produced various accounts that resonate with Sedgwick's work and point to the pervasiveness of the discourse of the closet.[7] Margot Backus and Joe Valente make a case for the pervasive importance of a violent form of knowing unknowingness that structured Irish sexual politics in the last century: "In Irish society, with its legacy of Jansenist Catholicism, a structure of vigorously buttressed ignorance, under-girded by a strict knowledge of what and where to overlook, has persisted through much of the twentieth century, making it easy to mis- or under-interpret the more subtle literary strategies of sexual representation" (55). This *vigorously buttressed ignorance* reprises key features of Sedgwick's theorization of how the discourse of the closet structures relations between knowledge and ignorance.[8] Valente explores an older double bind that defined Irish manhood in the nineteenth century through which Irish men were asked to control their purported passionate natures (read: not engage in organized political objection to their metrocolonial status) as proof of their manly control over baser instincts and thereby show themselves ready for self-rule. Yet thus resigning themselves, they only underscored the appropriateness of British governance over their lives.[9] These double binds were key to Irish gender and nationalist politics and anticipate the contradictions of sexual definition that Sedgwick exposes. Diarmaid Ferriter examines the power of the "seal of confession" as the Church sex scandals broke during the 1990s when people discovered not simply horrific *unknown* crimes committed by the clergy but discovered that Irish people in fact knowingly refused to know about what was going on (403). Their ignorance figured as what Sedgwick refers to as a glass closet. *Tender* offers its own critical analysis of these dynamics through an exploration of the discourse of the closet during the Tiger years. The novel unpacks the discourse of the closet in order to analyze the politics of sexual liberation that came with the boom, to reckon with the politics of paranoia and surveillance that dominated Ireland before, and to trace the restructured, but not completely dismantled, politics of repression that operated after the years of prosperity.

Coming out of the Closet in the Tiger Years

So what does it mean to say that the story of Catherine and James is about coming out of the closet? Their story is about knowing and not knowing, about saying and not saying, about hearing and not hearing, about seeing and not seeing, about being seen and not being seen. While it pivots on James's sexual orientation, the novel reveals that this is a story not just about James, and not even just about Catherine, but is about an entire society. The novel offers at least three moments of coming out of the closet: James's coming out to Catherine about his sexuality, James's coming out to his parents and in particular his mother, and Catherine's outing of James to her own parents, a scene which is equally a moment of her own coming out to her parents as someone who has a gay friend. All three of these scenes play with forms of social knowledge and expression and suggest that the closet organizes, as

James puts it "a way of saying something" and we might add a way of not saying certain things (66). Furthermore, the closet represents a way of structuring knowledge, what I have been referring to as a form of knowing unknowingness, or as Catherine phrases it, something that, "She knew but she did not know" (66). Finally, the novel reveals that the closet, as it polices visibility, is part of a broader society of surveillance. While the economy of the Celtic Tiger coincided with a certain sexual liberalization, particularly with the decriminalization of homosexuality, the novel implies that the new society of display and conspicuous consumption reconfigured and intensified rather than dismantled and dispelled older structures of surveillance and paranoia. McKeon suggests that the closet continues to be an important force whose dynamics frame more than simply questions of sexual identity.

Given the queer pleasure taken in language that yields to multiple senses—as we saw, for instance, in the term *tender*—the novel represents these acts of coming out as counter discourses—discourses that come to mark both pride and paranoia, display and surveillance, liberation and control. While readers might anticipate that coming out dispels ambiguity, Catherine reflects that James's initial coming out both does and does not provide clarity, even in retrospect: "James had suggested a walk down by the canal, and it was down by the canal that things became clear—finally, as Catherine thought of it afterwards, although at the time, this clarity did not feel like anything which was continuous with the things which had gone before" (60–61). As James edges towards his revelation, readers are given two coming out tales in the mounting tension—in the one, Catherine imagines that James is about to declare his love for her and even potentially propose marriage, and in the second, James explains why this would never work as he is not cut out for heterosexual marriage because he is gay. Catherine's expectations suggest a closeted social knowledge transmitted through silences, expectations, and taboos, and they repeat the closeted dynamics with which James struggles.

The closeted social knowledge of Catherine is most fully embodied by the figure of Pat Burke, a neighbor of her family, who sees James and Catherine holding hands on a train platform in Dublin. Catherine suspects that a report will be made to her family, and knows exactly what this report will represent. The surety of this knowledge becomes an ongoing joke between James and Catherine—"*Pat Burke is watching; Oh, that's one for Pat Burke, now; Good God, Catherine, what would Pat Burke say?*" (13). Her social intuition proves correct as during the fight with her parents—discussed more fully below—her father admonishes her, " 'We know plenty…We know that Pat Burke saw the pair of you'" (85). Catherine's reading of James's coming out is initially encoded with a similar sense of social knowledge: "This must be how it happened," she thinks to herself (63). And as his revelation draws near: "what was happening could not, surely, be happening, she told herself; they were eighteen years old—well, James was nineteen, but nineteen was *young*, too young—and they had met not even two months ago—and she did not, did *not* think of him that way—so this could not be happening, *could* not—but what had she stumbled into, what had she caused? *This! This! This!"* (65). Tender, if thought of as a governing trope for this scene, here qualifies her youth and naivety but it also suggests a form of social currency with which she is familiar—the romantic clichés that shape her expectations circulate within the broader society.[10] Tender points to her youthful misreading, or hopeful reading, of what's occurring, and indexes the social value, the abundance, the materiality, the currency, that James seems to introduce to her life: *This! This! This!*

James's coming out as gay, both to Catherine and to his roommates Amy and Lorraine, is similarly stamped by the already known, a mode of knowingness that is both potentially truly already known, but that is also a social pose. Amy and Lorraine, according to James, "said they already knew" when they are first told by James that he's gay (67). Catherine on the other hand, chooses to perform a kind of knowingness that exceeds James's euphemistic indication of his queer orientation. Her assumption of this posture offers a kind of politically progressive comfort to James, who is assured that his newly named orientation in a sense *doesn't matter*, as the cliché would have it, and is assured that he is still valued. Yet this posture also buttresses the social codes of surveillance. The paranoid dynamics of these codes insist that those who uphold them must always be on the lookout for threatening anomalies and yet they assure these vigilant subjects that they have achieved total social awareness:

> "It's a way of saying I won't be giving my mother a wedding. I'm not that kind."
> "OK," she said, dumbfounded.
> He looked at her. "I'm…different," he said slowly.
> "OK."
> "So that's how it is."
> She nodded: a rapid one-two. She knew but she did not know. (66)

Notice that the closet shapes not just expectations about queer sexuality but also sexuality more generally here. The discourse of the closet informs both Catherine's sense of impending heterosexual romance and James's half-spoken revelation about his queerness. *She knew but she did not know* describes her understanding both of heterosexual social codes and codes about queerness. This confluence suggests structures of power that operate with an intense violence against queers—and that violence then extends to broader forms of sexual identification and expression as the prose approximates the painful paranoia of Catherine's point of view. The novel pursues what Sedgwick terms a universalizing view of the politics of the closet that play out through coded forms of social knowledge.

While on the one hand Catherine's acceptance of James's sexuality is admirable and progressive, the novel begins to suggest in this scene the insidious mingling of sexual liberalization with newly liberalized forms of capitalism during the Tiger years. The text coins this in the argot of the middle class and its newly enriched worldview. When James warns Catherine that coming out to his mother will not go well, she tries to comfort him:

> "But your mother is so *brilliant*," she said, taking James's arm. As she said it, she was picturing Peggy as she had been at the kitchen table that morning, cigarette in hand, gold bangles jangling, freckles on the bridge of her nose, the V-neck of her cotton top. That was a nice top, a modern top, a top that not many women Peggy's age, Catherine thought, would wear. None of this she said to James; none of this could be helpful to him. But still, she said again, she was sure that his mother would be fine. Would, she said again, be *brilliant*. (67–68)

The colloquial *brilliant* stamps both an affective assurance, a kind of progressive optimism about how Peggy will react, and this attitude's connection to the consumerism of the boom years. Catherine's use of the term asks how the confident and youthful display of consumption could have any part in the destructive dynamics and homophobia of the closet? Brilliance in this case does not bring clarity, but rather a glare that distracts from the distortion and exploitation of neoliberal economics. The neoliberal abundance of the Celtic Tiger would have an Ireland of individuals who are young—both teenagers and their mothers—and fashionable, modern, socially open to gays, freckled from the sun, at ease and not at work, simply put, *brilliant*. Catherine's insistence on this reading of James's mother's reaction actually distracts from James's point that his mother's reaction will, in fact, not be brilliant. James is right, at least in the short term, while Catherine's optimism wins out in the end as his parents make the pages of the *New York Times* for his wedding announcement years later.

This brilliance, both does and does not operate as an example of what Lauren Berlant terms *cruel optimism*: "optimistic attachment is cruel when the object/scene of desire is itself an obstacle to fulfilling the very wants that people bring to it: but its life-organizing status can trump interfering with the damage it provokes" (227). Catherine's assurance that James's mother will be brilliant is at least in the short term ironically inaccurate—the sting that James receives after coming out is contrapuntal to the good cheer of Catherine's optimism. However, there is a historical context for the elaboration of Berlant's concept that does not line up well with the economic history of Ireland. Berlant explains that "in gathering up scenes of affective adjustment to material that mediates the ongoing present across the recent, the now, and the next, *Cruel Optimism* tracks the fraying relation between post-Second World War state/economic practices and certain postwar fantasies of the good life endemic to liberal, social democratic, or relatively wealthy regions" (15). In this, the timing of the Tiger is off: it emerges as a boom and disappears as a crash. Ireland did not enjoy the broad postwar prosperity that subtends the kinds of fantasies Berlant explores—indeed these "good life" fantasies would be more typically attached to emigration in an Irish context. However, Berlant's work does help us to read the cruelty in the insistence on the present in the years of the Tiger, the sense that "everything is grand now" glimmers in the word *brilliant*. The work of both Sedgwick and Berlant is helpful for understanding the politics of sexuality and economics during the Celtic Tiger. McKeon's novel gives us the lived history of those politics as language.

Expanding on these distorting dynamics, the novel deftly reveals the subtle exploitative connections between economics and affect as Catherine tries to account for her own response to James. What begins as an emotional conversation for James ends with Catherine capitalizing on the experience:

> Still, she was excited. There was this feeling—and she was far from proud of it—of having been given something. Or rather of discovering that she's had something all along, without realizing it; like those priests in Dublin who'd had no idea that the painting in their dining room was a Caravaggio....Feeling so warm towards James as he walked beside her; feeling such tenderness for him, such—it felt almost like gratitude. Because now—now what? Now she had one of her own? There it was, her own shallowness, and it was so depressing, and it was something that James could not know. That she was not good. Not—what was it? Not neutral. Not this solid ground for him, not for him, this safe trustworthy shore. (71)

The analysis of her feelings towards James and about their friendship operates through the language of economics. Her tenderness extended to him seems to have secured a new form of property or proprietorship, as she says, she *now has one of her own*. And instead of completely dismantling the closet, she reassembles a closet to possess a knowledge that she cannot reveal to James. Catherine struggles with this realization. On the one hand, she is thrilled by a novel possessiveness; on the other hand, she suspects that this is an exploitative, a *shallow*, response. The closet, the structure of secrecy and knowledge, has been reassembled in a way that also frames Catherine with its paradigmatic violence and force. As the closet comes into play, Catherine is at some level sensitive to a new relationship between emotional and economic modes. She is ambivalent. The distress of the closet brings that ambivalence into partial relief for herself and into an even clearer focus for the reader.

The spectacle of the closet relies on intensely monitored dynamics of social display. Catherine publicizes her support of James from the start, a gesture aimed at comforting James and securing her own social status:

> Show none of the fact that *This! This! This!* had now become *Gay! Gay! Gay!*— because that was wrong of her, utterly wrong. Nothing was more urgent now than

to keep all of this out, to keep her face soft with calm and with intelligence and with openness, the face of someone wiser, someone better, the face of someone that she wanted, so badly, to be. He was reading her; he was watching her face for the story of how he would be received—for the story, almost, of what he was. And she would not give him a face by which he could justify a tone any darker than the one in which he was speaking to her now. She was Amy, she decided in that moment. She was Lorraine. She was able. She was knowing. She was for telling... (70)

While on the one hand, her response represents a progressive attempt to make herself comfortable with his sexuality, on the other hand, we begin to see the reiteration of paranoia and surveillance in it too.

Catherine is well schooled in the paranoid discourses of the closet and this becomes clear in the next big coming out scene in the novel, Catherine's outing of James to her parents. This outing happens after we learn that James has come out to his own parents. The scene with Catherine's family has a double effect: it represents her challenge to her parents' authority and it reveals that this challenge itself is made possible by her interpellation into a society of surveillance for which the closet operates as a key figure. Catherine again attempts to dismantle a kind of closet and ends up reassembling other figurative closets. She both challenges authority and authorizes other modes of social control. Consider the moment when Catherine finally says directly that James is gay:

> "She doesn't know anything, Patricia," her father cut in. "You don't know how the world works yet," he said to Catherine. "Sure how would you? It's only natural. But your mother and I know, and it's our job to protect you. A young fellow has natural instincts, and if you go and put yourself in the way of them—"
> "Oh, for Christ's sake, that's *it*," Catherine said. It was not a tone she had ever used before with her father, but it was possible, she now realized, and it was somehow addictive. "For Christ's sake," she said again, and she looked at them both as they stared back at her. "James is not interested in my. There's a very simple reason for that."
> "You might think—" her father began, but Catherine held up a hand.
> "James is not interested in me because James is gay."
> There was a silence in the room for a moment... (88)

This challenge to authority is a progressive affirmation of James's sexuality. Catherine cuts through the muddled responses that authorize her parent's command of the scene—an authority based on nature (*natural instincts*), a form of worldly initiation (*you don't know how the world works yet*), and a mode of social labor (*it's our job to protect you*). In another way, the scene reveals just how well trained she is in the discourses of surveillance and paranoia. This is a point that an enraged James makes much later in the novel after Catherine attempts to disrupt his growing romantic relationship with Liam: "You learned your spake from the best of them. *People can hear?* Christ, you were taught and taught well" (345). She certainly challenges her parents' authority, but at the same time, she speaks their language, even going so far as using the same words when she declares to her friend Zoe that it's *her job to look after James.*

Catherine contemplates these structures of paranoia and surveillance as she describes the silent language of power that her family shares. Consider how she glosses the silent stares of her mother, pleading for Catherine to concede to her father: "full of the silent language that was spoken between them: *Just do what he wants, and we can work something out later. Just do what he wants now. Just say no more*" (85). Rather than follow the advice that she infers from her mother's silence, Catherine decides to challenge it: "'It's not *like* that!' Catherine said. She was shocked how fluent she had found herself to be in this language, this register, of standing in front of her father and telling him how it was. 'It's not *like* that, she said again'" (87). For Catherine, this is a moment that embodies new political sensibilities: *she was for knowing, she was for telling.* For her parents, the encounter is laced with class tensions and an urban threat to a rural worldview: "Is this the way you're going on in Dublin, going around with people like that? Is this what we sent you to Trinity for, so you can meet up with this kind of crowd?" (89). *Like that* points to a kind of shared social knowledge about sexuality and queers. Catherine challenges the power of that knowledge and the modes of abjection that it entails when she declares that James is gay. Yet the novel also reveals that she speaks the same coded language as her parents and in some sense shares their values.

As *tender* switches from a way of describing her sympathy with James to marking the hurt inflicted by the aggressive display of those sympathies, these oppositions—urban/rural, new generation/older generation, progressive/conservative, Catherine/her parents—are increasingly undone. The conservative rural and religious ideology espoused by her parents in the coming out scene is revealed as fractured and Catherine is revealed as more invested in the politics of paranoia and surveillance than she would like to admit. After James and Catherine start having sex, Catherine returns home for her grandfather's birthday. In a hilarious conversation with her mother and her aunts, her Aunt Fidelma offers advice for the young Catherine, advice that seems a far cry from the fidelity that rings in her name: "Ride all around you Catherine...and don't bother your arse marrying anyone of them. That's my advice to you" (245). It is true that in offering this advice Fidelma does not imagine the complications that attend James and Catherine's story, but it also presents a nuance that Catherine herself would not have foreseen. As her aunt takes to the dance floor, the language that describes the dance is haunted by the description of Catherine and James's first sexual encounter. Here is the dance:

> Here, on Murphy's dance floor, the couples all observed the unspoken rule [of not looking at each other in the eyes while they dance]—her father with her mother

> now, to "The Gambler," her grandfather with a neighbor woman, Uncle Matt with Fidelma, who was looking content and serene now, not at all like a woman who harbored a longing to go back to her unmarried years and fuck every man she saw. They moved quickly, with great skill, and they kept their eyes fixed on a point in the middle distance, which could not have been easy, since the pub was so small and so cramped; how, then, did they all find a point in the middle distance? And moving as fast as they were? (246)

The scene depicts a collective form of "life-organizing," as Berlant calls it, that includes the repressive regulation of vision, sexual desire (the desire at the heart of Fidelma's advice), and knowledge (how many knew the kind of advice that Fidelma had offered Catherine?), but also includes remarkable bodily fluency, agency, and know-how. It is not a scene of initiation for Catherine in terms of the dancing itself; Catherine never learned to dance, "always, it had been a disaster of knocking limbs" (246–47). It does initiate an awareness for her though as it replays dynamics from her first sexual encounter with James:

> And she knew why it was working for him. She knew why it was that he was able to do this. He did not stay hard the whole time, and she knew why this was, but it did not take him long to recover, and she did not mind—it did not occur to her to mind—that he did so looking not at her but elsewhere: at the ceiling, at the wall, it did not matter. Nothing mattered. She knew what this was. It was touch; he was desperate for it. With Nate—she pushed him instantly back out of her mind—it had been more than he could deal with, more than he could bear, but with Catherine, it was different. With Catherine, it was a deal. (236)

These representations are remarkably parallel: both organize bodily intimacies and pleasures, both repressively organize vision and by extension offer a kind of acknowledgement and a repression of knowledge, both contain notes of desperation, both involve repetition and skill. Finally, both figure social encounters through economics: "The Gambler" frames sociality in the first, setting up both participation and escape (*you've gotta know when to hold 'em, know when to fold 'em, know when to walk away, and know when to run*). In the sex scene, James and Catherine are *working out a deal*. The series of economic formulations that describe relationships in the text here suggest similarities between the modern society of the Celtic Tiger that Catherine imagines herself a part of and the rural, religious, and conservative society that she imagines she is escaping. Readers are invited to critique the repressiveness of village society but are not allowed to bask in what Michel Foucault refers to as "the speaker's benefit," that sense of holding a position outside of power, above the fray (6). Instead, *Tender* reveals Catherine as rightly opposed to homophobia but yet more invested in sexual repression than she may like to admit. The pain of life in the closet frames both scenes— it exposes the false optimism of the Celtic Tiger and reveals the violence of a reassembled repression.

Aesthetics Frames and Historical Questions

By tracking the enchained values of commerce and affect, the novel makes two modes of critique available to readers. One is an ideological critique of homophobia, and sexual repression more generally, organized by the discourse of the closet. For example, in the series of coming out scenes, we are invited to condone Catherine's tolerant embrace of James and to frown upon her parents' phobic responses. We are also invited to critique the discourse that frames both of these, the distortionary discourse of the closet, and in this critique Catherine's display of acceptance is revealed as a transposition of her parents' surveillance. As the novel proceeds, the violence of this distortion intensifies and develops into the kind of historical problem that Sedgwick argues both enabled and hampered queer theory in its development. Homophobic paranoia is generated by the violent distortions of the closet and was one of the most important early objects of study for a politicized queer theory. However, paranoia even as an object of study produces perverse effects and transformed from an object of critique to a methodology. As Sedgwick explains: "Paranoia thus became by the mid-1980s a privileged *object* of antihomophobic theory. How did it spread so quickly from that status to being its uniquely sanctioned *methodology*?" (126). Catherine embodies this transformation: at the outset of the novel her embrace of James's sexuality challenges the violent paranoia of her parents yet as the novel proceeds, her emotional display transforms into powerfully destructive surveillance. *Tender* offers this complex critique by tracking the dizzying transformations in the economies of affect and in the affects of the economic.

The novel tenders a second kind of critical tool, a kind of productive critical practice, particularly through its attention to the practices of representation. Recall that Catherine and James are depicted as learning modes of representation: Catherine, studying for an Arts degree, is being initiated into the disciplinary norms of literary and art criticism. She works for the college paper where she learns the ins and outs of journalism. She is learning how to relate poetry to both her school work and her own life as her reading of Ted Hughes's poems to Sylvia Plath both serves as the topic for a school essay and sparks uncomfortable parallels with her own relationship to James. Finally, she is learning a whole set of social modes of representation as she develops from the Longford country girl to the international journalist living in London who has all but shed her Irish accent.[11] James is similarly depicted as learning various modes of representation: although he is not in school, he has traveled to Berlin to train as a photographer, a training he continues when he returns to Dublin. Like Catherine, he is depicted as a budding critic and reader of literature. He is also shown developing from the country boy with the "culchie accent" (122) to a globe-trotting artist. He is learning how to represent himself and his queer desires. Finally, he is an initiate into the practices of male queer culture. While the novel recounts all of the unease of Catherine's awkward tutelage, James's initiation into queer culture, particularly during his time in Berlin, is only hinted at and perhaps never really grasped by Catherine.

An early scene at a Warhol exhibit, in which James returns to Dublin early and surprises Catherine, is key for both of their training—in particular, the discussion of Warhol's *5 Deaths*. Catherine explains the importance of the work: "I think the whole point is to be unsettled. It's not actually a photograph of a dead woman…It's a piece made out of a photograph of a dead woman." (109) The frame is the key—through the act of framing the artist produces something new, something connected to a particular material but yet in excess of that material. Similarly, *Tender* exposes a certain material: the society of surveillance and paranoia that continues to operate within Ireland. The novel also produces a new kind of queer knowledge, a sensibility that exposes the dynamics of paranoia but yet offers something beyond a paranoid exposure of paranoia. To use Catherine's explanation, the novel is not actually itself paranoid, it is a piece made out of a representation of paranoia. The final three chapters of the novel—"14," "Untitled," and "Freize (2012)"—mark the unraveling of Catherine and James's friendship, the passage of historical time from the Celtic Tiger to post-Tiger austerity, and the emergence of an aesthetic sensibility. In "14," a desperate and destructive Catherine attempts to out her sexual relationship with James in order to destroy his growing romance with another young gay man, Liam. Her attempts backfire violently and she finds herself isolated from James and a whole set of friends. To clear their heads, James and Liam set out to visit Omagh for the weekend where they are victims of the infamous bombing. James photographs the impact of this event and "Untitled" catalogues his efforts—"they were the photographs that made his name" (389). The lacuna between "14" and "Freize (2012)" enfolds over a decade of historical and personal transformations. Perhaps most important for the analysis of the ways in which the novel engages with the historical moments of the Celtic Tiger and post-crash austerity is that they both achieve a certain aesthetic training—James is a successful artist and Catherine is a successful art critic. Put another way, they both put the aesthetic framing that they discussed as students at the Warhol exhibit into professional practice. This framing of the novel itself offers a different kind of reading of James and Catherine's success. On the one hand, read simply as historical realism, there is a kind of anesthetized belief in neoliberal economics that underwrites the dazzling financial success of the two characters. There is very little austerity in the global resources of the two characters as they discuss jet setting from Venice to New York and their new lives as members of the global elite. On the other hand, there is a figurative reading, a sense that they have both become successful in thinking about frames and framing. What is unsettling, and perhaps liberating, is not that there are no questions by the end of the novel, but rather that there is a richer sense of an entangled past, and a more uncertain sense of the future. It is not the characters who must take up the tasks of this future, but rather the readers who are asked to account for how they will frame and write or rewrite their own histories.

No novel can exhaustively account for the events of any particular period. *Tender* examines a historical discourse and historical mentalities—the closet and the subjects articulated in relationship to it—with considerable formal dexterity, but it does not attempt an exhaustive inventory of its moment. When James breaks Catherine's framing of events by declaring that her reading of what happened was in part wrong, that those *were his things*, he interrupts the paranoid reading that produces the novel.[12] In this interruption, we can sense an entirely different novel that could have been or still might be in the hands of readers with different aims. The paranoia of the closet, as it marshals the details of the world to its logic, operates as a kind of austerity that prevents the generation of other possibilities. Sedgwick saw this and her response was in part the rebellious promiscuity and generosity of her writing. In that spirit, it is worth noting the historical transformations that this novel doesn't take up, but which might in this moment of interruption change the story again, reframe how we read it. Looking back on the 1990s, we note that the novel doesn't address the AIDS crisis, which given the centrality of James's exploration of queer sexuality seems important. Sedgwick's work on the closet was a direct engagement with this crisis as part of a long representational history of sexual politics. Looking to the present and the future, we can also ask how the gender and sexual politics the novel frames might help to think about the current movement to repeal the Eighth Amendment, Ireland's constitutional ban on abortion. Can *Tender*, through its intense examination of paranoia and surveillance, help us to imagine this other story and the political problems that might have been those of Catherine and James? The novel doesn't directly ask these questions, but suggests that we as readers can.

Notes

1. Catherine interviews McCabe in the novel, and given the dates, his most recent work would have been *The Butcher Boy* (1992).
2. For analysis of *The Butcher Boy* see "The Queer Labors of Patrick McCabe and Neil Jordan: Novel, Television, Cinema" in Mullen.
3. http://belindamckeon.com. Accessed on March 14, 2016.
4. As he notes, Valente here draws upon Slavoj Zizek's theorization of ideology.
5 Berlant explains the limits of "neoliberalism": "I suggested that critics interested in the ways structural forces materialize locally often turn to the heuristic 'neoliberlaism' into a world-homogenizing sovereign with coherent intentions that produces subjects who

serve its interests, such that their singular actions only *seem* personal, effective, and freely intentional, while really being effects of powerful, impersonal forces" (15).

6. See Mulhall's "The Republic of Love." http://criticallegalthinking.com/2015/06/23/the-republic-of-love/

7 For another example see Munt's "Introduction."

8 See her examination of ignorance 77–80.

9. See "Manliness and the Metrocolonial Double Bind," pages 19–25 in Valente.

10. Claire Bracken noted that Catherine recalls James's Joyce's Gerty from the "Nausicaa" episode of *Ulysses*—a reading that smartly marks Gerty's disability as a kind of tender. That is to say that Gerty also traffics (along with Bloom) in various clichés and that the circulation and exchange of these clichés rests in some way on perceived injury. Another literary precedent is the heroine of Jane Austen's *Northanger Abbey*, also named Catherine and also obsessed with generic clichés—gothic particularly. McKeon recalls Austen in her novel in the submerged storyline between Catherine and her sister Ellen. Ellen remarks that her older sister is "*Not even ugly*" (23), a phrase that echoes Austen's ironic treatment of her heroine.

11. We learn that while James seems to have retained his accent, Catherine has all but lost hers (365).

12. Sedgwick notes that despite the violence that it produces, the epistemology of the closet has been enormously productive for Western culture (68).

Works Cited

Backus, Margot; Valente, Joseph. "The Land of Spices, the Enigmatic Signifier, and the Stylistic Invention of Lesbian (In)Visibility." *Irish University Review: A Journal of Irish Studies*. 43.1 (2013): 55–73. Print.

Berlant, Lauren. *Cruel Optimism*. Durham: Duke UP, 2011. Print.

Ferriter, Diarmaid. *Occasions of Sin: Sex and Society in Modern Ireland*. Profile Books, 2010. Digital version.

Foucault, Michel. *The History of Sexuality. Volume 1: An Introduction*. New York: Vintage Books, 1990. Print.

McKeon, Belinda. *Tender*. New York: Little, Brown and Company, 2015. Print.

Mulhall, Anne. "The Republic of Love." *http://criticallegalthinking.com/2015/06/23/the-republic-of-love/*. Accessed on September 1, 2016.

Mullen, Patrick. *The Poor Bugger's Tool: Irish Modernism, Queer Labor, and Postcolonial History*. New York: Oxford UP, 2012. Print.

Munt, Sally. *Queer Attachments: The Cultural Politics of Shame*. Ashgate, 2012. *http://site. ebrary.com/lib/northeastern/detail.action?docID=10234643*. Accessed on September 1, 2016.

Sedgwick, Eve Kosofsky. *Epistemology of the Closet*. Berkeley: U of California P, 1990. Print.

——. "Paranoid Reading and Reparative Reading, or, You're So Paranoid You Probably Think This Essay Is about You." *Touching Feeling: Affect, Pedagogy, Performativity* Durham: Duke UP, 2003. 123–51. Print..

Valente, Joseph. *The Myth of Manliness in Irish national Culture, 1880-1922*. Urbana, Chicago, and Springfield: U of Illinois P, 2011. Print.

Gina and the Kryptonite: Mortgage Shagging in Anne Enright's *The Forgotten Waltz*

Rachael Sealy Lynch

Anne Enright's fifth novel, *The Forgotten Waltz* (2011), shares with other Post-Tiger fiction a focus on economic disintegration. Throughout the narrative, economic imagery is deployed in order to illustrate the apparent superpowers enjoyed by the citizens of Ireland, and indeed the entire EU, during the Celtic Tiger boom times. The Tiger period is characterized in the novel as post-human, featuring Dublin as a space inhabited by empty and shallow characters, devoid of connectedness, humanity, and ethical care. The narrator and main protagonist Gina Moynihan is deeply embedded in these contexts and functions as a symbol of her present time space. Enright acknowledges in comments to *The Guardian* Book Club her awareness that readers might not find the characters likeable, and her hopes of eliciting a complex response: "There is an amount of mischief in *The Forgotten Waltz*... . I was ... mischievous when I wrote the character of Gina. I wanted mixed feelings from the reader, not a sense of beautiful clarity, because although beautiful clarity may be what we have in books, mixed feelings are what we actually have about people in real life. Writing a contentious character also disturbs the smooth response of the literary snob" (6).

Indeed, *The Forgotten Waltz* has elicited "mixed feelings" from its reviewers, but one of the consequences of this is that the novel has also been underestimated by many of its readers. Reviews, when they first appeared, were frequently less than glowing. Edmund Gordon in *The Telegraph*, for example, opines that the novel lacks "narrative tension," although his review overall is fairly positive. Monica Carter agrees with him, writing in *ForeWord* that without Enright's "masterful stylistic prose and pitch-perfect distillation of the small moments between people, the book's lack of narrative tension would be difficult to overcome." Carter's view is that *The Forgotten Waltz* "is not as tidy as *The Gathering*." Even Hermione Lee, writing in *The Guardian*, who seemed to like the book, argues that the narrator's lover Seán is "not much of a person…and that blank at the centre makes this a thinner book than *The Pleasures of Eliza Lynch* or *The Gathering*." Most damning, perhaps, is Audrey Eyler's back-handed compliment in *The Irish Literary Supplement*:

Ultimately … Enright has done her job so well it's hard to care very much when we finally close the book on Gina, her lover Seán Vallely, his wife Aileen, daughter Evie, Gina's husband Conor, sister Fiona – on all the self-obsessed people Enright has exposed here. There's no later pleasure in calling them up as imaginary company. (22)

It is true that Gina Moynihan is not very likeable, at least until her retrospective narrative is well under way. However, what the critics have missed— and perhaps this is Enright tripping up the "literary snobs," as she puts it—is that she is not meant to be likeable; the point is that she is a contentious character. In other words, Enright's "mischief" signals that the novel requires effort from its readers. First, we need to understand that Enright is interrogating the Tiger's boom and bust economics by offering a meditation on the intersection of economic life with ways of living and being. Second, we must appreciate that Seán and Gina's affair pales in importance when compared to the relationship that is central to our understanding of Enright's project: the non-normative familial bond between Gina and Evie. By defining this crucial and growthful bond as non-normative, I am saying that it does not duplicate the relationships we traditionally expect to see within a heteronormative, traditional familial structure. Gina is not Evie's mother, yet they grow closer in some ways than Evie is to her biological mother. Gina also forms and overcomes a sibling rivalry with Evie as she compares her relationship with her father to Evie's with Seán's, as she learns to accept Evie's place in Seán's life and heart.

Despite, or maybe because of, the non-normative nature of Gina's relationship with Evie, it offers both participants the potential for emotional growth and maturation. When we leave Gina at the end of the narrative, she is a changed person with an impressive capacity for mature self-reflection. She declares that she loves Evie, and her love is neither possessive nor controlling; it just is. Enright's vision privileges interpersonal connection and community, suggesting alternative, non-traditional ways in which community bonds can be reimagined, while offering a sharp critique of the individualistic greed and possessiveness of the Tiger years.

In the essay that follows, I engage with two pertinent and applicable strands of posthuman critical thinking in order to frame Enright's radical ethical project. The first concerns itself with the connections between humans and machines. In my reading of *The Forgotten Waltz*, I explore the role of cyberspace in the characters' behavior, analyzing the (mostly destructive) ways in which, as Claire Lynch puts it, "technology forms part of the novel's landscape" (130). Gina's estranged husband Conor, for example, succumbs to "micro-electronic seduction," providing one of many examples in the narrative of "the fusion of human consciousness with the general electronic network" (Braidotti 90). Enright constructs her cyber-humans as emotionally flattened, "passive" (Lynch 131), and as disconnected from the materialities of life as they are connected to their digital devices.

The second and central engagement with critical posthumanism inter-rogates alternate ways of experiencing time and progress, and reimagines the concept of identity, privileging collectivity over individuality. In apply-ing these ideas, Gina and the conditions of her environment during and after the dehumanizing Celtic Tiger years must be thought of in terms of microcosmics, a shift that registers as a move from post-humanism to post-*humanity*, from ego-driven subjectivity to a focus on collective growth. This very shift is what is at stake in Rosi Braidotti's philosophical work on post-humanism, which offers a detailed road map to life beyond the self. She critiques "humanism's restricted notion of what counts as the human," defining it as a "doctrine that combines the biological, discursive, and moral expansion of human capabilities into an idea of teleologically ordained, rational progress" (16, 13). She further notes that the individu-alism that is so key to such a doctrine "breeds egotism and self-centredness" (30). Instead, citing Cary Wolfe's faith "in the potential of the post-human condition as conducive to human enhancement," she proposes new forms of subjectivity, "other versions of the self" (31, 38): "Post-human subjectivity expresses an embodied and embedded and hence partial form of accountability, based on a strong sense of collectivity, relationality, and hence community building" (49). These concepts of accountability, of non-teleological progress, and of "an enlarged sense of community" (191) are key to understanding Gina's changed perspective in the final pages of *The Forgotten Waltz*. In her developing bond with her pseudo-stepdaughter Evie, Gina "undergoes a process of redefining [her] sense of attachment and connection to a shared world, a territorial space," and in so doing she is "becoming posthuman" (Braidotti 193). Enright's novel therefore critiques Tiger post-humanism, replacing it with an ethical post-Tiger post-humanity, movingly embodied in this non-normative familial bond.

Lastly, the narrative structure of the novel signals to the reader that it is necessary to listen to the music. Every chapter heading is the title of a song, and Enright is offering us nothing less than signposts to a more livable future, to a post-Tiger post-humanity, proffered at a moment of desperate need. However, to transition successfully to the future, it is necessary to understand and learn from the past. For Gina, the time-machine enabling a return to the past is music. It is through the novel's staging of this return to and engaging memory that it establishes an alternative type of post-humanity for post–Tiger times, one that addresses the human in the way that it figures relationships and ties over singularity and insularity. Music therefore functions throughout the narrative as the most significant path back to the past, revealing a radical ethical potential embedded in the novel's core. Memories are evoked and brought to the surface, erupting in a non-linear fashion, through the music time-machine, enabling Gina to harness the past as she learns to step into the future free of the constraints preventing productive communication and growth.

Woman and Child, Present and Past

Kinga Földváry's reading in "In Search of a Lost Future: The Posthuman Child" attends productively to the figure of Evie. As Földváry notes, "Evie suffers from irregular epileptic fits, a condition often seen as a sign of divine visitation in biblical as well as secular narratives" (215). Drawing on "recent theoretical work on posthumanism"[1] encompassing "forms of existence ranging from mechanical creations to subhuman or superhuman creatures," she argues that

> Evie's character takes on such a vague and ungraspable peculiarity that her presence at certain events seems to be more decisive for Gina, the narrator, than the fact that she is committing adultery with Evie's father. This context is created by the very first sentence of the novel: 'If it hadn't been for the child then none of this might have happened, but the fact that a child was involved made everything that much harder to forgive' (Enright, 2011: 5). (215)

Földváry contends that Evie belongs to a group of child figures included in "a significant number of recent English prose writings … who can be interpreted as posthuman in the way they metaphorically embody the fears and anxieties contemporary European society feels about the future, and this despite their unquestioned physiological humanity" (207). While different from "the robots, cyborgs, or zombies that the technological branch of posthuman discourse focuses on, the uncanny child figures … serve as equally powerful signs of global anxieties" (209). Földváry reads Evie as emblematic of "an absence of a clear belief in a humanly comprehensible future, whether that of the individual or society as a whole" (208). There is no doubt that the figure of Evie is central[2] to the text and that she can be seen as the embodiment of anxiety. However, rather than placing emphasis on Evie as "the uncanny child figure," Enright directs the reader's focus towards the development of the bond between Evie and Gina, a bond that represents and embodies the hope for and path to a future that will be more, not less "humanly comprehensible" (208). Moreover, in order for Gina to recuperate her (post)humanity, she must allow herself to find strength in vulnerability, revisiting the past in order to move forward to the future. Gina must interrogate and try to comprehend her own family history, opening herself, through her relationship with Evie, to new ways of thinking about family.

Enright herself echoes Gina's love of Evie, indicating that the girl, and also the connection between adult and child, are pivotal to the entire project. She wrote in her response to *The Guardian Book Club* discussion of the novel that she was inspired to create Evie by "the figure of 'the girl'" in Ford Madox Ford's *The Good Soldier*. She says "[t]he soldier, Edward Ashburnham's final adulterous love is for his own ward, a girl just reaching adulthood, and this torments him beyond bearing. I thought it was wonderful, that love should be the best punishment for desire." She adds, "I am fascinated by the way we love children. It seems we have no option; children are mysterious creatures, and they magnify and distort our own deepest happiness, or lack of it. So I stole the figure of 'the girl' for my own uses and I called her Evie. She was there from page one, and the thing that surprised me, as I wrote the book, was how much I loved her" (6). Gina herself is surprised in a similar fashion. She progresses from jealousy and resentment of Evie's complicating presence in her life and her relationship with Seán to the realization that "I think I love her myself, a little" (258). Evie's presence in the narrative enhances Gina's life, growth, and posthumanity, showing her the way through the "fear and anxieties" engendered by the Celtic Tiger rather than embodying them (Földváry 207).

While Evie is central to Gina's ethical development, maturation, and movement towards the "unknowable of the yet-to-come" (Bracken 15), Enright also assigns vital importance to the eruptive, non-linear process of the recuperation of memory. Indeed, *The Forgotten Waltz* is a non-linear retrospective narrative. Gina's encounter with her lover Seán occurs in 2002, and the narrative then takes us back to her childhood, seen through the lens of both the height of the Tiger and its waning years, to 2009. The brash Dublin career woman *persona* Gina initially presents to the world masks a troubled family past, which we gradually discover as the narrative unfolds. The action takes place, for the most part, in the narrative past, and dwells within Gina's memory along with other key details, particularly in the realm of family dynamics. Many of these details (for example, Gina's memories of her father, and Evie's story) are not released until close to the novel's end. Significantly, the narrative loops around, bending time, beginning and ending in the narrative present, with Gina speaking to and of Evie. The first sentence of the preface, also part of Gina's first-person narrative, reads "If it hadn't been for the child then none of this might have happened" (5). Just four pages into her story, when Gina contrasts her "first sight of Seán" with "the stranger I sleep beside now," she describes her journey back through time and space in order to return to the beginning: "it's like I have to pull the whole planet around in my head to get to this garden, and this part of the afternoon and to this man, who is the stranger I sleep beside now" (13). At the end of the narrative, we have looped back, and forward, to the present, with Gina and Evie discussing what really matters to them both as they await Seán's return from a business trip on a snowbound Dublin day.

The past, including the traumas it contains, plays a key role in Gina's post-human construction, since an openness to vulnerability is an essential component of growth. The importance and workings of memory are recurrent components of Enright's fiction, and Denell Downum's compelling reading of *The Gathering* (2007) is equally applicable to its successor. Downum argues that the primary challenge for Veronica, the main protagonist in *The Gathering*, "like that of her country, is to learn how to live in the aftermath" (86). The answer to meeting this challenge is to return to central childhood places, "where all memory and all imagination begin" (85). Memory may be unreliable and "non-linear" in nature, but Gina, like Veronica, can only start to move forward "as she starts to understand her own past" (82, 86). Gina's project in her narrative is, above all, to become open to the memories lurking beneath conscious thought, and to try to understand where they take her. With Evie serving as her companion and guide, Gina needs to move back in order to move forward. Through the lens of her own and Seán's relationship with Evie, she revisits her relationship with her own parents, particularly her father, and the sibling rivalry she felt with her beautiful sister Fiona. She notes that she cannot compete with Evie in her conversations with Seán: *"He does not speak that way to me"* (237, italics Enright's). Yet it is through facing these hurts and resentments from her past that Gina evolves, discovering new feelings of love and understanding. Watching Evie's tender bedtime rituals with her father, Gina realizes that "I am suddenly passionate about Evie.... jealousy is a kind of loving too. Because when I was her age, my father was sitting up in his hospice bed enjoying the fact that all women were equally nameless to him now" (239). Instead of selfish competitiveness, Gina here expresses a generous sense of affection and she is happy that Evie is close to her father in a way that she was not.

The Eye of the Tiger

When we meet Gina in the first chapter (after her prefatory address to the reader) she is married to Conor, who increasingly succumbs to the "micro-electronic seduction" described by Braidotti (90). He "had just finished a Masters in multimedia; he was a happening geek. I was also in IT, sort of, I work with European communities mainly, on the web. Languages are my thing" (17). He is a solid, good-natured young man, from "a line of shopkeepers and pub owners in Youghal" (16), and Gina attests that in her pre-Seán days, "I loved Conor Shiels, whose heart was steady, and whose body was so solid and warm" (19). The couple buy an overpriced townhouse together and seem to be fairly content, until 2005 when Gina renews an earlier acquaintance with Seán Vallely. She finds him irresistible, despite (or maybe, as we discover, because of) his being eighteen years older than she (he was born in 1957 and she in in 1974, so he is a Baby Boomer to her Generation X). His presence is compelling, if a little menacing. He brings with him an "immediacy," a "copulatory crackle in the air," and Gina soon loses control of her emotions (29). Their affair leads to the disintegration of her marriage; all meaningful communication between Gina and Conor ceases. In the most profoundly posthuman moment in the narrative, reminiscent of "the robots, cyborgs, or zombies that the technological branch of posthuman discourse focuses on" (Földváry 209), Conor eschews human companionship and liaises instead with his computer, bathed by "the glow ... of [his] laptop ... sitting in the armchair, his face blue in the light of the screen, and nothing moves except the sweep and play of his finger on the mouse-pad and his thumb as it clicks" (81). Claire Lynch argues compellingly that Tiger Ireland is in thrall to technology: "By the late 2000s, it seems, the Internet was general all over Ireland," and Conor of course is no exception (133). Lynch points to his neglect of "his responsibilities as a husband to engage in childlike games – he plays rather than provides. More importantly, by retreating into cyberspace he becomes necessarily absent from the real world" (131). Lynch also pays attention in her analysis of *The Forgotten Waltz* to the ways in which technology speeds up the pace of life while simultaneously disrupting its users' attention spans. She argues that "Conor is like the web, in constant flux, perennially unfinished. Observations of Gina's brother-in-law go even further, merging man and machine by noting how he 'opened a bottle of red, sat on the rug and shut down, massively and at speed' (25)" (130).[3] I read what Lynch describes as a "convergence between body and computer" as a donning of numbing, protective post-human armor by the inhabitants of the emotionally barren landscape of late capitalist neoliberal Ireland (133). This arming process begins early in life as Lynch draws our attention to Séan's gift to his daughter: "her first laptop," on which she sends a redundant email to her father, "since father and daughter are within touching distance.... the child's first email captures the wider theme of frustrated communication on which the whole novel stands" (132). As direct interpersonal communication dwindles, so do the meaningful connections and the sense of community on which the health and vigor of a society depend.

The romantic, financial, and real estate parameters within which the action unfolds both define and reflect the novel's trajectory. As the *New Yorker* review puts it, "the move from romance to regret is also a metaphor for Ireland's recent economic struggles" (79). In 2002, when Gina first sets eyes on Seán, Ireland is riding a booze-fueled, materialistic, consumerist rollercoaster. In "Selling Tara, Buying Florida," Colm Tóibín provides some sobering statistics, reporting that "alcohol consumption between 1989 and

1999 went up by 41 percent" in the Republic of Ireland, while "wine sales also doubled between 2000 and 2005, having gone up by 300 percent between 1989 and 1999," and "sales of BMW cars went up 47 percent "during the same period" (15). Gina's wine consumption mirrors these facts; from Chardonnay at parties, to "120 euros' worth" of Krug consumed by Gina and Conor to celebrate the purchase of their townhouse in Clonskeagh (19), to "the cases of French wine" bought by Conor's family at Christmas to keep "themselves separate from the ordinary drunks of the town" (81), to the downing of entire hotel minibars, the Tiger economy apparently runs on copious amounts of expensive alcohol. Tóibín adds that in the same time period, "Ireland became the largest exporter of software in the world; 25% of Europe's computers and much of its Viagra would be made in Ireland" (15).

The rise in real estate prices noted by Gina is even more jaw-dropping.[4] At the height of the boom, with property values soaring by the minute, Gina and Conor engage with abandon in what she describes as "mortgage love. Shagging at 5.3 per cent" in their flimsy new house that "was going up by seventy-five euro a day … the wood of the new-laid floors would squeeze out paper money" (20). Every building in which Gina spends time during this period is somehow on steroids. Gina's rival in her initial pursuit of Seán is known only as Global Tax woman, and the pair face off in sumptuous surroundings in a hotel on the shores of Lake Geneva during an economic conference. Even Gina's office is larger than life, a weird combination of the functional space, the delicately exotic, and the jungle: it is "all stripped brickwork with industrial skylights … the foliage, which is everywhere and fabulous, from the bougainvillea going up the ironwork to the ivy cladding the bathroom walls. The Danes who did the refurbishment put in irrigation the way you might do the wiring so the place is a thicket …" (58).

Séan's New Year's Day brunch is perhaps the updated Tiger post-human equivalent of Joyce's famous gathering on the Epiphany in "The Dead": a flamboyant, drunken, superficial affair with undertones of desperation, a gathering of hollow, self-aggrandizing Masters of the Universe. The excesses of the consumer culture are on garish display; Séan's wife Aileen, and several other guests, call to mind "the robots, cyborgs or zombies" mentioned by Földváry: Aileen is "wearing a black Issey Miyake pleats dress edged with turquoise, and the collar stood up around her neck in a sharp frill" (92). It makes her look not quite human, but rather like "some soft creature, poking out of its beautiful, hard shell" (92).[5] The living room contained "Food at one end, drinks by the doors, a Filipino circling for the refill with a bottle in either hand" (94).[6] This is not a family party space; wheeling, dealing, and making an impression are the order of the day, and nothing of actual importance is ever discussed. Enright writes that while "The Enniskerry husbands stood about and talked property: a three-pool complex in Bulgaria, a whole Irish block in Berlin" (98), the women discuss plastic surgery. Gina comments that "a couple of women in the room had the confused look that Botox gives you, like you might be having an emotion, but you couldn't remember which one. One had a mouth that was so puffy, she couldn't fit it over the rim of her wine glass" (98). A heavily pregnant out-of-place wife lumbers hugely around the room, "as slow and hysterical as a turnip in a nervous breakdown," in between dozing off intermittently on the sofa (95). This scene offers a perfect example of the dehumanizing landscape described by Braidotti and Lynch, a world populated by emotionally flattened beings and in which rampant individualism "breeds egotism and self-centredness" (Braidotti 30).

Given the ostentatious display of materialism, Gina in contrast wears a cheap ring for the occasion that belonged to her mother, about which she offers the apparently casual observation that it was "a big plastic fake rock from my mother's dancing days, that might have been made of Kryptonite" (99). Kryptonite is, of course, a material from the Superman fictional universe, specifically the ore form of a radioactive element from Superman's home planet of Krypton. The Oxford Dictionary defines it thus: "(In science fiction) an alien mineral with the property of depriving Superman of his powers."[7] In Gina's case, the ring operates symbolically as an antidote to the poisonous atmosphere created by the Celtic Tiger, foreshadowing the superficiality of the entire Tiger enterprise and the illusory nature of the superhuman/posthuman sphere. It also heralds the cracking of Gina's armor, and her later journey back through her family history, delving into memory and the past, amidst the collapse and devastation of the Tiger economy. The Kryptonite ring thus serves as a sort of anti-capitalist currency, ostensibly worthless, but imbued with the power to render Gina vulnerable, to transport her back to the past and to fashion alternate and far more sustaining posthuman imaginaries than those offered by the Tiger Supereconomy.

Beyond Gina's Kryptonite ring, it must also be emphasized that the house also contains Séan's daughter Evie, who opens the door to Gina and then surprises Séan and Gina during a clandestine kiss upstairs, "barrel[ing] into her father and tilting her face up to receive a kiss from them both too" (107). These little encounters foreshadow Gina's later grappling with Evie's importance in her father's life, and, more importantly, her growing significance to Gina. The door is now open for their relationship to grow, the kiss perhaps foreshadowing the strength of the bond that will develop between them, despite the obstacles presented by Gina's initial jealousy and Evie's resentment of Gina's role in her parents' breakup.

After the bottom falls out of the economy and Gina and her husband have separated, mortgage shagging is replaced by "a whole litter of For Sale signs" that Gina and Seán have "loved…into being" (232) after the disintegration of both their marriages, and Global Tax woman reappears, unattractively drunk and middle-aged, looking "so old," and no longer of interest (177). Gina's sister Fiona and her husband Shay sell their beach house in Brittas, and Fiona reveals that Shay has been made redundant, a fact she tried to hide for as long as possible. At the same time she tells Gina that the "little fucker" Seán made at a pass at her before he moved on to Gina (209–10). Gina and Fiona cannot sell their mother's house, no matter how they drop the price: "The house had been on the market exactly a year. If you listened to the car radio, all the money in the country had just evaporated; you could almost see it, rising off the rooftops like steam" (233). Gina finds an online forum in which people "were laughing" at the still inflated price (204). At the end of the novel the house remains unsold. Shay reports that building has stopped, and that prices are in freefall (209–10). Seán, too, is enmeshed in real estate disasters: he needs to take care of the expensive needs of his ex-wife Aileen, and has no idea "whether he can break even in Budapest, or what is happening to his house by the beach, which is now up for sale too" (232). Even Gina's new office in Dundalk, after she "bailed out of Rathlin before it hit the buffers and started in the drinks industry" (168), stands in stark contrast to her previous botanically enhanced professional quarters: "The office, marginal in all respects, consists of a couple of rooms tacked on to a warehouse near the M1: grey walls, grey roof, blue carpet, red banisters, yellow cubes to set your coffee cup down…. [with just a] small meeting room" (170).[8]

Perhaps the fragility of both mortgages and marriages in the book is best exemplified by Gina's ring. I have suggested that the Kryptonite connection is no co-incidence, and it resonates symbolically throughout the narrative in two ways. The ring's junkiness points to Gina's vulnerability, foreshadowing the cracks in her illusory Tiger-given powers. Yet it also hints at the real source of strength, grounding, and personal growth for Gina: family connections, both normative and non-normative. The importance of these relationships, particularly those existing between adults and children, whether or not biological ties bind them, lies at the core of Enright's narrative. The ring, like "the cloying old glamour" (151) of *Je Reviens*, Mrs. Moynihan's favorite and aptly named perfume, represents a link to Gina's mother. Gina must grapple with a legacy of dysfunction in order to understand herself, her sister Fiona, and Seán as damaged children who have grown up and, in Seán and Fiona's case, become parents themselves. Of Fiona, before her world falls apart, Gina observes that "[n]ow she has a perfect life, my sister has taken to inventing a perfect past to match it. She doesn't think our father was a drunk – which makes two of them, I suppose – and she would certainly deny the memory" (191). Gina is realizing the critical need for human beings, if they are to grow, learn from, and move past their histories, to embrace rather than deny memory. Her ring serves as a potent visual symbol of this need, nudging her forth on her looping journey through the past towards a posthuman imaginary.

Familial Ties

Throughout the novel, Enright interrogates the destructive impact that parents can have on their children, but more importantly, through Gina and Evie, on the productive possibilities inherent in a non-normative adult-child relationship. When Fiona discovers Gina's and Seán's affair, Seán eventually leaves his wife, and he and Gina are forced to take refuge in Gina's family home after her mother's death, as the economy collapses around them. (This move of course results in Gina's ideal placement to recuperate the memories she needs to address on her journey forward). However, unlike Gina, who is childless, Seán comes with his complicated daughter, Evie, who is "nearly twelve" at the narrative's end, and who has a bedroom in Gina's family home (234). While Gina is technically "childless," she is not without a child in her life, and her lack of ownership of Evie frees them both to choreograph their own dance. This freedom from conventional parent-child parameters allows for dynamic and often productive, if unpredictable, encounters, enabling growth and change. For example, Gina demonstrates self-control in response to Evie's vicious *"You're not my mother!"* (252), because she recognizes that "I have no rights here" (252) but also because she is nevertheless prepared to answer to Evie's need. Her gentleness is further due to her belief that "[there] is something so formal about talking to children: you have to be very polite. It is the only thing they understand" (254). Gina's restraint represents a moment of communality, a sense of obligation and a willingness to engage with sensitivity despite (or because of) the absence of blood ties, in contrast with her father's highly insensitive treatment of her. In another encounter, it is Evie who is prompted to rise to the occasion. When she whines that Gina has finished all the mayonnaise, Gina, unburdened by any conventional maternal obligation to feed her young, responds, "Why don't you go and buy your own fucking food?" (246). Evie is clearly impacted by Gina's words, and carefully tempers her remarks later in the days so that they come out as "something that wasn't just a whine" (246). Not being a mother has its own importance; as the pair walk through the snow, Gina comments that "Evie slides along on the soles of her boots in a way that would annoy me, if I were her mother, but it does not annoy me much" (258). Clearly Enright places significant value on Gina and Evie's capacity to influence each other, and to build a unique relationship of their own.

Early in the narrative we learn that Gina is with Seán now, and that Evie "was a bit peculiar," but the only real early indication of Evie's later centrality in Gina's life is her unsupported comment on the first page that "the fact that a child was affected meant that we had to face ourselves properly, we had to follow through" (5). A fuller telling of Evie's story comes much later, when Seán acknowledges that Evie's childhood seizures and other neurological problems were caused, in part at least, and certainly not helped, by his and

Aileen's disastrous marriage and bad parenting; "I failed her," he says (182). And on the snowy Dublin day in 2009 of the telling of her story, Gina interrogates her own troubled relationship with her father. In the narrative present, both parents have died; Gina's father when she was much younger, and her mother recently, in 2007. Gina loved her mother and her grief is potent and sincere; speaking of her father's early demise, she remarks that "for the Moynihan girls – and this was our dirty little secret – it was the right parent who had died" (114). Her father was distant, drunken, and at the end demented, the result of "some funny bile thing that affected his liver and the toxins in his blood caused a quick kind of havoc in his brain" (188).

Gina also, significantly, mentions that her father taught her to Irish dance, and also describes how Séan dances with Evie. However, Mr. Moynihan was never around enough to parent his girls, to be a positive influence in their lives. Gina's greatest struggles are with the facts that Evie has a father while she did not, and that when it comes to Seán's love, she cannot compete with Evie, and she cannot "save" him as Evie can save him: "He does not hold me by the hand. He does not tango me down the hall, and arch me over backwards. He does not wake in the night, thinking of me" (237). And when Seán calls from overseas, it is Evie he calls first. Gina is consumed with jealousy until she learns to be glad that Seán is to Evie what her father never really was and cannot now be to her, and then she begins to move towards love for the girl, with Evie pushing Gina towards responsibility and accountability. Again the non-normative family relationship existing between Gina and Evie, initially expressed perhaps in the form of sibling rivalry, leads Gina towards growth and change. The last conversation in the narrative is between Gina and Evie, about Gina's role in the disintegration of Evie's parents' marriage. In response to Gina's insincere attempt to evade responsibility for her role in the break-up, "it could have been anyone, you know?" Evie replies, "But it wasn't… . It was you" (259). But by now Gina is ready to listen, and perhaps to live with her choice and its consequences.

Excess, the European economy, and the frozen moment make way for Gina's interior journey of self-discovery in this "snowed in" world of "frozen confusion, quiet chaos" (230). The snow opens up a space in which Gina can connect to her parents, feeling their presence in the house that was theirs, and also reach out to her lover's child. [9] Evie now spends some of her time in Gina's house, in the bedroom Seán has decorated for her. During their walk through the snow in the final chapter while Seán is still on his way home after a business trip, the pair dance awkwardly around their situation but actually achieve a few moments of genuine communication. Gina buys Evie some eyeliner and then, when they go for hot drinks, Evie speaks of her parents and the unpleasantness of her epilepsy, and Gina, remembering their first meeting, "when you were just a little thing… . long ago before anything," feels "an urge to kiss her" (256–57). Gina here finally allows herself to be completely vulnerable, to risk a love that must inevitably lead to loss. She understands the transience of the moment, acknowledging that "the snow will melt, the houses will sell ... and Evie will grow or be otherwise lost to me. Not that I ever had her, really" (259). Gina privileges the moment of connection, no matter what follows. Her post-human armor is crumbling on this snowy day, in a show of vulnerability first seen emerging in her wearing of the Kryptonite ring and linked to the recuperation of memory.

This relationship between Gina and Evie plays a key role in Enright's configuration of a new post-Tiger humanity, expressing "accountability, based on a strong sense of collectivity, relationality, and hence community building" and an ethics grounded in "the potential of the post-human condition as conducive to human enhancement" (Braidotti 49, 31). Evie's potent presence in Gina's life offers her a way forward, in part by taking her back to the very situations in her own childhood that initially caused such intense feelings of jealousy. However, the narrative also offers both Gina and the reader another way to access the deepest recesses of memory and comprehension: an embedded musical time-machine.

Listen to the Music

Music runs right through this novel, pulling us backwards and also propelling the narrative forward, allowing Gina to work her way through a constant undertow of musical references. The entire narrative is constructed upon a melodic frame, a musical time-machine which is by nature and design capable of slippage at any moment, and which like memory itself, requires activation in order to become effective. The musical references are dependent upon the attention and response of each reader. We are not specifically alerted to the fact that each chapter is named for a song, often an old one, unexpected perhaps in a novel about the frenetic Tiger boom times. The songs, like memories, are waiting for us to attend to them, to recuperate each melody in its entirety and investigate its relevance to Gina's narrative. They can easily be missed. Enright does not provide the lyrics, or even offer a clear indicator that she is quoting song titles. The reader must make this relevant connection, and then she can recall the songs from memory or research the lyrics and infer their significance to the text. Therefore, of course, a reader could pass over the references, never breaking the surface to realize that the chapter titles were song titles at all. Enright's brilliance in building this framework for Gina's journey through memory cannot be overstated. Form points to function, alerting us (if we take heed) as to how the narrative might be read. It is necessary to follow the trail backwards, so that we may be better prepared to proceed, allowing the lyrics underpinning the narrative to erupt from beneath the crust. Enright also deploys music for its power to awaken memories fraught with meaning, and the terminus of her musical time-machine is indeed truth, or at least Gina's best efforts to reach the truths embedded in her past. Furthermore, "a shallow present" is precisely what Gina and Evie must navigate in order to imagine a new posthuman.

The first chapter of *The Forgotten Waltz* is entitled "THERE WILL BE PEACE IN THE VALLEY" (9), followed by "LOVE IS LIKE A CIGARETTE" (16), establishing from the outset a pattern that runs right through the book. A study of the full lyrics to the song titles chosen by Enright for her chapter headings reveals her mastery and care in the composition of the narrative. The breathtakingly apposite lyrics reflect, support, and extend the details of Gina's story. To choose just a few examples, in the first chapter of the narrative, Gina describes her initial meeting with Evie and wonders, from the narrative present, whether she herself has herself "moved on" (15). Thomas Dorcey's "There Will Be Peace in the Valley" contains these words: "The host from the wild will be led by a Child / I'll be changed from the creature I am." Music of course leads to dancing, and Leonard Cohen writes of a continuing journey through the remnants of a damaged past in "Dance me to the End of Love": "Dance me to the children who are asking to be born / Dance me through the curtains that our kisses have outworn / Raise a tent of shelter now, though every thread is torn / Dance me to the end of love." Cohen's words haunt the chapter they introduce, in which Seán and Gina struggle through a weekend away that they mistakenly believe at the time to be the "close" of their affair (127). The lyrics also point to Gina's walk with Evie through the snow as a dance, one that will enrich them but also move them past love to loss. Gina knows that "whether her father stays with me or goes, I will lose this girl" (259). However, she is making a connection with Evie rendered all the more potent by the absence of possession, and she will retain the memory of this day, as she has of many earlier days.

Gina travels on a musical time-machine through memory to the reimagining of the forgotten waltz, the formative experiences of her life and the memories that make her who she is. We now understand why the novel is so named, and why Gina's mother's ring dates back, symbolically, to her "dancing days" (99); as Gina grieves for her mother in the days following her death, she envisages love as a dance and remembers that her parents would "go for drinks in the Shelbourne first, and dance after dinner, in the wooden centre of the carpeted floor, to Elvis covers and 'The Tennessee Waltz'" (150). The idea that love, and its memory, can be a painful, lonely dance, as it also was for her mother, comes up again when Gina is waiting for Seán to leave his wife: "The loneliness of it was, in its own way, fantastic. I lived with it, and danced with it" (203). Significantly, it is in the "SAVE THE LAST DANCE FOR ME" chapter that Gina describes, "on this night of snow" (187), how Seán finally opened up about Evie, and Gina herself faces the painful memories of her father and the damage he has wrought. She relates his drunkenness, his deterioration, and his terrible ability to hurt, remembering that "he did not forget, not to the very end, how to pitch one human being against the other. That he could do when all else was lost to him" (189). For example, comparing Gina to Fiona, "'A woman should be very beautiful or very interesting,' he used to say, when he was well. 'And you, my dear, are *madly* interesting'" (189). By thus objectifying and classifying his daughters, one as "beautiful" and one as "interesting," the girls' father is in fact robbing them of their individual humanity, their personhood, relegating them to a depersonalized space in which they are representative of a general attribute or a function and nothing more.

Moving Forward: From Post-Humanism to Post-Humanity

Victoria Justice's "THE THINGS WE DO FOR LOVE" headlines the final chapter, in which Gina and Evie take a slow walk in the snow: "Communication is the problem to the answer / You've got her number and your hand is on the phone / The weathers turned, and all the lines are down / The things we do for love, the things we do for love. / Like walking in the rain and the snow / When there's nowhere to go / And you're feeling like a part of you is dying / And you're looking for the answer in her eyes." So careful is Enright's interleaving of narrative and song that Gina's hand is indeed on her mobile phone in the midst of climatic conditions paralleling those in the song. Snow is once again "general all over Ireland," preventing locomotion, muffling electronic communication, and forcing a temporal slowdown enabling introspection and a return to interpersonal communication ("The Dead" 255). The temporal acceleration described by Lynch is here reversed; instead of speed and limited attention spans, "the sky ... was already dark and empty of planes" before evening even arrived (171). Gina obtains her news from the decidedly old-fashioned radio, where she learns that "[t]he entire country had bailed out of work early and was heading for home," and, in an interesting imagined disruption of linear time, "the port tunnel was so empty and pure it felt like the future" (171). Past and future here meet as they loop about the frenetic present. As Gina and Evie walk through their snow-bound world, Evie's "phone beeps" to let her know that Séan's plane has finally landed; it is, appropriately, buried deep in her bag rather than connected to her body, and it "takes her an age" to recover it. Its brief intervention prompts this parenthetical comment from Gina: "(I wait for my phone to jump but it does not)" (258). Gina's silent mobile clearly affects her, but the parenthetical nature of her thought is revealing. She dances past her hurt and looks—and finds—an answer, and a connection, in Evie's eyes. Enright is suggesting, in her inclusion and placement of the phone and other devices and machines (radios, landing planes) at the end of the narrative, the figurative possibility of a post-human world that privileges connection and relationality over armor. While electronic communication between father and daughter in the same room speaks more to separation than to engagement, the machine plays an important role in the contact of post-humanity, operating not to divide but to connect and communicate, just like the phone in the song "The Things We do for Love."

Of equal importance, as we interrogate Evie's importance to Gina's deepening understanding of familial ties and interpersonal connections, are the lyrics of The Drifters' "Save the Last Dance for Me," the title song of the novel's fourth to last chapter: "You can dance every dance with the guy / Who gave you the eye …" "But don't forget who's taking you home / And in whose arms you're gonna be / So darlin' save the last dance for me." Evie does take Gina "home" in her voyage of self-discovery, and Gina does save the last dance for her, concluding her narrative with their brief but powerful conversation. Their walk through the snow reinforces and emphasizes the non-normative relationship between the two that reveals itself in the end as the most important one in the novel. Evie's comment that "It was you," the final words of the narrative, can be read not only as a reference to Gina's breaking up of her parents' marriage but also as a recognition and an affirmation of Gina's importance to Evie (259).

Music, recuperation of a troubled family past through memory, dance, and the uncanny presence of Evie all pave the way for Gina to begin the process of understanding and healing from her many emotional wounds, and, perhaps, the formation of new familial, but non-normative, bonds. Yes, loving is a risky business; love is indivisible from involvement, pain, and loss. Perhaps "Evie started to disappear" from the Tiger landscape, slipping beneath the surface like the memory of a song, and resurfaces "clear-hearted," despite her mother's materialistic post-human nature, ready to walk home with Gina (240, 253). Memory provides a pathway to understanding who we were, who we are, and who we are becoming. In choosing to wear her mother's ring when her apparent superpowers appear to be at their zenith, Gina holds tight to her memories and her vulnerability, even if she does not yet at the time fully realize how much. The disruption of linear time in *The Forgotten Waltz*, through the ring, the music, and the blanket of snow, allows for the emergence of a post-Tiger posthuman ethics, grounded in such an understanding and in "a strong sense of collectivity, relationality, and hence community building" (Braidotti 49). Furthermore, Enright uncouples the concept of "the moral expansion of human capabilities" from that "of teleologically ordained, rational progress" (Braidotti 13). Gina travels backwards in time through the musical memory machine, and her travels equip her to resume her journey forward,[10] forging a new posthuman during chaotic times based on open communication, unselfish connections and familial ties. Gina's growthful relationship with Evie is one in which biological links and possessiveness are notably lacking, and in which Gina has nothing material to gain. Not only is the girl not Gina's, but Gina also cannot acquire or keep her. However, the fragility of this fruitful bond enhances rather than diminishes its potency; in Braidotti's words,

Gina is now possessed of the accountability and "enlarged sense of community" so lacking in Tiger times (191). This relationship is brought into its sharpest focus as the pair travel through the snow, sharing family memories as time stands still, and it embodies Enright's imagining of a post-Tiger ethics, placed in deliberate opposition to the shallow, empty materialism, possessiveness, commercial transactions, and strident individualism of the Tiger years.

Notes

1. Földváry references "the seminal texts of posthumanist criticism," noting that they "imply the necessity of the human as a vantage point for any investigation into the field of posthumanism." Citing Jean-Francois Lyotard's "well-known critique of the Enlightenment belief in the progress of history, she notes that "what I find particularly salient is his choice of the figure of the child to exemplify the double-edged sword of the notion of humanity and its controversial attitude to its own humanness." Following posthumanist discourse, she concludes that what we see in "young bodies" like Evie "is a clear reinforcement of the statements of critical posthumanism articulated in opposition to the liberal humanistic discourse. As Bart Simon argues, the notion of 'man' reenvisioned by Enlightenment narratives as 'rational, autonomous, unique, and free have in turn been challenged and deconstructed,' and as a result 'the posthuman subject is an unstable, impure mixture without discernable origins; a hybrid, a cyborg' (2003, 4)" (211–12).

2. Several of the best reviews of *The Forgotten Waltz* also recognize, albeit briefly, Evie's importance in the narrative. D.J. Taylor of *The Spectator* notes that "Plump, unpredictable, and engagingly farouche, Evie lurks at the proceedings' core" (33). Barbara Hoffert writes in *Library Journal* that "[t]hrough Gina's determined pursuit of their relationship, we see the stupefying nature of desire, which Enright deftly contrasts with the sometimes equally stupefying nature of parenting. Gina's big competition is not Seán's wife but his sweet, not-quite-right daughter" (70). Clare McHugh of *The Wall Street Journal* also stresses Evie's centrality: "Gina strives to hold Seán's affection, but she knows she is replaceable in a way that Evie never will be. True Love? Maybe it only happens between parent and child" (C.8).

3. Lynch also draws and builds upon Claire Bracken's discussion of the "body-machine compound" in Enright ("Modernity, Technology, and Irish Culture,"186). She notes that at the time of publication (2011), Bracken's claim that Enright privileges twentieth-century technology over the "digital and cyber technologies of the new millennium" (2011, 185) in her writing was accurate when made, it must be revised in the light of *The Forgotten Waltz*" (130).

4. Tóibín also discusses the property boom in "Selling Tara, Buying Florida," noting at the height of the madness (the article appeared in 2008) that "The Irish are buying second houses in both coastal areas and cities in Europe .... A Euro-Area lending survey reported in May 2007: 'A significant or considerable proportion of loans secured on property in Ireland was to buy further property, a higher proportion than the Euro average.' In other words, the Irish are spending and borrowing freely, but when they are investing, it is not in areas such as research and development that will create further wealth in the future but in property, which will depend on property prices to maintain their value" (24). Tóibín's words proved of course to be prophetic, as evidenced by the property crash of 2009.

5. Aileen's obsession with expensive clothing extends also to her insistence on armoring her daughter Evie in appropriately costly outfits, despite Evie's lack of interest and, indeed, outright dislike of such ostentation. Gina tells us that "Aileen looks in the cheap shops to see what she will wear and tries to match it in something a little more expensive" (233). Evie is also equipped with an ill-fitting bra. Gina remarks that Evie is "hugely uncomfortable in her bra – for which she has my sympathy, it's a life sentence" (236). For a thought-provoking discussion of the "representation of the girl-in-bra," see Claire Bracken, *Irish Feminist Futures*, 82–87.

6. "There were little bowls of glazed nuts, and dried mango slices that had been dipped in dark chocolate. Really dark. At least 80 percent" (97). The parallels between this scene and the dinner scene in "The Dead" are remarkable. The feast in "The Dead" features "a large green leaf-shaped dish with a stalk-shaped handle, on which lay bunches of purple raisins and peeled almonds, a companion dish on which lay a solid rectangle of Smyrna figs, a dish of custard topped with grated nutmeg, a small bowl full of chocolates and sweets wrapped in gold and silver papers, and a glass vase in which stood some tall celery stalks" (224).

7. Superman's susceptibility to poisoning from Kryptonite radiation has entered popular usage as a metaphorical reference to an individual's vulnerability. I want to acknowledge here my debt of gratitude to my student Clint Kantor. Without his having drawn attention during a lively class discussion to the composition of the ring, I, neither a US native nor a reader of comic books, would probably have noted it in passing but not dwelt on the very suggestive details.

8. For detailed treatment of the Post-Tiger years, see David McWilliams's *The Good Room* and Fintan O'Toole's, *Ship of Fools: How Stupidity and Corruption Sank the "Celtic Tiger."*

9. In another echo of "The Dead," the blanket of snow offers the possibility of regeneration. Hermione Lee draws a parallel between the "snowbound" streets of Dublin and 2009 and those in "The Dead," seeing "a faint tribute to the end of Joyce's great story of love, loss, family, and nation." While time constraints prevent a full interrogation here, Enright's tribute to Joyce is not a faint one. Most important perhaps is that for both Gretta and Gina, music disrupts the temporal progression through linear time, enabling a return to the past, while Gabriel and Conor are firmly planted in their present.

10. Backwards travel in the book is also portrayed as non-linear. Remembering takes place as a rupture, set in motion by a "tremor" like Gina's recall, in the silence of a snowy night, of her father "listening to classical music in the dining room" (187), initiating her return in the time-machine or the silence of a snowy evening and the extended reliving of her childhood.

Works Cited

Bracken, Claire. "Anne Enright's Machines: Modernity, Technology, and Irish Culture." *Anne Enright*. Eds. Claire Bracken and Susan Cahill. Irish Academic Press, 2011: 185–204. Print.
_____. *Irish Feminist Futures*. Routledge, 2016. Print.
Braidotti, Rosi. *The Posthuman*. Polity Press, 2013. Print.
Carter, Monica. Review of *The Forgotten Waltz*. *Foreward*, 17 May 2011. go.galegroup.com. ezproxy.lib.uconn.edu/ps/i.do?&id=GALE|A272994759&v=2.1&u=22516&it=r&p= LitRC&sw=w&authCount=1
Cohen, Leonard. "Dance Me to The End of Love." www.azlyrics.com/lyrics/leonardcohen/ dancemetotheendoflove.html
Dorcey, Thomas A. "There Will be Peace in the Valley For Me." www.negrospirituals.com/ songs/peace_in_the_valley.htm

Downum, Denell. "Learning to Live: Memory and the Celtic Tiger in Novels by Roddy Doyle, Anne Enright, and Tana French." *New Hibernia Review* 19.3 (2015): 76–92. Print.

Enright, Anne. *The Forgotten Waltz*. Norton, 2011. Print.

_____. "Anne Enright on Writing *The Forgotten Waltz. *" Review/response to John Mullan in *The Guardian Book Club. The Guardian Review Pages*, March 17, 2012, p.6. www.theguardian.com/books/2012/mar/16/book-club-forgotten-waltz-enright

Eyler, Audrey Stocklin. "Brilliant indictment." Review of *The Forgotten Waltz* by Anne Enright. *Irish Literary Supplement* 32.1 (2012): 22. Print.

Földváry, Kinga. "In Search of a Lost Future: The Posthuman Child." *European Journal of English Studies* 18.2 (2014): 207–20. Print.

Gordon, Edmund. "*The Forgotten Waltz* by Anne Enright: Review." *The Telegraph*, 28 April 2011. www.telegraph.co.uk/culture/books/bookreviews/8480088/The-Forgotten-Waltz-by-Anne-Enright-review.html

Henigan, Julie. "'The Old Irish Tonality': Folksong as Emotional Catalyst in 'The Dead.'" *New Hibernia Review* 11.4 (Winter 2007): 136–48. Print.

Hoffert, Barbara. "Enright, Anne. *The Forgotten Waltz. *" Review, *The Library Journal*, July 2011, 70. Print.

Joyce, James. "The Dead." *Dubliners*, with an Introduction by John Kelly. Alfred A. Knopf, 1991, 199–256. Print.

Justice, Victoria. "The Things We Do For Love." www.azlyrics.com/lyrics/victoriajustice/thethingswedoforlove.html

"Kryptonite." *Oxford.dictionaries.com.* www.oxforddictionaries.com/us/definition/american_english/kryptonite

Lee, Hermione. "*The Forgotten Waltz* by Anne Enright – review." *The Guardian*, Sunday 1 May 2011. theguardian.com/books/2011/may/01/forgotten-waltz-anne-enright-review

Lynch, Claire. *Cyber Ireland: Text, Image, Culture*. Palgrave Macmillan, 2014. Print.

McHugh, Clare. "Review — Books: The Ways and Woes of Illicit Love." Review of *The Forgotten Waltz* by Anne Enright. *The Wall Street Journal* Oct. 15, 2011, C.8. search.proquest.com. ezproxy.lib.uconn.edu/docview/898389367?rfr_id=info%3Axri%2Fsid%3Aprimo

McWilliams, David. *The Good Room*. Penguin Ireland, 2012. Print.

Meaney, Geraldine. "'Waking the Dead: Antigone, Ismene, and Anne Enright's Narrators in Mourning." *Anne Enright*. Eds. Claire Bracken and Susan Cahill. Irish Academic Press, 2011:145–64. Print.

O'Toole, Fintan. *Ship of Fools: How Stupidity and Corruption Sank the "Celtic Tiger."* PublicAffairs, 2010. Print.

Review of *The Forgotten Waltz. The New Yorker*, 28 Nov 2011, 79. Print.

Taylor, D.J. "Doomed to Disillusion." Review of *The Forgotten Waltz* by Anne Enright. *The Spectator*, 7 May 2011, 33. Print.

The Drifters. "Save the Last Dance for Me." www.azlyrics.com/lyrics/drifters/savethelastdanceforme.html

Tóibín, Colm. "Selling Tara, Buying Florida." *Éire-Ireland* 43.1&2 (2008): 11–25. Print.

White, Harry. *Music and the Irish Literary Imagination*. Oxford UP, 2009. Print.

Waking the Feminists: Re-imagining the Space of the National Theatre in the Era of the Celtic Phoenix

Emer O'Toole

Waking the Nation

In October 2015 Ireland's national theatre, the Abbey, announced its 2016 program, entitled Waking the Nation. 2016 constitutes the centenary of the Easter Rising and the proclamation of the Irish Republic—powerful political events that would culminate in Ireland's partition and the independence of the South from Britain. While the seeds of this moment lie in far deeper historical soil, birth of the nation rhetoric abounds in relation to 1916, and the centenary year was characterized by reflections on the history and current state of the Republic. It saw re-enactments, parades, processions, speeches, an outpouring of pride in Ireland's independence movement, as well as critical debates on Irish history and where the nation is headed next.

The Irish national theatre has long been understood as a "mirror up to nation" (Murray), due, in part, to its central role in the cultural nationalist movement that informed the Easter Rising. Though the first nationally endowed theatre in the English-speaking world, the Abbey is no mouthpiece for the state. For example, in 1926, just ten years after the Rising, it staged Seán O'Casey's *The Plough and the Stars*, a tragi-comedy about 1916 that critiques blood sacrifice and laments the death of socialism in the Irish nationalist movement as well as the effect of the rising on women and protestants. The play provoked outcry from government officials, nationalists, and the relatives of those who died in the rebellion (Morash 163–71). Theatre scholar Patrick Lonergan notes that *The Plough and the Stars* firstly, "established that the function of the Abbey in an independent Ireland would be to analyze the nation's sense of itself," secondly, "allowed the Abbey to emphasize its importance to—but independence from—the new Irish state," and thirdly, "provoked a series of protests that were based on the belief that national theatre is worthy of serious debate and contestation" (62). This legacy remains vibrant today.

It was to be expected, therefore, that in announcing the Waking the Nation program, Fiach Mac Conghail, then artistic director of the Abbey, promised to "interrogate rather than celebrate the past" and encouraged Irish people, "in a year of national introspection," to "ask urgent questions about the safely guarded narrative of our nation" (www.abbeytheatre.ie, "Waking"). Arguably, it was also predictable that the centenary program showcased more writers by the name of Murphy than it did women. Ninety percent of the plays were written by men. Female directors did not fare much better: eighty percent of the plays were directed by men. As columnist Úna Mullally noted in the *Irish Times*,

> If the Abbey Theatre announced that 90 per cent of its 2016 programme was made up of plays written by women it would be viewed as extraordinary. It would be a 'statement.' Yet when the national theatre announced its programme celebrating the 1916 centenary, 90 per cent of the plays programmed are by men. That is not a 'statement,' it's just the norm.

If little interrogation of masculine domination in Ireland was present in the Abbey's centenary reflections, there was little distortion either. At the time the program was announced, 84% of Dáil Eireann consisted of men; 72% of voices on current affairs radio programmes were male voices (Walsh, Suiter and O'Connor 35); over 90% of board members of Irish private companies were men (Barry 11); men comprised 79% of broadsheet byline writers (Deane and O'Mahony); 82% of those at professorial level at University were men (and there has yet to be a female president of any Irish university) (O'Connor 24–25); 87% of produced screenplay writers in the Irish film industry were by men (Liddy 903); and men, of course, comprised 100% of bishops in the Catholic church, an organization that continues to have immense influence over Ireland's education and health sectors.

The Irish Republic faces into its second century at the same time as it climbs out of the economic recession that followed the Celtic Tiger, a recovery some call the Celtic Phoenix (*The Economist*). While the European Central Bank, the European Commission, and the German government have argued that Ireland's political commitment to the austerity measures imposed by the Troika in the wake of the crash have been central to its recovery, Aidan Regan and Samuel Brazys argue that it is more likely attributable to the cultivation of Foreign Direct Investment (FDI) in the technology sector by Irish political elites ("Capitalist Diversity"). Further, the narrative of economic progress under austerity, on which Enda Kenny's Fine Gael party sought to capitalize during the 2016 general election with the slogan "Keep the Recovery Going," was rejected at the ballot box, and Fine Gael was forced into an uncomfortable coalition with rival Fianna Fáil. This signals an awareness on behalf of the electorate, which can be backed up by empirical research (Regan and Brazys, "Phoenix"), that the "leprechaun economics" of Ireland's recovery benefit those within FDI sectors, many of whom are skilled EU workers, and leave low-to-middle income workers hit by austerity measures behind (9–29). Public sector and social welfare cuts have meant that austerity measures have disproportionately affected women, particularly working class women and lone parents (Spillane). Ursula Barry and Pauline Conroy show that gender equality policy was "a victim of the recession and crisis management of the Irish economy" (204).

This moment is indeed a time for national introspection. As Ireland "recovers," how can women challenge narratives of nation—cultural, economic, and political—that continue to exclude them? Drawing on theories of protest as performance and the performative re-constitution of space, this paper will introduce the feminist movement, Waking the Feminists (WTF), that arose in response to the Abbey's centenary Waking the Nation program. It will place the questions raised and the methods employed by WTF in the context of historic and ongoing struggles to articulate a place for feminism in the face of appeals, from enemies and allies alike, to ostensibly higher ideals— whether appeals to aesthetic merit or economic recovery, appeals to class politics or republicanism—showing that the questions raised by WTF are important not only for women in Irish theatre, but for many feminist movements struggling to change patriarchal national and political narratives. It will confront what I term the "logic of lack" that justifies female exclusion from artistic and political movements through analysis of two contemporary female-authored theatre pieces, THEATREclub's *Heroin* and ANU Productions' *Laundry*, productions that undoubtedly "interrogate rather than celebrate" Ireland's past. Ultimately, I will argue that both WTF and the moment of recovery demand more than just recognition of female artists; they demand the restructuring of the architecture of the national theatre and the redistribution of its cultural capital to all the people of the nation.

Waking the Feminists

Fiach Mac Conghail might be considered an ally to the Irish feminist movement. For example, his 2016 Abbey conference program, Theatres of Change, was unmistakably and confrontationally pro-choice. Yet, when Mac Conghail was first questioned on the exclusion of women from his Waking the Nation program, he infamously responded (on Twitter): "Them's the Breaks." He drew on a defense that combined the primacy of aesthetic merit over feminist concerns with what I call the logic of lack, which holds that work by women of sufficient aesthetic quality simply does not exist. He tweeted: "All my new play choices are based on the quality of the play, form and theme." Further, he claimed that decisions were not based on gender, but, rather, on, "who [he] admired and wanted to work with." The Waking the Nation program featured new work by David Ireland, Seán P Summers, and Phillip McMahon; it featured canonical work by Shakespeare, Tom Murphy, Frank McGuinness, and Seán O'Casey; it featured a play by Mutaz Abu Saleh about Israel and Palestine; and a staged reading of an adaptation by Jimmy Murphy. The only play by a woman was Ali White's *Me Mollser*, a monologue for children. Though the quality of White's work is not in question here, it is telling that women tend to be afforded more recognition in the Irish arts when the work is aimed at children. Mathematically speaking, the probability that a gender selection of 90% men would occur at random is very tiny (Prasad; Martin). Add the fact that the Abbey program was no anomaly, but representative of an Irish theatre scene in which men dominate the main stages and festival line ups, as well as an Irish public sphere in which men dominate media, politics, the arts, the academy and religion, and the failure of Mac Conghail's rationale is clear to see.

Lian Bell, a freelance Dublin-based theatremaker, took to social media to issue a clarion call, while Maeve Stone, associate producer of Pan Pan Theatre Company coined the hashtag #WakingtheFeminists (#WTF), under which protest began to mobilize. Journalist Úna Mullally articulated the anger women felt in a rallying column for *The Irish Times*. Others with media platforms, such as Belinda McKeon, Sara Keating, and Aoife Barry, followed her lead. Celebrities around the world, including Meryl Streep, Debra Messing, and Wim Wenders posed with signs showing their support. On social media platforms, on the airwaves, and in public discourse, the conversation and frustration continued to grow. In response to this furor, Mac Conghail and the Abbey apologized for the intemperate initial reaction, admitted that the 2016 program did not represent gender equality, and offered its stage for a public meeting to discuss the marginalization of women in Irish theatre. Five hundred tickets were sold in less than 10 minutes—the fastest selling show in Abbey history.

Performance scholar Baz Kershaw suggests the importance of dramaturgically analyzing popular protest. This requires alertness to both the aesthetic assumptions underlying radical action for social change and to what he terms the "*knowing* performativity" (91) of direct political action. If, to draw on Judith Butler, performative acts create what they name, performative acts of protest are deeply conscious of this creative force. Dramaturgies of protest have, of course, changed over time, and Kershaw asks for our attention to what different forms signify at "moments of crisis in history, when radical social and political change is, or appears to be, immanent" (92). It is perhaps telling that the WTF inaugural meeting was not only knowingly performative but also allied to performance in the theatrical sense; in taking to the Abbey stage the movement signalled consciousness of the power of representation, of the vital relationship between what is seen and what is believed.

The dramaturgy of the inaugural meeting showcased the maximum number of women's stories possible within its timeframe. Thirty invited speakers had 90 seconds each to share their observations about working as women in the Irish theatre. No one received a privileged time slot due to her prestige or place within the movement. Senator Ivana Bacik chaired, opening the event with remarks linking the lack of female voices on the Abbey stage with women's lack of visibility in public life. Lian Bell delivered WTF's mission statement: demands for sustained policies in achieving female inclusion in the arts, equal championing of female artists by Irish arts institutions, and economic parity for women working in the sector. Women's stories followed. If, as Kershaw suggests, we should look for the connections between dramaturgies of protest and moments in history when change appears to be immanent, then it is crucial to keep in mind that—as I argued above—at the moment of ostensible economic recovery the ideology of austerity is celebrated for its role in resuscitating the "Celtic Phoenix" while its deleterious effects are still felt by the majority of the population, and disproportionately by women. Change is certainly immanent, though the form it will take is uncertain: Ireland could become a two-tier society, where those working in favored FDI sectors live elite lives while the majority of the population live under neoliberal precarity (an economic and political arrangement which, Regan and Brazys argue, would be unstable, as many of the skilled workers in the tech industry are EU citizens who do not have a vote in Ireland); or the country could reject exclusionary national narratives, finally forging the feminist and socialist Republic by and for its people imagined by the 1916 proclamation.

Austerity, Helen Davies and Claire O'Callaghan remind us, is both a fiscal and ideological system, which "produces and enables socio-cultural politics as well as financial policies" (227). The archetypical values of this system, such as competition, the profit motive, and eradication of weakness, can be "coded as traditionally masculine" (227), while feminism's commitment to social justice is challenged by austerity's individualist and privilege blind logic. The dramaturgy of the meeting powerfully opposes this worldview, emphasising collectivity, community, equality, and—through personal testimony—the barriers to opportunity faced by those marginalized within the system. Its semiotics offer a rejection of a Republic for the few and not the many, implying an embrace of socialist feminism, which, in feminist theatre scholar Michelene Wandor's characterization, "proposes changes both in the position of women as women, and in the power relations of the very basis of society itself—its industrial production, and its political relations" (138). As director Laura Bowler pointed out at the meeting, when you only listen to half of the world, "you only get half the story." Speakers also addressed Ireland's lack of attention to regional and Irish language theatre. Many referred to the Abbey as "my" or "our" theatre, while actor Kate Gilmore gestured to the centenary as a symbolic moment at which real change can happen. The WTF meeting was not about slotting privileged women into traditionally male roles; it was about uncovering the other side of the national narrative; it was about restructuring the sector; it was about radical transformation and the validity of public claims on national institutions.

Many of the feminist contributors to the event demonstrated a keen aware-ness of Kimberlé Crenshaw's intersectional observation that subordination is "frequently the consequence of the imposition of one burden that interacts with pre-existing vulnerabilities to create yet another dimension of disempower-ment" (1299). Playwright Rosaleen McDonagh, a woman of Traveller ethnicity with a disability, spoke to the importance of preventing the replication of patterns of exclusion within feminist movements. Director Catriona McLaughlin reminded the auditorium that "being fair takes work" and encour-aged people to look around and see who's missing—not only in terms of gender, but also in terms of other modes of marginalization. Dramatist of color Mary Duffin offered the affecting testimony that stories based on her life experiences will only be staged if she makes the characters white. Echoing the consciousness raising tactics of second wave women's movements, the contributions were personal. Women spoke with conviction, anger, and plenty of humor about the discrimination they have faced working in the Irish arts. Some, including veteran theatremakers Noelle Browne and Gina Moxley, spoke of the fear that speaking out would brand them, that men with power over whether or not they are cast or commissioned would not want to work with "difficult" women. Writer and actor Erica Murray, playwright Lisa Tierney-Keogh and actor Derbhle Crotty gestured to the innumerable talented women they know working in the theatre: a riposte to those who want to paint patriarchy as a meritocracy. Many explicitly tied the situation of women in Irish theatre to the position of women in the Republic. They noted the constitutional slurs on Irish women's autonomy, which enshrine their place in the home and deny them access to abortion; all thirty women spoke from the deep conviction and knowledge, which as an Irish theatre scholar I share, that women's work is of national importance too.

These intersectional, personal, and political critiques were underscored by the protest's use of space. Thirty chairs were arranged facing the auditorium, on which the speakers sat until it was their turn to take one of the podiums downstage left or downstage right. In a bold sense, this physically placed women artists centre of the hallowed stage from which they have been so excluded. In a more subtle register, it created two audiences, including all those in attendance in the dramaturgy of the protest. In her analysis of the global anti-capitalist movement, Sophie Nield interrogates the forms of space materialized by seemingly theatrical political interventions. She shows that activist theatre can inhabit "provocative borderlines," including those between "the real and the representational; and between dominant and resistant materialisations of the contemporary world" (53). Nield argues that "the battle is ultimately between two possible spaces: that imagined and produced by power in its domination and organisation of social activity, and that imagined, foretold and *temporarily materialized* in the theatrical moment of opposition"(53). If Ireland's patriarchal culture produced an

Abbey in which men speak and women listen, WTF's protest temporarily materialized a space where women's stories were deemed to be of national importance too. The raucous auditorium, spatially framed as part of the spectacle, breaking into whoops and even, at the end, dance, implicated society-at-large in this temporarily materialized possibility. Further, the spatial framing of the audience troubled the relationship between representation and the real, drawing attention to the material work that needs to happen to make WTF more than just a theatrical gesture, to give the movement the radical potential to permanently transform the space of the national theatre, if not the nation.

Waking the (Socialist) Feminists

The centenary year also marked the implementation of a new political quota system to ensure that 30% of the candidates each Irish political party put forward for the general election were women. It was also a time when the campaign to Repeal the Eighth amendment, Ireland's constitutional ban on abortion, was in full swing. Drawing again on Kershaw, who asks us to find the links between dramaturgies of protest and actual or immanent social change, it is notable that WTF coalesced with Irish women demanding greater rights and representation on social and political stages. WTF also came at a time of renewed feminist vigor internationally (Cochrane). As Susan Faludi's work on feminism in the media has shown, these moments can create backlash. Our current political moment demonstrates that this backlash can come from both left and right of the political spectrum. It is no mystery how conservative factions react to gender quotas, abortion rights, or women playwrights. However, critique from ostensible feminist allies can be more insidious, positioning gender equality as a consideration secondary to the bigger picture of (as we have seen in relation to the Waking the Nation program) aesthetic integrity, but also to national, class, anti-austerity, or anti-establishment politics. The questions that are raised by WTF in terms of how women can gain access to the artistic, cultural and political movements of our nations are important not only for Irish women and artists, but for all socialist and intersectional feminists working at this time of frightening gains for the right and dismaying fracturing of the left.

Such questions are not new. We know that the marginalization of women within the New Left was part of the impetus behind the second wave of feminism (Evans 156–92), and that the insistence on the inclusion of women, queers and people of color fractured working class support for the US democratic party in the 1970s (Teixeira and Abramowitz 8–9). Similar issues have played out within academia and within feminist discourse for decades. For example, Christine Delphy, writing in the 1980s, insisted on an accessible materialist feminism that accounted for patriarchy, while Marxist Feminists

Michèle Barrett and Mary McIntosh insisted that patriarchy was superstructural, and that the feminist mode of analysis adopted by Delphy excluded her from the project of Marxism. Delphy's defense feels almost as urgent today as when it was published in 1980. She says:

> What bothers the left is when women apply to their own situation a materialist analysis; when they reject the ideology which says that they are naturally inferior or the victims of a culture which happens, unhappily but mysteriously (i.e. without any material benefits for anyone), to be sexist. But women are now saying 'there is no mystery: we are oppressed because we are exploited. What we go through makes life easier for others.' And the left is afraid that women will call a spade a spade, the economic economic, and their own sufferings exploitation. (100)

Delphy refuses to subsume her materialist analysis of gender oppression under a materialist analysis of capitalism. For her, these are different modes of oppression and have different beneficiaries; where capital exploits labor, men under patriarchy exploit women. She roundly condemns feminist theoreticians knitted to the letter of Marx who attest that addressing one mode of oppression will automatically erase another; she encourages vigilance against modes of thinking that hold women's liberation secondary to anti-capitalism.

Yet there are dangers to a feminism alienated from a holistic politics of the left. Work by Nancy Fraser and Angela McRobbie offers vital critiques of the kind of feminism arising in the '80s that has, variously, distanced itself from socialism or been co-opted by capitalism. Frasers maps a shift of focus "from redistribution to recognition" (108) within feminism in the 1980s, concurrent with the rise of neoliberalism. She attributes this, in part, to the ways in which neoliberalism "changed the terrain on which feminism operated" (108) by recuperating feminist critiques of "bureaucratic paternalism" intended to transform state power into a vehicle of social justice (112), using them instead to legitimate marketization and state retrenchment. Writing following the global economic recession of 2008, at a moment of crisis for neoliberalism, Fraser is hopeful about the role of feminism in contesting what she terms the "successor society" (114). In explaining the "dangerous liaison" she maps between feminism and neoliberalism, she invokes the critique of traditional authority common to both (115), which, she argues, led the movements to converge. McRobbie, writing just before the moment of feminist resurgence to happen in the second decade of the twenty-first century, critiques the "post-feminism" of the 1990s and early 2000s, detailing the neat ideological trick whereby the language of feminism in terms of empowerment and choice was co-opted by neoliberalism, replacing structural critique with a narrative of agency as a "substitute for feminism" (1; 24; 48; 155). She worries about "the suspension of the critique of capitalism that has always been such a defining feature of the tradition of socialist-feminist scholarship" (3).

While grateful for the valuable insights of Fraser and McRobbie, I remain skeptical that feminism and socialism have been disentangled to the degree they claim. If feminism has been less visible within the socialist movement, certainly socialism has been plainly legible within the feminist movement. In the columns of popular feminist media outlets, in publishing houses, and in the academy there are reams of writing and activism from the 1990s and 2000s challenging the co-option of feminism by capitalism and arguing against bourgeois, postfeminist, and antifeminist ideology. As I have argued above, WTF as a movement is informed by socialist ideals. As I will argue below, women's theatre work in Ireland is often intimately concerned with issues of class and economic inequality, and strives towards radical restructuring of social systems and social space. And yet much public discourse about WTF, as well as Mac Conghail's initial response to feminist critique, revolved around the need to avoid a politics of recognition: the need to avoid programming women just because they are women. It is very easy to invoke "identity politics" or the politics of recognition to delegitimize and misrecognize the structural nature of feminist critiques of under-representation as well as the extent to which women are already carrying out crucial political and creative work.

Further, if the rhetoric of feminism has found its way into popular culture in a somewhat superficial way, this potentially offers a base from which to recruit people to a more robust analysis. 1990s cultural products such as the pop group the Spice Girls and the television show *Sex and the City* might function as "gateway drug" just as easily as "substitute." I also feel protective of the work of womanists, queer feminists, working class feminists and feminists with disabilities to ensure an intersectional politics, and am sensitive to the degree to which intersectionality is miscast as the politics of recognition by some historical materialists (see Bernstein 49–53). However, to the degree that feminism and socialism became disarticulated in the 1980s, 1990s, and early 2000s, it seems vital to acknowledge that there might be reasons that some feminists looked rightward that cannot merely be explained as a convergent critique of traditional authority: namely, abiding gender oppression inscribed at a fundamental ideological level on the left. For many Marxists and socialists, economic redistribution, which concerns the economic base, comes first, and the liberation of women, which is superstructural, is secondary. If real change comes from the base (the definition of which often fails to convincingly account for the domestic) then to insist on women's inclusion is to attack socialism with "identity politics," putting the good of one group before the good of all. Meanwhile, the neoliberal right, with its logic of individuality and meritocracy, becomes attractive to feminists precisely because, if it does not ideologically recognize the patriarchal causes of women's oppression, it does not slap feminist wrists when they insist on women's interests either. This is not simply about recognition; it is about redistribution. There is a significant body of evidence showing that women in positions of political power, whether left or right of the political spectrum, attend to issues affecting women and children substantially more than their male counterparts. Beth Reingold's review of this literature in the American context finds that "across time, office, and political parties, women, more often than men, take the lead on women's issues, no matter how such issues are defined" (130). This redistribution of political and economic resources from men to women is as important to many feminists as redistribution of political and economic resources from the bourgeoisie to the working class. More, it does not in any way preclude redistribution of resources to the working class. In fact, to the extent that women as a demographic are more left-leaning than men, it potentially encourages it.

In a hopeful article on the place of feminism in three emergent UK sites of anti-austerity activism (Left Unity, The People's Assembly, and Occupy) Bice Maiguashca et al. identify:

> increased presence and visibility of women and self-identified feminists in all three political spaces, the efforts of activists within each to engage with feminist theory and ideas – although notions of capitalism and class continue to dominate left discourse – and at the level of practice, the implementation of formal and informal policies/practices aimed at strengthening gender parity. (52)

Despite this conclusion, the descriptions of the organizations indicate that the work of creating a practically functioning feminist socialism is in its beginning stages. In all three of the case studies, the scholars found that gender oppression, patriarchy, and sexism were less than central to the groups' diagnoses of inequality and prescriptions for a better society. This is despite the particularly deleterious effects of austerity on gender equality and on women. Feminist concerns were often relegated to "safer spaces" policies, and lacking from press releases, founding statements, or official ideological visions. Also, the work of including feminist analysis in the movements often appears to be women's work (carried out in separate women's assemblies and caucuses) which, arguably, further marginalizes women from the central operations of the organizations, while also providing analytical labor to which the men (who numerically dominate) can gesture as evidence of equality. In short, even while Maiguashca et al. find an increased feminist presence and ideology on the left, it is clear that this ideology is secondary to what many socialists and Marxists quite simply see as the bigger picture. Perhaps we have not really come so far from the moment in the 1960s where the women's movement emerged from the New Left. Like nationalist narratives, like Mac Conghail's Waking the Nation program, like Ireland's story of recovery, and, of course, like patriarchy, contemporary socialism positions women as secondary. In the meantime, socialist commitment to radical restructuring of material conditions is integral to some of the most exciting female-authored theatre work being made in Ireland. Perhaps, ultimately, women's access to the national theatre means significantly changing the space of the national theatre, and perhaps, ultimately, it is women's work that can do this.

Women's Work

According to the logic of Mac Conghail's initial defense, Irish female artists of sufficient quality and national importance weren't excluded from the centenary program, they simply didn't exist: they were lacking. Doreen Massey points out that space and the feminine are "frequently defined in terms of dichotomies in which each of them is most commonly defined as lack" (73)—women are castrated; space is empty. Yet, the dramaturgy of the inaugural WTF meeting showed the power of manipulating space to make women appear. Thematically, the meeting was characterized by a strong sense that while the work on the Abbey stage is branded as important, the most exciting work is happening elsewhere.

This is one contention of the WTF movement that has met with much skepticism in public discourse, in, for example, the comment threads beneath newspaper articles on the movement. "If Irish women are so good at making theatre, why haven't I heard of any Irish female theatremakers?" seems to be the refrain. Answering this is important, because WTF needs the public to attend work by women if its objectives are to be realized. For the skeptical, then (and in the awareness that academic attention confers cultural capital) I offer two case studies of contemporary Irish theatre for consideration in the context of 2016, productions which might also be read as dramaturgies of protest; productions which thread discourses of class and gender through the national narrative; productions which speak to Ireland's history, but gain even more urgency as Ireland's recovery narrative threatens to overwrite the ongoing effects of austerity on society's most vulnerable.

First, take *Heroin* (2010), directed by Grace Dyas. Dyas is a founding member of THEATREclub, an experimental company that works with marginalized groups to produce aesthetically challenging and politically provocative work, the dramaturgy of which is in itself a kind of protest against both oppression and the kind of art that perpetuates or ignores it. In 2009, Dyas began two years of workshops and outreach with recovering and current addicts at the Rialto methadone clinic. Dyas saw clear throughlines between economic and social deprivation, sexual abuse, failed social housing projects, and drug addiction. She felt there was a story the public simply did not understand in terms of how planning and infrastructure created and then ossified the problem. A theatre piece, *Heroin*, emerged to tell the story of heroin addiction in Ireland over the last five decades. This process of making—community-engaged, generating creative material collaboratively with demographics that have a lived stake in the material—itself disrupts what Davies and O'Callaghan locate as traditionally masculine "archetypical values" of austerity. What Rustom Bharucha calls in a postcolonial vein "the cult of the maestro" (40)—that is, the Western elevation of the artist to a godlike status because of his (and I use the male pronoun deliberately) supposed individual genius and the concurrent relegation of complex communally authored and sustained artwork to the status of raw material for his experiments—is challenged by work like *Heroin*, which rejects the notion of sole authorship. Dyas often contradicts attempts to single her out as the author of theatre pieces she has directed or co-directed, pointing to her fellow artists in THEATREclub as well as to the contributions of workshop collaborators.

The aesthetic content of the work mirrors the politics of the production process. The task of telling the story of addiction in Ireland over five decades is a daunting one, and, rather than writing a well-made play to present a coherent and comprehensive narrative, Dyas and her collaborators created an experimental dramaturgy that foregrounded the impossibility of painting the full picture. Three interrelated timelines played out at once. First, the three actors, Barry, Ger, and Lauren, were involved in a game. Barry tried to tell the story of heroin addiction in Ireland, getting the others to help him; Ger was required to do everything Barry said, while Lauren could do anything she liked. This game created an affective sense of the futility of trying to keep a narrative, a purpose, or a life together when faced with architecture that by its nature disallows it. The production also displayed a keen intuitive grasp of Henri Lefebvre's observation that to change the social you must change space (289–91). The three actors built the set on stage each night, starting with a bare stage and slowly enclosing themselves in a ramshackle apartment. This was THEATREclub's attempt to represent the impact of design on the situation. The third and final timeline was that of addiction, which often follows a pattern of experimentation to initiation to isolation. These three timelines manifested and interwove with each other differently every night, but, like addiction, followed a familiar pattern, ensured by fatalistic structures. Drawing on George Ikishawa, Augusto Boal notes that

> The bourgeois theatre is the finished theatre. The bourgeoisie already know what the world is like, *their world*, and is able to present images of this complete, finished world. The bourgeoisie presents the spectacle. On the other hand the proletariat and the oppressed classes do not know yet what their world will be like; consequently, their theatre will be the rehearsal, not the finished spectacle. (120)

Heroin's experimental dramaturgy offers its audiences a piece that can never be fully finished; the frustration of the actors/characters as they operate within eternally unwinnable games confronts not only Ireland's ongoing crisis of addiction, but also a bourgeois complacency that expects mimetic order, not aesthetic challenge. *Heroin* temporarily materializes not the utopian spaces found by Nield in Occupy's theatrical interventions, but, rather, an argument in space and time that gives form to the problem and stages the necessity of new spaces, new rules, a new Republic.

Heroin was made in the depths of the recession, about people whose lives the economic boom never touched, about people who are certainly now being left behind as official Ireland celebrates its recovery; it is work that combines an Aristotelian fatalism with a shrewd social conscience: the situation has been designed, not by uncaring Gods, but by mundane civil engineers. It is inherently a piece about the project of the Republic of Ireland, true to the experimental nature of the Abbey's roots. As Ireland recovers, *Heroin* might compel audiences to pay attention to those eternally excluded from the narrative of nation. The piece also offers some evidence as to why work by women is deemed "not ready" for the national stage. If ready means work by a sole maestro, work finished for Bourgeoise consumption, THEATREclub consistently challenges the very definition of nationally important art. Is the Abbey for all the children of the nation, or, like the Republic celebrating its economic recovery, are its benefits for a privileged class? Whose stories are told at the national theatre? Who feels welcome to participate? If we are honest in our answers to these questions, it becomes clear that encouraging work like THEATREclub's is not just about representation; it is about redistribution.

Second, let's consider Lisa Lowe's work *Laundry* (2011). Lowe's site-specific theatre company ANU Productions makes innovative use of space and place to immerse audiences in social worlds and Irish histories that exist beneath the public consciousness. Based in a working class area of Dublin's North Inner City known as the Monto, ANU animates the urban environment in ways that are interdisciplinary, collaborative, and committed to active spectatorship. As Brian Singleton argues, what singles ANU's work out from other site specific companies is "their engagement with the social history of the sites they choose to revisualise and reanimate" (23), an engagement in which the site becomes a "social archive" (23). Bringing their often middle class theatre audiences into these working class areas has a provocative politics, which, Singleton argues, resists asserting the authority of the theatrical over the environment (35); Singleton points to a "sense of ownership of the area by the community, including all activity, social, anti-social or theatrical that occurred there" (35) as well as the propensity of residents to write themselves into the production (35). Like *Heroin*, this is work that confronts bourgeois theatre with its own biases, necessary work as the narrative of recovery threatens to blinker those set to benefit from Ireland's FDI sector to intersectional modes of exclusion.

Laundry brought spectators into a building in the Monto that had been used as a Magdalene Asylum.[1] Lowe's piece blended performance art and installation with intimate, sometimes one-on-one performances and real testimonies, confronting audience members with choices and rendering them complicit in the fate of the women: would they help the penitents; would they listen to them; would they remember their names? Miriam Haughton, in her detailed examination of the landmark production, suggests that representation and the performance of silence function as strategies of power in *Laundry*. She argues that the "silencing of outcast women supported the representation of pure Irish womanhood that was critically bound up with the representation of the Irish state" (68) and, further, that the production succeeds "not only in its interrogation of past wrongs but in its realisation of present wrongs" (90). These functions map neatly onto Mac Conghail's professed aims for the Waking the Nation program. It might be argued, of course, that if the functions of the work map neatly onto the Abbey's centennial aims, the nature of the site specific and immersive dramaturgy is harder to align with its architecture. Here I am reminded of Catriona McLaughlin's important statement at the WTF inaugural meeting: being fair takes work. While a bourgeois feminism, defined by Wandor as the kind of feminism that "accepts the world as it is, and sees the main challenge for women as simply a matter of 'equalling up' with men" (136), might see the challenge of equality in the Irish arts as simply inserting female artists into conservatively individualist auteur roles and bourgeois spaces, a socialist feminism demands systemic change. We need to understand how the institution of the national theatre can evolve to encompass some of the most important women's work happening in the Republic. Whether reimagined for the space of the Abbey or forming part of the program while retaining its site specificity, a work like *Laundry* might have reminded the audience that 2016 marks another anniversary of immense importance to the Republic: the 20th year since the closure of the last Magdalene laundry. Haughton observes, "It is interesting to note that, in the early days of independence, the nation was referred to as the Irish 'Free' State. Evidently, some sections of society enjoyed this new national freedom, whereas others were hidden, silenced, and imprisoned" (90). Surely work of this quality, commemorating the fate of those abused by an independent Ireland in the name of self-representation might befit a moment of national introspection. Certainly, I would be more convinced of this logic than of the Abbey's decision to stage *Othello* because the tale of femicide is, apparently, a "state of the nation" play. And, while I am delighted that Waking the Nation program chose Mutaz Abu Saleh's play, "New Middle East," increasing the diversity of the program and making links between Irish occupation and ongoing modes of colonialism, it seems pertinent to note the play's description in the Abbey's promotional material:

> A masked soldier stands beside an open pit. He is burying a woman alive. The soldier is fulfilling his duty and the woman must be his victim.
> Who is he? Who is she? What has she done?
> (www.abbeytheatre.ie, "New Middle East")

With all this symbolic male-authored femicide being used to interrogate the state of the nation, surely there is a need to acknowledge the actual violence that independent Ireland has enacted on women's bodies. At the very least, *Laundry* speaks to the presence of visionary female theatremakers who might have been commissioned to reflect the history and present of the nation in 2016.

In considering the deeply political, historically engaged, aesthetically daring art made by women in Irish theatre, art which foregrounds the experiences of the marginalized, art which seems to prove that in asking for female representation we are asking not merely for recognition but for structural change and redistribution, it becomes apparent that WTF is more than a protest about the exclusion of women from the Abbey's centenary programme. It is also an interrogation of women's place in Irish history; it is a meditation on how women were written out and how they can regain access to the artistic and political movements of their eras and nations. If prosperity is once again in store for Ireland, WTF asks: prosperity for who? How can the egalitarian ideologies of feminism shape the next century of the Republic?

WTF just Happened

Women were integral to the artistic and administrative early years of the Abbey, just as they were integral to Ireland's independence movement. Yet, for many feminists of the time, the national question took precedence over the women's question (Ward; Cullen-Owens). Without a united women's movement to insist on the project of women's liberation as equal to the project of Republicanism, "post-partition Ireland was able to implement, with little resistance, highly reactionary policies in relation to women" (Ward 35). The feminist conviction that freedom from the colonizer and Gaelic revival would mean gender equality was proved false, and, as too often happens after a revolutionary moment in which socialists, feminists, and other artists are a driving force, post-independence Ireland was co-opted by a repressive, religious right. In 1937, the Irish constitution, Bunreacht na hÉireann, enshrined both the special place of the Catholic Church within the Irish state and the special place of Irish women in the home. Female revolutionaries were written out of history. Single mothers were incarcerated in state-funded, church-run laundries. Married women had to leave state jobs. And between the years 1934 and 2014 only an estimated 1% of the plays on the Abbey's main stage were female-authored (Lonergan, "Women Writers"). The theatre once again held a mirror up to the Irish nation.

WTF arose in response to this male domination of Irish theatre and Irish society. Happening at a time in which austerity (the archetypical values of which can be coded as traditionally masculine) continues to victimize society's vulnerable even while global institutions and Irish politicians celebrate the Celtic Phoenix, WTF refuses to pretend that women, the working class, and other marginalized demographics have risen from the ashes; rather, the movement challenges these masculine values and the neoliberal threat of a new kind of divided Ireland. WTF is not only about recognising female artists, but also about redistribution of cultural capital and the restructuring of public institutions. The dramaturgy of the initial meeting emphasized collectivity and barriers to inclusion, countering faux-meritocratic claims of austerity and neoliberalism. It temporarily materialized an intersectional feminist space within the national theatre, and, to the extent that the Abbey is the nation's mirror, within the Republic.

Linking the exclusion of women from the (in many ways anti-hegemonic) Waking the Nation program with the exclusion of women from national and political movements, I explored the extent to which feminist demands for structural change are miscast as mere demands for recognition or even special treatment. I hope the dangers of this for socialist and artistic movements are apparent. As the right adopts an alluring language of faux-feminism, the left is weakened by failing to recognise intersections of class and gender; as artistic movements and institutions continue to define merit as masculine, they become aligned with neoliberalism and disarticulated from the projects of interrogation that they profess, and which, I would argue, make art valuable to a nation, relevant to citizens, and a force for speaking truth to power.

Tracing uses of space in *Heroin* and *Laundry* uncovers cutting analyses of class and gender: the dramaturgies of these pieces function as a kind of performative protest, rejecting the semiotics of bourgeois theatre spaces, foregrounding the impact of design on gender and class inequality, and decentring the neoliberal agent of the "maestro," whose ostensible genius merits his privilege. Making space for these kinds of productions does not just mean a women's name on the publicity posters; it means an entirely different kind of national theatre.

In the wake of the inaugural meeting, the Abbey promised to redress the gender imbalance in its 2016 program by staging female artists in its Autumn/Winter season. This program included Dyas's *Heroin*. When WTF met on November 14 2016, a year after the first explosive meeting, Bell recounted the movement's successes: the Abbey has committed to guiding principles on gender equality that set a new national and international standard; a member of the Waking the Feminists team is now serving on the Abbey board; the Arts Council has funded research into women and the arts, meaning that the personal stories shared at the first meeting can now be backed up with statistics, and progress towards equality will be measurable. Waking the Feminists has also liaised with other major arts and theatre companies and institutions beyond the Abbey. On November 29, 2016, the Abbey, under the new artistic directorship of two men, Neil Murray and Graham McLaren, announced its 2017 program. Fifty percent of the directors were women. Female writers fare less well at just under 20 percent.

Nonetheless, it is certainly an improvement, and the Abbey has committed to achieving equality by 2020. Given the current gendered power structures in Irish theatre, that would be revolutionary.

What really excites me about these developments is not just women's representation in the arts (although this is undoubtedly a step towards greater equality in and of itself) but the faith I have that greater women's representation will lead to an Abbey that serves the many, not just the privileged few. If the dramaturgy of the WTF protest and the work of ANU and THEATREclub are indicators of what is to come, I can imagine a national theatre which actively challenges masculine austerity ideology, sexism, classism, patriarchy, racism, and ableism, while pushing at the aesthetic boundaries of what theatre art can be and the social boundaries of to whom it can and should speak.

The year of WTFs extraordinary energy came to an end in November 2016, and the activists who spearheaded it stepped down to focus on their own art and their lives. If the promises that were made hold, and WTF manages to achieve gender equality in this one Irish institution, in this one symbolically vital area of Irish society, and in just five years, imagine what else is possible. The Abbey Theatre is a mirror up to the Irish nation, so what would it mean if it held an image of an equal society? In 1916, the proclamation spoke of equal rights and opportunities to all Irishmen and Irishwomen. When I asked one of those women, Grace Dyas of THEATREclub, what she wanted to happen in the next 100 years of the Irish Republic, she said: "I want it to happen. At all. It hasn't actually started yet. There hasn't been a Republic." WTF offers hope that it might finally be starting.

Notes

1. Magdalene Asylums for unmarried mothers or other "fallen women" were institutions in which penitents were incarcerated and worked, unpaid, in industrial laundries run by the Catholic Church but supported, the McAleese report confirmed in 2013, by state structures.

Works Cited

Abramowitz, Alan, and Ruy Teixeira. "The Decline of the White Working Class and the Rise of a Mass Upper-Middle Class." *Political Science Quarterly* 124.3 (2009): 391–422. Print.

Barrett, Michele, and Mary McIntosh. "Christine Delphy: Towards a materialist feminism?" *Feminist Review* 1 (1979): 95–106. Print.

Barry, Ursula. "Policy on Gender Equality in Ireland Update 2015." Policy Department C: Citizen's Rights and Constitutional Affairs. Brussels: European Parliament. Sept. 2015. Print.

Barry, Ursula, and Pauline Conroy. "Ireland in Crisis 2008-2012: Women, Austerity and Inequality." *Women and Austerity: the economic crisis and the future for gender equality*. Ed. Maria Karamessini and Jill Rubery. Oxon; New York: Routledge, 2013. 186–206. Print.

Bernstein, Mary. "Identity Politics." *Annual Review of Sociology* 31 (2005): 47–74. Print.

Boal, Augusto. *Theatre of the Oppressed*. 1979. London: Pluto Books, 2008. Print.

Butler, Judith. "Performative Acts and Gender Constitution: An Essay in Phenomenology and Feminist Theory." *Theatre Journal* 40.4 (1988): 519–31. Print.

Cochrane, Kira. *All the Rebel Women: The Rise Of The Fourth Wave Of Feminism*. Vol. 8. London: Guardian Books, 2013. Print.

Crenshaw, Kimberlé. "Mapping the Margins: Intersectionality, Identity Politics, and Violence against Women of Color." *Stanford Law Review* 43.6 (1991): 1241–99. Print.

Cullen Owens, Rosemary. *A Social History of Women in Ireland, 1870–1970: An Exploration of the Changing Role and Status of Women in Irish Society*. London: Gill & Macmillan, 2005. Print.

Davies, Helen, and Claire O'Callaghan. "All In This Together? Feminisms, Academia, Austerity." *Journal of Gender Studies* 23.3 (2014): 227–32. Print.

Deane, Lughan and Patricia O'Mahoney. "Diversity Audit of Irish Front Pages." IMPACT. Impact.ie. Sept 30 2016. Web. Accessed Jan 10 2017.

Delphy, Christine. "A Materialist Feminism Is Possible." Trans. Diana Leonard *Feminist Review* 4 (1980): 79–105. Print.

Evans, Sara Margaret. *Personal Politics: The Roots Of Women's Liberation In The Civil Rights Movement And The New Left*. London: Vintage, 1979. Print.

Fraser, Nancy. "Feminism, Capitalism, and the Cunning of History." *New Left Review* 56 (2009): 97–117. Print.

Faludi, Susan. *Backlash: The Undeclared War Against American Women*. New York: Broadway Books, 2009. Print.

Haughton, Miriam. "From Laundries to Labour Camps: Staging Ireland's 'Rule of Silence' in ANU Productions' Laundry." *Modern Drama* 57.1 (2014): 65–93. Print.

Kershaw, Baz. *The Radical In Performance: Between Brecht and Baudrillard*. London: Routledge, 1999. Print.

Lefebvre, Henri. "The Production of Space." *The People, Place, and Space Reader*. Ed. Gieseking, Jen Jack, et al. New York: Routledge, 2014. Print.

Liddy, Susan. "Open To All And Everybody"? The Irish Film Board: Accounting For The Scarcity Of Women Screenwriters." *Feminist Media Studies* 16.5 (2016): 901–17. Print.

Lonergan, Patrick. "More Thoughts (and stats) on Women Writers at the Abbey." Patricklonergan.wordpress.com. Jan 22 2014. Web. Accessed Jan 10 2017.

———. *Theatre and Globalization: Irish Drama in the Celtic Tiger Era*. London: Palgrave Macmillan, 2009. Print.

Mac Conghail, Fiach. "Personal Tweet." Twitter.com. 29 Oct 2015. Web. Accessed 10 Jan 2016.

Maiguashca, Bice, Jonathan Dean, and Dan Keith. "Pulling together in a crisis? Anarchism, feminism and the limits of left-wing convergence in austerity Britain." *Capital & Class* 40.1 (2016): 37–57. Print.

Martin, Jennifer L. "Ten Simple Rules To Achieve Conference Speaker Gender Balance." *PLOS Computational Biology* 10.11 (2014): 1–3. Print.

Massey, Doreen. "Politics and Space/Time." *New Left Review* 196 (1992): 65. Print.

McAleese, Martin. "Report Of The Inter-Departmental Committee To Establish The Facts Of State Involvement With The Magdalen Laundries." Dublin: Department of Justice and Equality, Ireland (2013). Print.

McRobbie, Angela. *The Aftermath Of Feminism: Gender, Culture And Social Change*. London: Sage, 2009. Print.

Morash, Chris. *A History Of Irish Theatre* 1601-2000. Cambridge: Cambridge University Press, 2002. Print.

Mullally, Úna. "Abbey Theatre celebrates 1916 centenary with Only One Woman Playwright." *The Irish Times*. 2 Nov 2016. Web. Accessed 30 May 2017. http://www.

irishtimes.com/opinion/una-mullally-abbey-theatre-celebrates-1916-centenary-with-only-one-woman-playwright-1.2413277

Murray, Christopher. *Twentieth-Century Irish Drama: Mirror up to Nation.* Syracuse: Syracuse University Press, 1997. Print.

Nield, Sophie. "There Is Another World: Space, Theatre And Global Anti-Capitalism." *Contemporary Theatre Review* 16.01 (2006): 51–61. Print.

O'Connor, Pat. *Management And Gender In Higher Education.* Oxford: Oxford University Press, 2014. Print.

Prasad, Aanand. "Conference Diversity Distribution Calculator." Aanandprasad.com. N.d. Web. Accessed Jan 10 2016.

Regan, Aidan and Samuel Brazys. "Celtic Phoenix or Leprechaun Economics? The Politics of an FDI-led Growth Model in Europe." *New Political Economy.* 2017. Forthcoming.

Reingold, Beth. "Women as Officeholders: Linking Descriptive and Substantive Representation." *Political Women and American Democracy.* Ed. Christina Wolbrecht et al. Cambridge: Cambridge UP, 2008. Print.

Singleton, Brian. "ANU Productions and Site-Specific Performance: The Politics of Space and Place." *That Was Us': Contemporary Irish Theatre and Performance.* Ed. Fintan Walsh. London: Oberon, 2013. 21–36. Print.

Spillane, Alison. "The Impact of the Crisis on Irish Women." *Ireland Under Austerity: Neoliberal Crisis, Neoliberal Solutions.* Ed. Colin Coulter and Angela Nagle. Oxford: Oxford UP, 2015. 151–70. Print.

The Abbey. "Waking the Nation 2016 at the Abbey Theatre." Www.abbeytheatre.ie. Oct 2015. Web. Accessed 10 Jan 2017

———. "New Middle East." www.abbeytheatre.ie. 2016. Web. Accessed 30 Mar 2017.

The Economist. "Celtic Phoenix: Ireland Shows There is Economic Life after Death." *The Economist.* 19 Nov 2015. Web. Accessed 30 Mar 2017. http://www.economist.com/news/finance-and-economics/21678830-ireland-shows-there-economic-life-after-death-celtic-phoenix

Walsh, Kathy, Jane Suiter and Órla O'Connor. "Hearing Women's Voices: Exploring Women's Underrepresentation in Current Affairs Programming at Peak Listening Times in Ireland." National Women's Council of Ireland & Dublin City University. Nov. 2015. Print.

Wandor, Michelene. *Understudies: Theatre and Sexual Politics.* London: Methuen, 1981. Print.

Ward, Margaret. "'Suffrage First, Above All Else!' An Account of the Irish Suffrage Movement." *Feminist Review* 10 (1982): 21–36. Print.

A Girl is a Half-formed Thing?: Girlhood, Trauma, and Resistance in Post-Tiger Irish Literature

Susan Cahill

On 28 August 2016, the courtyard of the Irish Museum of Modern Art (IMMA) hosted the culminating performance of the School for Revolutionary Girls, an exciting ten-day project co-ordinated by artist Suzanne Lacy and historian Liz Gills. Fifteen young women between the ages of 14 and 17 were invited to take part in the School, to participate in "an artistic 'consciousness-raising' process that uses group discussion, performance, and social media. Imagining the world as it is for them as young women, and as it could be, they explored issues important for their present moment, developing creative expressions of their own unique 'public voice'" (*The School for Revolutionary Girls*). The initiative was part of IMMA's larger 2016 project *A Fair Land*, a dynamic installation which aimed to "examine the function of art" in a similar manner to the "role played by artists in creating and articulating a new vision for Ireland pre-1916" by creating a model village in the space of the museum (*A Fair Land*). During the ten days of the School for Revolutionary Girls, the young women met feminist groups such as Waking the Feminists, discussed sexual assault, consent, feminism, reproductive rights, and wrote their own proclamation for their revolutionary future, performed at the IMMA on the 28 August.[1] Thus, the young women proclaimed:

> In a fair land women would feel safe when they are walking home. In a fair land no one will suffer in silence. In a fair land persons who suffer from mental health issues are equal to everyone else and will not be viewed as lesser than others. In a fair land women will not need protection against rape or assault. In a fair land our happiness and self-worth will not depend on the things we buy. [...] In a fair land we will all treat people according to their personal struggles, experiences, and circumstances rather than according to their body image, gender or colour of skin. In a fair land we stand together with everyone not just as our own separate entities. In a fair land we will have the power to make a difference. @revgirlschool

Such a dynamic performative intervention by young women marks a significant moment in Ireland's post-Tiger climate, one that highlights teenage girls' voices, visibility, energy, and feminism, and that echoes literature of the period both for and about the teenage girl herself. Such initiatives also signal a shift in representation of the teenage girl, a wresting of control of her image, and a countering of dominant portrayals of her in the Celtic Tiger period, portrayals that positioned her as sexualized commodity.

In 2006, at the height of Ireland's Celtic Tiger, journalist Ailish Connelly bewailed the state of the young women she encountered in a nightclub, appalled by both the pornification of their appearance and their sexualized behavior on the dancefloor. In contrast to Claire Bracken's sympathetic awareness of the contextual pressures of the "dictates of body regulation that intensified during the Tiger period and [...] the imbrication of girls within such a regime" (63), Connolly lays the blame squarely on the shoulders of the girls themselves:

> By the late teens, early 20s, the tables have turned. Because the Celtic Kittens are in control. The ultra thin girls with their knowing ways, their hint of decadence and whiff of the burlesque have their boyfriends by the short and curlies. The boy-friends are property developer wannabees, or junior bankers or lawyers. Something with money, because you will need serious dosh to keep up with these ladies. God bless them, you'd nearly feel sorry for the lads. Stalked and hunted ruthlessly, the guys give up and give in. They haven't a hope…[T]he girls had learned the lessons of the feminist movement, albeit in a fashion not anticipated by the original leaders of the movement. They had turned feminism on its head. They use the tools of modern Ireland to get their own way, to move through life on their terms … Perhaps it's the boys we should be more worried about.

Connelly's analysis of the young women of the Celtic Tiger is part of a wider discourse that vilifies the girl for her heedless consumerism, her overt sex-ualization, and her emasculation of men, also significantly situating the girl in a position of agency and power: "the Celtic Kittens are in control." Femininity became increasingly constructed in postfeminist neoliberal terms such that female empowerment became coded as the freedom to consume (Ging; Tasker and Negra). In many despairing critiques of Ireland's economic boom and its failures, young women and girls are made to carry the burden of the excesses of the Tiger, encouraged to consume yet simultaneously pilloried for their excessive consumption. The power and control that these "Celtic kittens" supposedly hold is the power to spend money: "you will need serious dosh to keep up with these ladies," and the power to appear sexually attractive: "ultra thin girls with their knowing ways, their hint of decadence and whiff of the burlesque." The young woman is blamed for the rampant consumerism and for the money-driven culture, while also being denied access to the structures of power— it is her boyfriend who is the property developer, banker, or lawyer. The figure of the girl has a long history of carrying and symbolizing social anxiety, particularly when that anxiety circulates around questions of consumerism, modernity, and sexuality—and this figuration becomes especially potent when these anxieties intersect. As girlhood scholar Catherine Driscoll points out, "the emergence of feminine adolescence is historically coincident with a move from industrial to commodity capitalism" (108). Indeed several critics have noted the considerable (and continued) overlap among conceptions of girlhood, commodity culture, and the commodity itself (Leonard; Lindner; McRobbie, "Young Women and Consumer Culture"; Stoneley). Driscoll continues: "But more specifically in capitalism the girl has represented ideas of consumption or commodification. Analogies between girls and commodities are widely promulgated and commodities are often aligned with girls (and their desirability)" (109).[2]

In the context of an Ireland rapidly undergoing major social, economic, and cultural transformation, it is no wonder that the girl becomes both the figure around which such anxieties about the new Ireland circulate and the personification of the negative aspects of twenty-first century Irish consumerism. I am especially interested here in the ways in which girlhood is figured, constructed, and symbolized in the context of Ireland's recession, officially declared in 2008. The recessionary climate in Ireland sees a shift from the Tiger shaming and blaming of the girl as too closely tied to the commodity to a more feminist critique of the commodification of girlhood in post-Tiger texts, specifically in texts aimed at teenage girl readers themselves. Furthermore, these recessionary era texts explicitly link girlhood, trauma, language, and resistance in ways that challenge dominant representations of the girl in the Tiger period. These more overtly feminist representations of the girl in the post-Tiger period insist that we pay attention to her—indeed they situate her at the nexus of their powerful feminist critiques.

Significantly, the recession in Ireland has seen an increase in visibility of feminism and women's rights, illustrated in the emergence of powerful grassroots activism circulating around women's reproductive freedoms (Repeal the Eight campaign), representation of women in theatre (Waking the Feminists), and marriage equality. Diane Negra and Yvonne Tasker point out that "[i]n a moment characterized by widespread public anger at and lack of trust in corporations, [...] political questions about equality are deservedly acquiring a new centrality" (Negra and Tasker 3). Claire Bracken's recent plenary for the Mid-Atlantic Regional ACIS Conference addressed this very phenomenon, arguing that a recessionary climate of scepticism towards neo-liberalism co-exists with and indeed facilitates a dynamism in feminist movements. She identifies "an affective mood of neo-liberal suspicion in Irish cultural life of the post-Tiger period and in the specific context of gender and sexuality [...] an energized and popularized feminist activism both on the streets and online, a collective incantation of outrage and a calling for necessitated change" ("Austere Times"). The affective mood that Bracken identifies here is significant as it marks the recessionary texts about girlhood that I will discuss: *A Girl Is a Half-formed Thing* by Eimear McBride, and *Only Ever Yours* and *Asking For It* by Louise O'Neill all immerse the reader in the consciousness and experience of the teenage girl in highly affective and radical ways. These radical elements become all the more crucial not only because they powerfully critique how the Irish girl was exploited during the Tiger period, but also because of Irish literature's long-standing tendency to ignore the experiences of the teenage girl.

Where growing scholarship on Irish boyhood is evident, girls suffer from a critical invisibility. And indeed, in general, girls tend to suffer from invisibility across twentieth- and twenty-first century literary life. Fintan O'Toole, in a 2010 *Irish Times* column on the prevalence of coming of age narratives in Irish literature, observed that "youth was the comfort zone of Irish fiction." He cites four significant works of Irish fiction from that year, Emma Donoghue's *Room*, Paul Murray's *Skippy Dies*, Claire Keegan's *Foster*, and Colm Tóibín's short story collection *The Empty Family*, all of which feature narrators or significant characters who are children or adolescents. O'Toole goes on to list major works of Irish literature that concentrate on young characters or narratives of growing up, yet significantly, the vast majority of these texts focus on young men or boys:

> It is certainly arguable that the novel of growing up, from James Joyce's *A Portrait of the Artist as a Young Man* to John McGahern's *The Dark* and Edna O'Brien's *The Country Girls*, is the quintessential Irish form. The archetypal Irish short stories, Frank O'Connor's *My Oedipus Complex* and *My First Confession* [sic], are told from the point of view of children. Two of the great narrative voices of 1990s Irish fiction, Roddy Doyle's eponymous Paddy Clarke and Patrick McCabe's Francie Brady in *The Butcher Boy*, are young boys. (O'Toole)

Scholar Jane Elizabeth Dougherty argues that while Ireland boasts some of the most notable examples of literary boyhoods (Joyce's *Portrait of the Artist as a Young Man* is, as she points out, the exemplary *bildungsroman*), narratives of female development are rare and obscure (Dougherty 50). For Dougherty, "childhood," in an Irish context, "has become a male genre" (Dougherty 54). As outlined in my previous work this elision is structural, as "Girlhood is [...] written out in national terms, in which the boy represents the idealized, heroic future of the nation and woman the passive producer of this future (Cahill, "Where Are The Irish Girls" 215). And despite Dougherty's claim that Irish literary girlhoods are rare and obscure, what is instead apparent from my research on turn-of-the-twentieth-century literature for girls is a proliferation of fiction by Irish women writers aimed at girl readers and featuring the development of Irish female characters (Cahill, "Making Space"; Cahill, "Where Are The Irish Girls"). The issue is not that these narratives do not exist. It is rather that the Irish literary canon fails to take account of them, an elision that continues into the twentieth century.

Indeed, when thinking about canonical twentieth-century Irish literature, the teenage girl becomes difficult to locate, and when we do see female adolescence in Irish literature of the twentieth century, representations of the teenage girl are generally characterized by crisis and trauma. Edna O'Brien's Baba and Kate in *The Country Girls* negotiate a vulnerable space of adolescence—they are subject to sexual predatorship rather than rebellious transition—and the novel was indeed banned for the girls' expressions of desire. The pregnant teenage girls of Roddy Doyle's *The Snapper* and O'Brien's *Down By the River* (based on the X Case),[3] Peter Mullan's film *The Magdalene Laundries*, and Margo Harkin's film, *Hush-a-Bye-Baby* all situate teenage girlhood as an anxious space, lacking protection, subject to invasion, so much so that when teenage girlhood is encountered in twentieth century Irish literature it carries with it this constant threat. When reading Éilís Ní Dhuibhne's 1999 novel *The Dancers Dancing*, set in the 1970s concerning four teenage girls who travel to Donegal to attend summer Irish college, the reader is on constant alert for the terrible thing that is surely imminent, which unusually, in this narrative, does not happen. The novel is, however, conscious of the nation's disregard for girls "Boys were boys or lads or fellas. Girls were just young *ones*: they did not merit a generic name of their own" (Ní Dhuibhne 79). And the novel also gestures towards darker undercurrents of crisis pregnancies: Orla, the protagonist, discovers a cillín, a burial space for unwanted babies, a dark history of infanticide literally underfoot.

The Dancers Dancing operates as an interesting marker of a shift in representation in the Celtic Tiger years operating alongside the texts mentioned above that are constructed around crisis and trauma. Aware of this prevalent mode of threatened girlhood, *The Dancers Dancing* plays on and disperses these expectations while acknowledging the difficulty of female adolescence. For example, when one character, Pauline, breaks into a teacher's cottage and surprises him, the novel makes explicit the potential dangers that such a scenario elicits: "She wonders, if he will murder her, or do some worse, nameless thing to her. The room vibrates with potential danger" (Ní Dhuibhne 170). However, the novel rapidly dispels this potential, as the teacher, although (and somewhat ironically) called Killer Jack, offers her orangeade and crisps and nothing happens beyond a brief conversation: "She is not to be a hapless victim after all. She is not to be a mangled corpse, a girl child wronged" (Ní Dhuibhne 170). Kelly J.S. McGovern observes in her astute reading of the ways in which girlhood functions in the novel, "*The Dancers Dancing* portrays girls as weighed down by their own and their culture's overfamiliarity with received narratives," and I would add that an inability to uncouple girlhood from crisis and trauma is the strongest of such narratives (McGovern 248). However, as I've noted, the novel refuses this outcome as a narrative strategy, while still keeping the possibility in focus. Interestingly, Marian Quinn's 2007 film, *32A*, which also focuses on teenage girls in the 1970s, similarly frustrates audience's expectations that narratives about teenage girls are inevitably structured around trauma. Indeed, Roddy Flynn's review of the film critiques it for "featur[ing] less incident than that contained in a typical episode of *Sex and the City*" and goes on to unfavourably compare it to *Hush-A-Bye-Baby*, Gus Van Sant's *Elephant*, and Rian Johnson's *Brick*, the latter two which "suggest a much more troubled (and troubling) undercurrents amongst contemporary youth" (Flynn). Flynn's issues with the film seem partially to do with its lack of trauma enacted on the female protagonists.

This is not to suggest that Irish literature's dominant mode of traumatized or threatened girlhood is no longer prevalent in the Celtic Tiger period.[4] However, what is significant is the space that is given in texts like *The Dancers Dancing* and *32A* to a girlhood that does not have to be character-ized by damage. The decisions of both texts to locate this girlhood in the 1970s rather than in their Celtic Tiger present, nonetheless, does raise some interesting questions about whether conceptualizing contemporary girlhood outside of trauma and damage is possible in an Irish context.[5] While the Celtic Tiger period, then, offers a potential space through which to concep-tualize the teenage girl outside of models of trauma and crisis (although, as discussed, this space seems to exist mostly in the 1970s), what we see in the post-Tiger literary landscape is a marked increase in registering trauma and vulnerability within the contemporary moment, to use, in Bracken's terms, an "affective immersion" of these states for the reader. These texts demand us to inhabit the consciousness of the teenage girl and to experience the effects of her damage in immediate and affective ways. This is often also coupled with an explicit feminist consciousness and critique, particularly in texts aimed at teenage girls themselves.

Eimear McBride's 2013 debut novel *A Girl Is a Half-formed Thing* plunges us directly into the consciousness, or rather, the pre-consciousness of an unnamed teenage narrator. In a remarkable similarity to the shifts in repre-sentations of girlhood from invisible to visible (albeit with trauma), McBride's novel languished unpublished for ten years before being published in 2013. Written during the period of Ireland's economic boom but pub-lished during the recession by independent British publisher Galley Beggar Press, in many ways, the novel's appearance in post-Tiger Ireland marks a moment in which the girl becomes powerfully visible, although her visibility is marked by an intensity of negative feeling. One could argue that the climate of the Tiger, with its drawing away from trauma-inflected narratives of girlhood, was not a sympathetic climate for this intense and subversive novel, which instead finds its place in a recessionary climate. Significantly, the intensity of a return to narratives in which girlhood is structured by damage, trauma, and vulnerability in the post-boom period, such as *A Girl Is a Half-formed Thing* and Louise O'Neill's YA novels, is also expressive of the ways in which the recession itself is experienced as traumatic for the culture at large. Negra and Tasker identify the complexity of the post-boom's emotional register, "involving competing discourses of anger, nostalgia, denial, and loss" (Negra and Tasker 15). The novels I will explore here engage these affects of anger and loss, allowing no room for denial or nostalgia, to powerfully feminist effects.

While the novel's narrative is entirely familiar, its style is astoundingly innovative. *A Girl Is a Half-formed Thing* charts the consciousness of the unnamed "A Girl" from womb to birth to adolescence. The bulk of the narrative is aligned with the girl's teenage years, in an unspecified time and place in Ireland, although certain references situate the events as taking place in rural Ireland in the 1980s or 1990s. Her father dies early in the novel and she is raised by her cruelly religious mother. Her older brother, suffering from brain damage as the result of a tumor, is the "you" of the novel, and the love felt for her brother is one of the (perhaps the only) positive emotional affects of the novel. It is a difficult novel to read, stylistically and content-wise, for the thirteen-year old narrator becomes the victim of sexual abuse by her uncle by marriage, warping her sexual development. For her, sex becomes about momentary assertions of power and sustained self-harm, completely devoid of any expression of pleasure. Similarly, the stream of consciousness style of the novel immerses the reader in a space of language formation that seems to exist before articulation. A Girl's thoughts occupy the same space as snippets of other people's conversations and habitual phrases from, for example, religious discourse. Her birthing moment, for instance, includes the doctor's announcement of her sex as well as her own fractured and viscerally evocative thoughts:

> Scream to rupture day. Fatty snorting like a creature. A vinegar world I smelled. There now a girleen isn't she great. Bawling. Oh Ho. Now you're safe. But I saw less with these flesh eyes. Outside almost without sight. She, asking after and I'm all fine. Hand on my head. Her hand on my back. Dividing from the sweet mother flesh that could not take me in again. (McBride, *A Girl Is a Half-Formed Thing* 5)

One of the effects of this style, which I will come back to, is the immediate porousness of A Girl's consciousness and the ways in which her process of articulation is always already vulnerable to invasion.

The stream-of-consciousness style that the novel employs, which, to a certain degree, matures with its protagonist, has invited comparisons to Joyce since its publication. Indeed, McBride identifies her reading of *Ulysses* as a kind of epiphanic moment, commenting in an interview: "I started reading the book, got off at Liverpool Street, and just thought: that's it. Everything I have written before is rubbish, and today is the beginning of something else" (Cochrane). McBride also situates herself consciously within the traditions of European modernism. As Michael Gorra points out in his consideration of McBride's two novels:

> They are modernist or rather neo-modernist attempts to get under the skin of thought, indeed to find the point at which thought and physical sensation prove

inseparable. As such they stand as self-conscious throwbacks to the way that Joyce in particular presents the inner life. (Gorra)

However, McBride's style—its broken, staccato phrasing—highlights the problematics of the teenage girl both literally and representationally in a much more brutal and immediate way than the stream of consciousness of *Ulysses*. Where Gerty McDowell in the Nausicaa episode can negotiate the difficulties of her life through the language of the sentimental romance narrative, the unnamed narrator of *A Girl* does not have those (or any) narrative strategies available to her.

And unlike the ways in which the style of Joyce's *Portrait of the Artist as a Young Man* "grows up" with its protagonist Stephen, the narrative of A Girl remains at a fragmented pre-articulate state, mirroring the ways in which the "I" of the novel is damaged by the patriarchal and stifling climate she grows up in. If this is a portrait of the artist as a young girl, the novel reveals the ways in which patriarchal religious Ireland refuses the girl expression, so much so that the only revenge is a destruction of language and self, manifested in this scene from a rape which occurs towards the end of the narrative:

> Doos the fuck the fuckink slatch in me. Scream. Kracks. Done fuk me open he dine done on me. Done done Til he hye happy fucky shoves upo comes ui. Kom shitting ut h mith fking kmg I'm fking cmin up you. Retch I. Retch I. Dinneradntea I choke any. Up my. Thrtoat I. (McBride, *A Girl Is a Half-Formed Thing* 193)

The sucking away of the vowels here highlights the sucking away of self, the claustrophobia of violation. There is an almost entire absence of the comma in this novel and a heavy use of full stops, unlike Molly Bloom's soliloquy, which revels in lack of punctuation but includes no full stops. Commas connect while periods separate and this grammatical fragmentation in *A Girl* can be aligned with the isolation experienced by the narrator combined with the failure to maintain separation through the violation of bodily and emotional boundaries that she experiences. As Gorra points out, "McBride writes in the first person, but the narrator's voice contains other voices, snatches of the things she hears other people say, always presented without typographical distinction" (Gorra). The porousness of the narrative voice, then, highlights the difficulties of articulation of the female subject in an imaginary governed by fictions of the coherent self.

A Girl Is a Half-formed Thing highlights girlhood's difficulty in an Irish context. McBride makes this difficulty poetic, immersive, yet unbearable to us as readers— as well as to A Girl herself who drowns herself at the end of the novel, dissolving her untenable subjectivity. The last words of the novel, "My name is gone," highlight Irish literature's unease with the figure of the girl. She is most grammatically articulate at the moment of her destruction. The novel as a whole—and in particular its linguistic experimentation—gives space to the preconsciousness of the girl but also draws our attention to the inhospitality of our culture to the articulation of the young girl and the ways in which her sexuality, desire, and emotion are distorted in our current modes of representation.

However, the novel is also an important intervention against the writing away of the adolescent woman, for the novel forces us to occupy her consciousness and embodied experience in immediate and immersive ways and indeed the porousness of her narrative voice contributes effectively to the ways in which the novel asks us to extend our consciousness into hers. As McBride acknowledges, "I didn't want the reader to feel separate from her or in a position to pass judgment on her actions. I wanted them to feel they *were* her, and that what was happening to her, and inside her, was also happening within themselves" (McBride, "Eimear McBride") Asking a reader to *be* a teenage girl is a profoundly radical move, especially in the contexts of Irish literature where she is rarely glimpsed. However, as I argue, the particularities of the recessionary climate render girls visible in intense and immersive ways, and a novel like McBride's forces us to confront and inhabit the embodied experience of the teenage girl and makes explicit the problematics of representation attendant to these experiences. In other words, *A Girl Is a Half-formed Thing* alerts us to the ways in which Irish literature refuses to see or hear the teenage girl.

We can then think about McBride's text of immersive girlhood as an indicator of a more visible presence of the teenage girl in the post-Tiger era, confirmed in a marked increase in Irish Young Adult fiction and the success of writer Louise O'Neill's two powerfully immersive YA novels about teenage girls. Irish Young Adult literature is currently experiencing an extraordinary boom with the emergence and success of authors such as Sarah Crossan, Paul McVeigh, Sarah Moore Fitzgerald, Sarah Bannan, Elske Rahill, Sheena Wilkinson, Claire Hennessy, Deirdre Sullivan, and Sarah Maria Griffin. The most successful YA breakthrough in Ireland has been that of author, Louise O'Neill, whose two novels to date are explicit in their feminist engagement with the conditions of the teenage girl. In a recent interview O'Neill states proudly "To be honest, I just love teenage girls. There's something about that age that is so painful and so raw. God, I remember it so well. Teenage girls are just the best. This is why I get so angry when people make fun of fangirls. Teenage girls bring passion and real sense of engagement to everything, whether that is books or bands" (Eric-Udorie). O'Neill's championing of the teenage girl and her passions is strikingly unusual in discussions about female adolescence, and, like *A Girl Is a Half-formed Thing*, O'Neill's novels require the reader to occupy the consciousness of their teenage first-person narrators. While both her novels are marketed as YA, they have also been published in "adult" versions (meaning different marketing, book covers, and positions in bookshops) due to their crossover popularity, speaking to an increasing public articulation of both feminism and teenage subjectivity in Ireland. O'Neill's two novels powerfully articulate the reduction of the teenage girl to commodity in a neo-liberalist economy while also offering the teenage reader a vocabulary with which to critique such a positioning. In contrast to McBride's novel, then, which is interested in the problematics of representation, O'Neill's novels render the experiences of the teenage girl in stark focus in order to stimulate feminist critique.

Only Ever Yours, published in 2014, imagines a future dystopia in which female children are no longer born but genetically engineered in accordance with rigid standards of beauty and are schooled in submission and constantly reminded of their own lack of significance. The novel is a searing exploration of the objectification of women, eating disorders, and internalized and externalized misogyny. Inculcated from birth in the belief that self-worth lies only in appearance and the performances of behaviors that will satisfy men, the novel is a study of the damaging effects of sexism on the psyche and the ways girls are pitted against each other in an economy of appearance. In a ceremony on their seventeenth "design date," the girls, known as "eves" are divided into companions (those who will bear children), concubines (those who will satisfy the sexual desires of the men), and chastities (those who will run the schools). Narrated in the first person by sixteen-year-old frieda, we are given intimate access to the internalization of misogyny and the damage that it enacts on the teenage girl's consciousness. What is brilliant and terrifying about O'Neill's novel is that every aspect of the dystopia is an explicit manifestation of the more insidious sexisms of our own culture. One boy, for example, is given the ultimate put down: "You can be such a *girl* at times, Darwin," his father says dismissively (O'Neill, *Only Ever Yours* 367). A classroom scene in which a teacher circles a girl's perceived bodily imperfections in red ink is a physical realization of familiar magazine spreads like this. The reality TV shows that the girls watch, "America's Next Top Concubine" and "Chilling with the Carmichaels," are thinly veiled versions of our own.

In the novel, the girls are manufactured into commodities that the naturally-born male children will consume, in an astute comment on the ways in which men are codified as universal and individual, and women (particularly teenage girls) are categorized as artificial and collective, indeed almost indistinguishable from each other. The manufacture of the girls also functions as a commentary on those discourses that associate and align the young woman with commodity culture, indeed with the commodity itself, especially potent in the climate of the Celtic Tiger, as outlined above. That this novel emerges in a post-Tiger Ireland is significant and its success speaks to the ways in which recessionary neo-liberal suspicion and feminist activism coexist, as outlined by Bracken. O'Neill herself is an outspoken advocate of the teenage girl, feminism, and sexual politics, and indeed has instigated important public conversations, particularly around issues of consent and rape culture (see her hashtag #NotAskingForIt and her involvement in the Not Asking

For It campaign launched by University College Dublin), which are the subjects of her second novel.

Asking for It is a profound and brutal exposé of rape culture and questions of consent, set in a small town in Ireland, and narrated through the voice of popular and beautiful eighteen-year-old Emma, highly conscious of her sexuality and appearance as oriented towards men, rather than her own pleasure. O'Neill's rendering of Emma's voice is perfectly pitched, highlighting the complexity of the pressures and performances of teenage girlhood:

> I nod at the girls passing who call my name, say hello, ask me where I got my sunglasses, or what lip gloss I'm wearing, or how I'm feeling about our Irish exam today. I smile, telling them, 'Thanks, you're such a pet,' and doling out compliments in return. I imagine them whispering to themselves once I'm out of earshot about how nice I am, how genuine, how I always seem to have time for everybody, how it's amazing that I can still be down to earth when I look the way I do.
>
> By the time the final bell rings, I am exhausted. I have to smile and be nice and look like I care about other people's problems or else I get called a bitch. (O'Neill, *Asking For It* 12)

The immersive quality of the teenage girls' voices in both of O'Neill's novels, as well as the concern with rape and sexual assault in *Asking For It*, link them with *A Girl Is a Half-formed Thing*, although stylistically the novels operate in very different ways: McBride's focuses explicitly on questions of articulation and representation, while O'Neill's provoke readers into feminist engagement.

O'Neill does not allow us the comfort of an easy reaction to Emma. She is an imperfect victim—she is vain, bitchy, yet also intelligent and often self-aware—so that we are forced to examine our own complicity in the question: was she "asking for it?" When she drinks, takes drugs, and hooks up with a local football star at an extraordinarily realistic depiction of a teenage party, she is then gang-raped, dumped on her front porch, and then subjected to a series of online posts and photos of her naked and unconscious body during the rape as well as vicious victim blaming from her friends, family, and anonymous strangers. Like *Only Ever Yours*, every incident in *Asking for It*, finds its inspiration in real life, from the echoes of international incidents such as the Steubenville High School rape case, as well as Irish instances such as "Slane Girl" (in the novel Emma becomes the Ballinatoom Girl), and the priest who shakes the hands of the accused.[6] Structured in two parts, one the week leading up to the rape, and the second depicting the same week a year later, the novel shows the devastating and lasting effects of the trauma, and the stylistic device of repetition, particularly with phrases such as "(pink flesh) (Splayed legs)," highlights the relentless and dehumanizing effects of a rape culture that reduces women's bodies to objects. Moreover, the bracketing of such phrases adds to the effect in which women's bodies are depicted as sexualized parts, and the novel thus brilliantly depicts the pervasiveness of rape culture. Emma has internalized its logic, using its derogatory language, "the dirty slut" (O'Neill, *Asking For It* 21), and silencing a friend who has been raped: "*Let's just pretend it didn't happen, I told her. It's easier that way. Easier for you*" (O'Neill, *Asking For It* 86). Emma initially denies the claim of rape in her own situation, barely able to use the word, and attempting to distance herself from the accusation in an attempt to "fix it" and to be the "good girl." Emma imagines her parent's thoughts: "*We thought we could trust you to be a good girl. Emma. We thought we had raised you better than this*" (O'Neill, *Asking For It* 163). It's a chilling reminder of the narrowness of our culture and legal system's conception of what constitutes such an act, because Ireland has no legal definition of consent, and the ways in which the voice of the teenage girl is not heard or only heard in ways that she has no control over. As Emma remarks: "I don't have anything to say but they want to hear it anyway. Journalists from Jezebel, from xoJane, from the Guardian, from the *New York Times*. Everyone wants me to tell my story. I don't have a story" (172). In a similar manner to *A Girl* we witness the ways in which representation of the teenage girl's story is difficult and complicated in a misogynistic culture that denies her voice and structures her responses. These novels and McBride's bring that problem into stark and important focus.

The endings of O'Neill's two novels are particular in their adherence to the internal logic of the cultures depicted and their refusal to comfort the reader or allow any sense of catharsis. In *Only Ever Yours*, frieda's failure to perform her obedience adequately results in the ultimate punishment: "*You know what we do with girls who break the rules, don't you? We send them Underground*" (O'Neill, *Only Ever Yours* 390). "Underground" is revealed at the end of the novel to be a laboratory in which defective eves are kept asleep to facilitate research into non-conforming behaviour: "I look at the naked bodies marinating in the clear containers. Some of them look so familiar, evoking memories of high jinks and raucous misbehaviour, dropped trays in the Nutrition Centre, raised voices screaming at the chastities" (390). The conclusion of the novel sees frieda join their ranks, forced into an ultimate obedience, her personhood effectively obliterated: "I am ready to feel nothing, forever" (390). *Asking For It* ends on a similar note, with Emma choosing obedience, dropping her charges against her rapists as the pressures of going through with a court case in the face of vicious victim-blaming become too much for her: "And I walk downstairs, dragging my mouth into a smile so that I can look normal. It's important that I look normal now. It's important that I look like a good girl" (317). What both of O'Neill's novels highlight is the ways in which young femininity is heavily regulated through precise technologies of power; limited power as gained through adherence to particular performances of femininity. Failure to obey brings punishment through public shaming (see the Slane Girl phenomenon in which discourses of shame are heaped on public sexual acts if performed by a girl. There is no Slane Boy, for example.) or the discrediting of her voice and story.

Sue Jackson and Amanda Lyons outline constructions of the "girl" in postfeminist popular culture to identify "constructions of femininity as 'empowered' yet heavily constrained through the reinvigorated regulatory force of an (over) 'emphasised' and 'good' femininity" (Jackson and Lyons 229). In this, they draw on Angela McRobbie's analysis of "a new sexual contract" in *The Aftermath of Feminism* in which she outlines new "technologies" of femininity that offer freedom and power, yet only within the context of an adherence to a neoliberal subject position deeply imbricated in consumer culture. McRobbie outlines four technologies of femininity that operate in such a way: "the immaculately groomed young woman in masquerade, the sexy adventurous phallic girl, the (hard) working girl and her 'pleasing' global counterpart" (McRobbie, *The Aftermath of Feminism* 8). O'Neill's novels can be read as laying bare the technologies that produce the girl characters—frieda as the "postfeminist masquerade" and Emma as the "phallic girl"—and they offer a searing critique of the illusions and limitations of power afforded to the girl in neoliberalism.

That both of O'Neill's novels emerge in a recessionary climate points to the complex intersections between the politics of recession and feminist interventions, as well as registering larger cultural currents of trauma and loss associated with the post-boom era. In *Asking For It*, Emma decides to withdraw her complaint when she overhears her father telling her mother that he will be transferred to a different bank and demoted from manager to assistant manager. Emma reads this as her fault: "I have done this. I have done this to us all. I am ruining their lives" (O'Neill, *Asking For It* 294). That Emma's decision is tied to her perception of her culpability in the economic systems that demote her father speaks to the ways in which the politics of austerity and discursive productions of capitalism are profoundly gendered. As Penny Griffin argues, the financial sector is deeply structured by a masculinist discourse:

> The tropes of invasion, occupation, and colonization in contemporary financial discourse outlined by Ling (echoed also in De Goede and Hooper's work) should not be underestimated, not least because they are fundamental to casting 'capitalist investment as masculine conquest of virgin territories,' wherein financial transactions are understood as the operations of masculine agents called on to act boldly in the face of panic, irrationality, and 'exuberance.' (Griffin 13)

Particularly interesting here are the ways in which these constructions of finance and masculinity are subtended by a feminine which waits to be conquered, which operates passively in the service of a "masculine agent" which functions to tame female "irrationality." Emma's father is a bank manager, linking him explicitly to the financial sector that operates in these specifically gendered ways. However, the making public of and drawing attention to Emma's rape refuses the masculinist discourse of global capitalism that would render her as something to be acted upon, to be used, and to be consumed and, importantly, that this goes without saying. That the publicity of her story affects her father's job in this sector reveals the ways in which investments in particular constructions of female silence structure such discourses. Emma's only words of consent in the novel; her only significant use of the word "Yes," occurs when she confirms her withdrawal of the complaint:

> My father looks at me, right in the eye, for the first time in months. "Is this what you want?"
> I can feel the word in my mouth. It feels as if it's drawing blood from my tongue. It feels as if this word is a sacrifice.
> He and my mother look at me, *say yes, say yes, say yes*, and I can almost taste their fear that I might change my mind.
> "Yes," I say. "Yes. This is what I want." (O'Neill, *Asking For It* 304)

Indeed, Emma's consent to silence, her consent to obedience to the system that produced her as object, is a profound sacrifice.

What O'Neill's novels starkly reveal are the ways in obedience to these technologies of gender work precisely to produce girls as consumable objects (freida's literal positioning in *Only Ever Yours* and the use of Emma's body in *Asking For It*) and the bleak endings of the texts insist on laying bare the ways in which submission to these systems obliterates personhood, revealed especially starkly in the novels' conclusions. We can also see this operating in the ending of McBride's novel in which A Girl's subjectivity has become so untenable that she performs the ultimate act of immersion by drowning herself:

> There now. There now. That just was life. And now.
> What?
> My name is gone. (McBride, *A Girl Is a Half-Formed Thing* 203)

The last lines of these novels ("My name is gone" (*A Girl Is a Half-formed Thing*), "I am ready to feel nothing, forever" (*Only Ever Yours*), and "It's important that I look like a good girl" (*Asking For It*)) profoundly illustrate the damaging and totalizing effects of consenting to these technologies of gender.

O'Neill's novels position the reader in particular ways at their conclusions, primarily in terms of affect. The immersion in the teenage girl's psyche via first-person narrative allows O'Neill to lay bare the damaging effects patriarchy enacts on this psyche and also to starkly reveal the sexist injustices of its systems, such that the reader becomes deeply invested in the potential (or hope) that justice might be served and that these characters might achieve some level of agency. However, such hope is robustly denied in the novel's conclusions, producing as a result powerful affects of anger, fury, and frustration, forcing the reader to examine their own behaviour, their own complicity in patriarchy, and asking us to use that affect to be disruptive of those systems.[7] In *Only Ever Yours* the girls are told that "All eves must manage their behaviours and conduct themselves in a manner that is ladylike at all times. Emotional behaviour can be off-putting to men and must be controlled" (287). O'Neill's novels instead ask you to revel in emotion, and to channel that emotion into trampling on the patriarchy, to rebel. As Sara Ahmed writes in *The Cultural Politics of Emotion*, "Feminists who speak against established 'truths' are often constructed as emotional, as failing the very standards of reason and impartiality that are assumed to form the basis of 'good judgement'" (170). Thus, the highlighting of emotion as a form of suppression also reveals the subversive powers of affect, "off-putting" to the patriarchy. Similarly, the affect released upon the novels' conclusions also has powerful potential as a mode of feminist activism. Indeed, for Ahmed, drawing on Audre Lorde, anger is one of the most powerful affects for a feminist politics. "Anger is creative;" she writes, "it works to create a language with which to respond to that which one is against, whereby 'the what ' is renamed, and brought into a feminist world ... Anger ... moves us by moving us outwards " (Ahmed 176). Both of O'Neill's novels are "moving" in Ahmed's terms, offering us a productive and dynamic anger, dynamic in its resonances beyond the boundaries of the text, in excess of the worlds and characters of the novel, and creating a language with which to challenge the silencing of and violence against the girl. In a similar way, the internalized seething and frustrated rage, that destroys language in McBride's novel, forces us to experience the damage enacted on a teenage girl in a culture that refuses her voice and representation. This anger is offered to us, the readers, to do something with.

O'Neill's novels are part of a wider feminist energy, particularly powerful in post-crash Ireland. Bracken identifies the intensification of visibility of feminist activism in post-Tiger Ireland, such as the Marriage Equality Campaign, Waking the Feminists, and the Repeal Movement, arguing that "evident in all this feminist activity and communal action is a collective incantation of outrage and critique, a call for change" ("Austere Times"). Teenage girls have also made space for themselves in these feminist energies as we can observe in the example that opened this essay: The School for Revolutionary Girls, which acknowledges and explores the role that young women played in the events of the Rising, is part of a conversation to counter the erasure of women's involvement in nationalist politics. Such an event argues that the turn of the twentieth century marked a potentially fertile moment of girlhood in Ireland, which however cannot take hold in the climate of a conservatively Catholic state, only interested in girls in terms of their purity or potential motherhood, one that hides girls who deviate from these roles in Magdalene laundries and mother and baby homes. This is a state that fails to protect the vulnerable, that will allow a fifteen-year-old girl to die in childbirth in 1984, to choose one example, or will force a young asylum seeker to undergo a forced Caesarean section in 2014,[8] or that fails to legally define consent. Such inhospitable climates for the teenage girl find their expression in literary representations that highlight trauma, crisis, anxiety, and suffocation, which increase in intensity in the postboom era. The girl *is* a half formed thing, denied protection and articulation. However, the success of novels that insist on affective and immersive engagements with the teenage girl, that force us to confront misogynies—especially those levelled against young women—connect us back to the imagined revolutionary girls of the IMMA performance. O'Neill, for example, is actively working to engage teenage girls in feminist conversations by visiting schools, speaking publically on issues relating to consent and body image, and creating communities of young women through her social media presence and the emotional affects of her novels. What these three novels share is a taking seriously of the teenage girl's consciousness, asking us to inhabit that space no matter how uncomfortable it might seem, but also harnessing the intensity of teenage affect in order to influence change in a climate of austerity. As the School for Revolutionary Girls proclaim: "In a fair land we will have the power to make a difference."

Notes

1. Follow @revgirlschool and #SchoolRevGirls for more information and videos of the final performance.
2. The longevity of these anxieties connecting girls to commodity, sexuality, and consumerism can be observed in this mid-nineteenth-century example: Eliza Lynn Linton's famous diatribe against "The Girl of the Period," published anonymously in *The Saturday Review* in 1868. In it, Linton admonishes the modern girl for her "immoral" investment in fashion, elaborate dress, artificial beauty, and consumerism, which, for her, brings the girl into dangerous alliance with overt sexuality and the commercial sphere. "The girl of the period," Linton writes, "is a creature who dyes her hair and paints her face, as the first articles of her personal religion; whose sole idea of life is plenty of fun and luxury; and whose dress is the object of such though and intellect as she possesses. Her main endeavor in this is to outvie her neighbours in the extravagance of fashion... Men are afraid of her; and with reason" (Linton 340).
3. The X case refers to a 1992 Supreme Court Case in which the Attorney General sought an injunction to prevent a fourteen-year-old girl, pregnant as a result of rape and suicidal because of the pregnancy, from travelling to the UK to terminate the pregnancy. The Supreme Court overturned the injunction ruling that the threat of suicide was legitimate ground for granting the right to seek an abortion, although legislation was not put in place. A referendum followed which allowed for the freedom to travel for a termination and the freedom to obtain information about such. See timeline of the events here: O'Carroll.
4. See for example the texts under discussion in Bracken's *Irish Feminist Futures*: Ursula Rani Sarma's play *Blue*, which circulates around the death of a teenage girl, and Leanne O'Sullivan's poetry collection, *Waiting for my Clothes*, which explores the effects of an eating disorder.

5. Bracken's reading of the texts (*32A, Blue,* and *Waiting for my Clothes*) offers some potential for reimagining the ways in which girlhood functions, arguing that while the texts stage critiques of the difficulties of girlhood experience in the climate of the Celtic Tiger, they generate alternate models of selfhood and relationality, models, I would add, that are not marked by threat. For Bracken, these texts challenge a neo-liberal rhetoric of isolation, privileging instead collectivity and selfhoods characterized by connection, immersion, and affective relations. She notes that "affective immersion, relationality, and queer collectivity [...] all operate as mechanisms through which to engage a feminist reflection on and critique of constructions of girlhood, as well as provide imaginative hope, ultimately figuring connective selfhood as a model for a fluid becoming-woman, the about-to-be of the girl figure" (86).

6. The Steubenville High School rape was the sexual assault of an unconscious sixteen-year-old girl by two high school football players whose friends filmed and photo-graphed the acts, then posted them to social media sites, resulting in the public shaming of the victim. "Slane Girl" refers to the 2013 case in which a seventeen-year-old girl was photographed performing oral sex on a young man at an Eminem concert. The photos and a video were posted to social media sites with the hashtag #Slanegirl and the public shaming the occurred resulted in her hospitalization and sedation. There was no hashtag #Slaneboy. The final case referred to here occurred in 2009 at a case in the Circuit Criminal Court in Tralee in which a convicted sex offender, waiting for his sentence, was publicly supported by around fifty people, including the parish priest, who all shook his hand while the twenty-four-year old woman he had raped watched. See Oppel Jr.; Wiseman; Hickey Tralee.

7. I recently taught *Asking For It* to a group of undergraduates and they were unanimous in their feelings of rage and frustration at the novel's conclusion, while understanding the importance of its effects and affects. I would like to thank my 2016 "Narrating Irish Childhoods" class for the stimulating discussions of this novel which have informed my analysis here.

8. For a timeline of this case, see Holland.

Works Cited

@revgirlschool. "The final proclamation: 'In A Fair Land...'" *Twitter*, 28 Aug. 2016, 5:13 a.m., https://twitter.com/revgirlschool/status/769915800757084160

A Fair Land. http://www.imma.ie/en/page_237103.htm. Accessed 30 Aug. 2016.

Ahmed, Sara. *The Cultural Politics of Emotion.* Edinburgh University Press, 2004. Print.

Bracken, Claire. *Irish Feminist Futures.* Routledge, 2016. Print.

Cahill, Susan. "Making Space for the Irish Girl: Rosa Mulholland and Irish Girls in Fiction at the Turn of the Century." *Colonial Girlhood in Literature, Culture and History, 1840-1950,* edited by Michelle J. Smith and Kristine Moruzi, Palgrave Macmillan, Forthcoming.

_____. "Where Are The Irish Girls Girlhood, Irishness, and L.T. Meade." *Girlhood and the Politics of Place,* edited by Claudia Mitchell and Carrie Rentschler, Berghahn Books, 2016, pp. 212–27. Print.

Cochrane, Kira. "Eimear McBride: 'There Are Serious Readers Who Want to Be Challenged.'" *The Guardian,* 5 June 2014, https://www.theguardian.com/books/2014/jun/05/eimear-mcbride-serious-readers-challenged-baileys-womens-prize.

Connelly, Ailish. "The Celtic Kittens Are in Control." *Irish Times,* 11 Dec. 2006, p. 16.

Dougherty, Jane Elizabeth. "Nuala O'Faolain and the Unwritten Irish Girlhood." *New Hibernia Review,* vol. 11, no. 2, 2007, pp. 50–65. Print.

Driscoll, Catherine. *Girls: Feminine Adolescence in* Popular Culture and Cultural *Theory.* Columbia University Press, 2002. Print.

Eric-Udorie, June. "Louise O'Neill: 'I Just Love Teenage Girls. There's Something about That Age That Is so Painful and so Raw.'" *New Statesman*, Oct. 2015, http://www.newstatesman.com/culture/books/2015/10/louise-o-neill-i-just-love-teenage-girls-there-s-something-about-age-so.

Flynn, Roddy. "32A." *Estudios Irlandeses* 4 (2009): 174–76. Print.

Ging, Debbie. "Culture on the Edge: The Postfeminist Challenge." *Theory on the Edge*. Eds, GiffneyNoreen and Margrit Shildrick, Palgrave Macmillan US, 2013. 209–220. *link. springer.com*, doi:10.1057/9781137315472_15.

Gorra, Michael. "Eimear McBride's Toolkit." *Times Literary Supplement*, Sept. 2016, http://www.the-tls.co.uk/articles/private/bodies-of-evidence-2/.

Griffin, Penny. "Gendering Global Finance Crisis, Masculinity, and Responsibility." *Men and Masculinities* 16.1 (2013): 9–34. Print.

Hickey Tralee, Donal. "People Queued to Shake This Sex Attacker's Hand." *Irish Examiner*, 17 Dec. 2009, http://www.irishexaminer.com/ireland/people-queued-to-shake-this-sex-attackers-hand-108061.html.

Holland, Kitty. "Timeline of Ms Y Case." *The Irish Times*, 4 Oct. 2014, http://www.irishtimes.com/news/social-affairs/timeline-of-ms-y-case-1.1951699.

Jackson, Sue, and Amanda Lyons. "Girls' 'New Femininity' Refusals and 'Good Girl' Recuperations in Soap Talk." *Feminist Media Studies* 13.2 (2013): 228–244. Print.

Leonard, Garry. "Women on the Market: Commodity Culture,' Femininity,' and 'Those Lovely Seaside Girls' in Joyce's *Ulysses.* " *Joyce Studies Annual* 2.1 (1991): 27–68. Print.

Lindner, Christoph. *Fictions of Commodity Culture: From the Victorian to the Postmodern.* Ashgate, 2003. Print.

Linton, Eliza Lynn. "The Girl of the Period." *Saturday Review of Politics, Literature, Science and Art*, vol. 25, no. 646, Mar. 1868, pp. 339–40. Print.

McBride, Eimear. *A Girl Is a Half-Formed Thing*. Galley Beggar Press, 2013. Print.

_____. "How I Wrote A Girl Is a Half-Formed Thing." *The Guardian*, 10 Sept. 2016. *The Guardian*, https://www.theguardian.com/books/2016/sep/10/guardian-book-club-eimear-mcbride-how-i-wrote-a-girl-is-a-half-formed-thing.

McGovern, Kelly J.S. "'No Right to Be a Child': Irish Girlhood and Queer Time in Éilís Ní Dhuibhne's The Dancers Dancing." *Éire-Ireland* 44.1 (2009): 242–264. Print.

McRobbie, Angela. *The Aftermath of Feminism: Gender, Culture and Social Change*. SAGE, 2009. Print.

_____. "Young Women and Consumer Culture." *Cultural Studies* 22.5 (2008): 531–550. Print.

Negra, Diane, and Yvonne Tasker. "Introduction: Gender and Recessionary Culture." *Gendering the Recession: Media and Culture in an Age of Austerity*, 2013, pp. 1–30. Print.

Ní Dhuibhne, Éilís. *The Dancers Dancing*. Blackstaff Press, 1999. Print.

O'Carroll, Sinead. *Twenty Years on: A Timeline of the X Case*. 6 Feb. 2012, http://www.thejournal.ie/twenty-years-on-a-timeline-of-the-x-case-347359-Feb2012/.

O'Neill, Louise. *Asking For It*. Quercus, 2016. Print.

_____. *Only Ever Yours*. Quercus, 2014. Print.

Oppel Jr., Richard A. "2 Teenagers Found Guilty in Steubenville, Ohio, Rape." *The New York Times*, 17 Mar. 2013. *NYTimes.com*, http://www.nytimes.com/2013/03/18/us/teenagers-found-guilty-in-rape-in-steubenville-ohio.html.

O'Toole, Fintan. "Why Irish Writers Don't Grow out of Adolescence." *The Irish Times*, 6 Nov. 2010, p. C8. Print.

Stoneley, Peter. *Consumerism and American Girls' Literature, 1860-1940*. Cambridge University Press, 2003.Print.

Tasker, Yvonne, and Diane Negra. "Introduction: Feminist Politics and Postfeminist Culture." *Interrogating Postfeminism: Gender and the Politics of Popular Culture*, edited by Diane Negra and Yvonne Tasker, Duke University Press, 2007, pp. 1–26. Print.

The School for Revolutionary Girls. http://www.imma.ie/en/page_237159.htm. Accessed 30 Aug. 2016.

Wiseman, Eva. "The Slane Girl Twitter Scandal Proves That Women Can't Make Mistakes." *The Guardian*, 1 Sept. 2013. *The Guardian*, https://www.theguardian.com/lifeandstyle/2013/sep/01/slane-girl-twitter-scandal-women.

Melatu Uche Okorie: An Introduction to her Work and a Conversation with the Author (with Preface: 2020 Update)

Sara Martín-Ruiz

Preface: 2020 Update

The conversation that follows took place at the beginning of 2017. Since then, Melatu Uche Okorie's work has blossomed, and her name has become better known, both in an Irish and in an international context. While not changing its subject matter or style, her writing, which had until then been always published in small, and often migrant-focused media, has slowly but surely moved closer towards the canon of Irish literature. After the publication of her short story "This Hostel Life" in *LIT: Literature Interpretation Theory* in 2017, in the same issue in which this interview originally appeared, Okorie published "Under the Awning" in *College Green Magazine* in 2017. With her characteristic nuanced and ironic tone, "Under the Awning" skilfully exposes the many ways in which racism affects a black woman living in Ireland, as she shares a partially auto-biographical story in a creative writing workshop and her white colleagues diminish her experience. Thus, "Under the Awning" reveals how the acceptance or rejection of fiction written by immigrant or ethnic minorities in Ireland is a reflection of the degree to which Irish society as a whole is ready to accept the many ways in which racism is present in Ireland today, going from the macro (institutional racism is at the heart of Irish migration policies, citizen-ship rights, and refugee law) to the micro level (as illustrated by the implicitly or explicitly racist comments and attitudes that the protagonist of the story has to endure).

2018 marked a turning point for Okorie's writing career, with the publishing of her debut volume *This Hostel Life* by the newly founded Skein Press, which, as stated on their website, "was established in June 2017 to publish writers whose work is fresh and thought-provoking and features outlooks and experi-ences not often represented in Irish publishing". Okorie's *This Hostel Life* was Skein Press' first project, and the book included two previously published short stories ("This Hostel Life" and "Under the Awning"), and the new "The Egg Broke", which retells an Igbo superstition from the point of view of a mother of twins whose newborn babies were taken away from her. The three stories are preceded by an "Author's Note," in which Okorie denounces the Direct Provi-sion system in which many of her stories take place and in which she started to write during her eight-and-a-half-years stay in the Irish asylum system. The collection ends with an academic essay by Liam Thornton, in which the legal aspects of Irish asylum law are explained.

Melatu Uche Okorie's *This Hostel Life* provided the author with unprecedented success. It was shortlisted for the An Post Irish Book Awards Sunday Independent in the category of New Comer of the Year. In 2019, it was republished in the UK by renowned feminist Virago Press. That same year, in September, the Irish National Opera offered an experimental opera adaptation of Okorie's debut book. Since then, it seems that Okorie's work, once forced to remain at the margins of Irish society, a reflection of the institutional isolation forced upon the characters it portrays, is finally achieving the space it deserves in Irish literature. In 2019, "BrownLady12345" was included *in Being Various. New Irish Short Stories*, an anthology edited by Lucy Caldwell, published by Faber & Faber, and which includes other trending authors such as Eimear McBride, Sally Rooney, Kevin Barry, and Lisa McInerney. "BrownLady12345" focuses on Joseph, an asylum seeker who strives to come to terms with their gender identity and their queer sexuality while living in Direct Provision, a fact that aggravates their struggle as institutionalised isolation, sanctioned poverty, and lack of privacy further complicates Joseph's attempts to unravel their traumatic past and meet and date Irish people.

In October 2020, Okorie's "Under the Awning" has been included in Sinead Gleeson's *The Art of the Glimpse: 100 Irish Short Stories*, published by Head of Zeus. In this monumental work, Gleeson seeks to expand the Irish canon, making renowned names such as Bram Stoker, Edna O'Brien, or James Joyce share space with others such as Chiamaka Enyi-Amadi, Oein DeBhairduin, and Melatu Uche Okorie. As Gleeson notes in her introduction to the volume, "an anthology is an interesting means of taking the temperature of a nation" (Gleeson 2020). Hence, the inclusion of Okorie's stories in recent anthologies of Irish literature can be taken as a two-fold positive sign. On the one hand, Melatu Uche Okorie is being recognised as what she is: one of the most talented and innovative short story writers in contemporary Ireland. On the other hand, the inclusion of a writer like Okorie in general anthologies of Irish literature, traditionally dominated by white, settled, and usually male, authors, speaks of a willingness to open the idea of Irishness to something more faithful to the polyphonic and varied experiences that shape what Ireland is today. It is my wish, then, that the ongoing acceptance and inclusion of these stories into the canon of Irish literature will open up and contribute to the debate of what it means to be Irish, and that the challenge of such restrictive, monolithic, and exclusionary notions of Irishness in the cultural arena will bring forward a social and political reconsideration on matters such as Direct Provision or the 27th Amendment to the Constitution.

An Introduction to Okorie's Work

Melatu Uche Okorie was born in 1975 in Enugu, in the Igbo-speaking region of Nigeria. She obtained a BA in English from the University of Port Harcourt in her native country. In 2006, she arrived in Ireland as an asylum seeker. In 2009, still living in Direct Provision,[1] Okorie won the *Metro Éireann*[2] Writing Award for her short story "Gathering Thoughts." Obtaining the first prize of this literary competition (judged by best-selling Irish writer Roddy Doyle) was just the beginning of Melatu Uche Okorie's writing career. She later obtained an MPhil in Creative Writing from Trinity College, Dublin. In 2010, her story "Shackles" was published in the Irish Writers' Exchange[3] anthology *Dublin: Ten Journeys, One Destination*. This compilation included ten short stories by writers living in Ireland, and the stories all revolve around the city of Dublin. Some of the authors are Irish-born, like the critically acclaimed writer Nuala Ní Chonchúir, while others are born in places as diverse as Sweden, Germany, the United States or, as in the present case, Nigeria. A year later, Okorie's short story "If George Could Talk" was selected for publication in the anthology *Alms on the Highway* (2011), which compiled short stories, poetry and drama written by postgraduate students of the MPhil in Creative Writing of Trinity College. Nowadays, she lives with her daughter in the West of Ireland, where she combines her full-time job as a mother with her writing sessions, as well as with her work as a board member of AkiDwa[4] and the occasional teaching of creative writing to children.

Despite being a very prolific writer, as attested by the abundance and quality of her unpublished materials, Melatu Uche Okorie's publications are relatively scarce.[5] However, her four published stories (five, if we include "This Hostel Life" published in this special issue) already indicate that her work is developing in very interesting directions. Roddy Doyle has underscored Okorie's skilled style,[6] which combines the expressive orality of her characters with subtly poetic descriptions of their surroundings, while also highlighting the most prosaic aspects of their precariousness. To this one has to add that the subjects narrated in Melatu Uche Okorie's short stories are of crucial relevance in Ireland, a multicultural country with extreme forms of institutional racism, as epitomized by the system of Direct Provision. Hence, the importance of Okorie's work is not only due to its literary quality, but also because of her representations of the harsh realities for asylum seekers—realities which are often made silent or invisible. Furthermore, while representations of the so-called "New Irish" in fiction, written by Irish-born authors such as Roddy Doyle, Anne Haverty, Hugo Hamilton, Oona Frawley, or Róisín O'Donell, have received widespread media and scholarly attention, it is high time that the literary voices of immigrants themselves are finally heard.[7]

In her award-winning "Gathering Thoughts" (2009), Okorie vividly narrates the story of Lagos-born, 14-year-old Angela when she and her 12-year-old sister travel with their parents to their father's birth place, Amagunze, for the first time in their lives. Instead of the dream-like village that had been transmitted to Angela by her parents' childhood memories, the narrator meets a very strict, matriarchal family, ruled by her paternal great-grandmother Ugochi, who is not happy about their urban and westernised lifestyles. Angela's father will soon become the new "Igwe"—Amagunze's traditional ruler—and he will have to prove his value by accepting the matriarch's abuse of his wife and children, including the genital mutilation of his two daughters. The story narrates, through the eyes of naïve Angela, how her father's unquestioning embrace of tradition, as imposed by the matriarch Ugochi, drastically affects Angela's, her sister's and her mother's lives. With an abrupt and open ending, "Gathering Thoughts" complicates the role of women, positioning them as both victims and perpetrators of tradition, and Okorie emphasizes the very few possibilities the protagonist faces regarding her future.

In her following publication, "Shackles" (2010), Okorie again raises questions about the protagonist's uncertain future by placing his home of origin in conversation with his new, unstable home in Ireland. This is Okorie's first story entirely set in Ireland—more specifically, in a fictional Direct Provision centre in Dublin.[8] The narrator and protagonist of this story is Osita, a Nigerian asylum seeker who has been living in DP for eight years. He shares a room in the hostel with his heavily pregnant girlfriend of five years, Mary, and his seven-year old daughter Uju, from a previous relationship. When he receives the news of his mother's death back in Nigeria, he is faced with the dilemma of how to fulfill his duty as a son. Osita is obligated to enter the illegal job market in Ireland in order to obtain the necessary money to pay for his mother's funeral, as well as to appease his mother's relatives, as is tradition in Nigeria. Yet his decision to comply with these obligations risks his family's future in Ireland, because if the authorities find out about his illegal employment, it would mean immediate deportation. Hence, similarly to "Gathering Thoughts," "Shackles" addresses the suffocating role of tradition in Nigeria, but this is further complicated by an imperialist, neoliberal world system which has replaced colonialism and empire. For example, the important role the Catholic Church continues to play in daily matters in the story cannot be separated from its colonial roots (with the work of the missionaries, often Irish Catholics, in Nigeria) and the pressures that the global economy has put on the global South ensures that its natural and human resources are exploited for the benefit of the North. The pressure of this mutual reinforcement of old and new systems of oppression cannot be escaped even when one lives abroad, as Osita laments: "It is a waste of time trying to explain to any of my relatives in Nigeria that I am only an asylum seeker here in Ireland and not a millionaire with trees made up of Euro leaves in my backyard" (2010: 146). At the same time, the story is also a harsh critique of life in Direct Provision, perhaps best summarized in the narrator's observation: "I am running away from persecution, but I'm being persecuted in the country that is meant to provide safety for me" (2010: 144). Read in juxtaposition with "Gathering Thoughts," one can only think of the extremely precarious situation Angela might find herself in if she decided to flee Nigeria and seek refuge in Ireland.

Okorie continues to provide depth to the trajectory of migration, from a hazardous present in Nigeria to an uncertain future in Ireland, in "If George Could Talk" (2011).[9] In this story, the author presents the reader with the lifestory of Jumi, a Nigerian-born woman by the story's conclusion arrives in Ireland as an asylum seeker. "If George Could Talk" begins with Jumi's preparation for her *Umu-Ogbo* ritual, which marks her entrance into a very narrowly defined concept of womanhood. It is at that moment that the narrator is given the "George," traditional Nigerian clothing that has been passed on from mothers to daughters for generations. However, this particular George has skipped a generation, since Jumi's mother died during childbirth (before the George was given to her). Hence, it is Nene, Jumi's grandmother, who passes on the George to her. In Okorie's story, the George functions as a symbol of the weight of traditional gender roles that will accompany Jumi throughout her treacherous journey. Throughout the story, Okorie adroitly uses different reflective surfaces to offer glimpses into the characters' minds. One example of this are the small mirrors sewn into the George, which give "fat reflections of people's faces" (134), as a reference to the "fattening houses" to which Jumi refuses to go, where she would learn "practical things, like how to please my future husband" (135). There is also a "cracked mirror leaning against the wall" (135) in the room where Grandmother Nene and Auntie Ugo help Jumi prepare for her *Umu-Ogbo* ceremony; its broken reflection suggests the physical and psychological damage that the protagonist will suffer when she is forced to accept her imposed female role. Despite the narrator's attempts to escape her proscribed role as a woman, the death of her protective grandmother shatters her dreams of independence. Jumi is then forced to abandon her studies and to marry Captain Izuekah, a violent man who abuses her and their two children. When Jumi's husband takes part in a failed *coup d'état*, the protagonist and her children flee the country to escape the death penalty. One of the very few belongings that the narrator manages to take with her is, however, the George. Curiously, the George survived the fire that killed Jumi's grandmother precisely due to the protagonist's defiance to tradition: she took it with her to college despite the fact that Nene had told her not to. Already in Ireland, another reflective surface, this time a television screen in a shopping mall, locates Jumi's utter sense of displacement and isolation. The narrator observes Captain Izuekah's execution in Nigeria broadcasted on CNN, "[w]hile people chatted, laughed, shoved and pushed around me" (143). The story ends with Jumi's arrival in Ireland seeking refuge, although it does not elaborate on her life as an asylum seeker in Ireland.

To a certain extent, "This Hostel Life" continues on from that moment of arrival, albeit with a different character, and focuses on a female experience in Direct Provision. In this story, Okorie continues her trend of using a first-person narrator as she offers a realistic, polyphonic representation of life in a Direct Provision centre, where a literal and metaphorical taste of honey is systematically denied to asylum seekers. However, "This Hostel Life" also supposes a departure from her previous publications in several aspects: it features a Congolese, not a Nigerian, protagonist; the kind of English used throughout the story is very experimental, as the author will confirm in our conversation; and it has certain comedic elements which are not present in the previously published stories. All in all, Okorie's publications to date offer a non-linear *continuum* of the lives of asylum seekers in Ireland, both pre- and post-arrival. Each narrative defies temporal logic, refuses definitive answers, and provides a snapshot of possible and plausible stories.

In the interview that follows, Melatu Uche Okorie talks about her writing, the obstacles of publication in Ireland for migrant women, and the impact of the "recession" on migrant women like herself living in post-Celtic Tiger Ireland.

A Conversation with Melatu Uche Okorie

SMR: **You have a BA in English from the University of Port Harcourt in Nigeria. This reveals that your love for literature is long-lived and has been cultivated throughout your education. Did you already write fiction while living in Nigeria, or was it something that you started once in Ireland? In an interview,[10] Ifedinma Dimbo shared with me that she did not actually start writing until she became an asylum seeker in Ireland, as writing became her coping mechanism. Was that the case for you, or did you already have some writing experience before arriving to Ireland?**

MO: Yes, it's true I have a BA in English from Nigeria, and I have always loved literature; however, my love has always been as that of a reader. I've always loved stories, whether being told orally or through books. I've always enjoyed reading, but I had never written. I was a scribbler, though – you know, one of those people who scribbled throughout conversations. I would say that, like Ifedinma, I started writing when I came to Ireland, although I wouldn't say it was a form of coping mechanism, or maybe it was but I never looked at it like that. For me, it was just having these stories playing around in my head that I suddenly started putting down. I didn't give it too much thought; I certainly didn't think it would last this long, but here we are today.

SMR: **With such a long history as a reader, could you please tell me which authors might have had an influence on your writing? Have you discovered any Irish writers who have make an impression on you?**

MO: Oh, I read everything readable as a young child; from the school recommended literature books of – Flora Nwapa, Mariama Ba, Chinua Achebe, Wole Soyinka, Shakespeare – to the crime detective novelist at that time – James Hadley Chase. And I was one of those readers who remembered the tiniest detail, if there was a red door, I would pick up on it and store it somewhere, if there were tiles on a bathroom floor, I would remember. Have there been Irish writers who have made a lot of impression on me? Most definitely…where do I even start to name them? …Colm Tóibín, Paul Murray, Roddy Doyle, Hugo Hamilton, Emma Donoghue, Joseph O'Connor, Nuala O'Faolain, Dermot Bolger, John Banville, Sebastian Barry… I'm sure I've forgotten someone important whose work I love.

SMR: **You also mentioned the oral telling of stories in your first response…Orality is a very important feature of the transmission of culture in Nigeria, isn't it? Do you think this oral quality has somehow influenced your writing?**

MO: I'll say it has. I would say it come across in my dialogues. I especially like to work on the voices of my characters. I want their voices to be distinctive. I want their life to be reflected in their voice.

SMR: **The Call For Papers for this journal emphasised that women have often been one of the most negatively affected by this "new era of recession" in the Post-Celtic Tiger era. However, you arrived to Ireland in 2006, when the Tiger was still alive and kicking, yet, as an asylum seeker, you did not get to enjoy any of the prosperity often associated with the Celtic Tiger. What does this post-Celtic Tiger recession mean for women like you?**

MO: This is an interesting question. I think recession is a normal way of life for women like myself. During the Celtic Tiger years, we were left on the sideline, we were hearing of this new prosperity, but we never partook of it. In retrospect, it is a good thing because you don't miss what you never had, but, the strange thing about this particular time in Irish history is that if you ask your ordinary Joe on the street who he blames for the crash of the Celtic Tiger years, he would point to the refugees and asylum seekers.

SMR: **If one thinks of non-white and/or non-Irish born female authors during the post-Celtic Tiger period, it is hard to underscore the challenges that are faced in terms of visibility, publishing, and so on. Would you say that publication in Ireland has been harder for immigrant women like yourself?**

MO: Publication has definitely been harder for immigrant women, and there are several reasons for that. First, there is the local knowledge. When a place is your town and you speak the lingo, life is a bit easier to navigate. Second, to pursue publication takes a lot of dedication and hard work. For some of the migrant women, the hard work is there, but the dedication comes with a price.

SMR: **What is that price?**

MO: Day to day survival…

SMR: **In the Foreword to the anthology *Alms on the Highway* (2011), where your story "If George Could Talk" is included, Kevin Barry states: "getting the work down on that tyrannical white page is only the start of it. Getting the work out into the world is every bit as difficult, and every bit as critical to a writer's fruition" (2011: xi). Until now, your work has only been published in smaller, often migrant-led and migrant-focused media.[11] Do you think that the "fruition" of immigrant women writers in Ireland like you has been blocked by the severe difficulty to have your work published?**

MO: What I said above also stands here. I think for every writer, publication is a sort of affirmation, a form through which you know someone thinks what you have to say is worth hearing. So, a "severe difficulty" in getting one's work published can definitely knock back confidence, and I think that some part of that difficulty comes from some people feeling that if you're not a certain way, look a certain way and speak a certain way, then automatically, your writing is poor.

SMR: **You have only published short stories so far, but I know that there was once a stage production of "If George Could Talk." Could you please tell me more about this play?**

MO: I think the idea of the play was spontaneous. It didn't come from me though. A friend of mine read the short story and asked for my permission to stage it. She had the story transcribed into a play, found the actors and director. She did the whole work and all credit deservedly goes to her. They performed the play at some DP hostels. It was a small, fun, thing; nothing major by any means.

SMR: **However, I was wondering whether you have also written in formats other than the short story. Have you tried writing your own plays? Have you ever thought of maybe writing a novel? Or do you feel more at ease with short stories?**

MO: I have written a couple of other plays. One was while studying at Trinity, and the other quite recently, actually. I like writing plays. Yes, I probably would agree that I feel more at ease with writing short stories. I love reading novels, but I find short stories more concise as a writer.

SMR: **I know that you sometimes teach creative teaching to children. Could you tell me more about this experience? Does the experience of teaching how to write creatively somehow affects your own writing?**

MO: It does. I always learn new things! I love working with children in this form. They remind you that it's all about the story; and it comes so easily to them. I've never done a creative writing workshop with children and come out of it not smiling. There's always this sense of wonder and gratitude that they had let me into their world and you get to see that they are dealing with the same kind of issues that we adults are contending with!

SMR: **I would like to focus now on your published work so far. There seems to be certain leitmotifs that cross all your *oeuvre*, both in style and in content. In terms of style, all your stories have first-person narrators. In terms of content, it would seem that they all touch on topics which either you know first-hand, or are very familiar and close to you. Is that so? Do you only write about things that have affected you directly?**

MO: Well, I don't think all of my stories are in first person. I do write in third person, and I think I have a short story that I wrote in the second person. They just haven't been published yet…You're probably right that I write about things that are close to me, maybe not affected me directly, but certainly things that I have observed close to me. I know a lot of my stories centre around life in DP, but you know what, I don't think I have scratched the surface in terms of writing about DP. I know I owe it a novel, and maybe when I stop dittering around, I'll sit down and write that novel. I have it in bits and pieces, it's just putting it all together into a full story that is left to do.

SMR: **I definitely can't wait to read that novel! Continuing with certain trends in your stories…There is also something that the narrators of your stories have in common: they are all Igbo characters who seem to be very critical of traditions. It seems to be especially so in** the case of female characters. In "Gathering Thoughts" (2009), Angela wonders: "was this what customs and traditions were all about? Humiliating an innocent woman?" (2009: 13). Could you comment on this critical attitude to tradition of your characters?

MO: Aren't we all critics of tradition? I think some traditions are hindrances. Some people may argue that it gives us a sense of identity, but it also cripples us, and it is mostly used when there's an expectation to "toe the line."

SMR: Another topic which is repeated in your stories is the representation of different Nigerian rites of passage into female adulthood. In the case of "Gathering Thoughts," Angela and her sister suffer female genital mutilation, which, the narrator is told, "is a rite that every woman in Amagunze must go through before they can get married" (2009: 13). Jumi, on the other hand, wears the George for the first time for her *Umu-Ogbo* ceremony, which marks her officially coming of age, meaning that she can get married and have children. The consequences of both narrators' becoming adult women are terrible. Are you somehow suggesting, through these stories, that the traditional female roles in Nigeria are becoming outdated for the current generation of young women?

MO: Oh they are indeed. More slowly in Nigeria than they are in some other parts of the world. Sometimes, this doesn't necessarily translate into a good thing, because from what we can see, it does feel like once an ill is abolished, another takes its place. But that's by the way. I definitely believe that the traditional female roles in Nigeria are becoming outdated. Now, there's a common Igbo saying which goes, "*Nwoke gaba ogu, nwanyi enwere akuko*," which means that "the man goes to war, the woman tells the story." That tells you the role of the woman - that of the one who stays home and gossips, while the man is the breadwinner. But that is simply untrue with the current generation. Every time I look around me, I see women who left their home countries, families, husbands...to me they are warriors. I see a lot of women parenting alone. Where are the men? The women are the ones going to war now, while the men are the ones who stay home to tell stories.

SMR: In your stories, there also seems to be a great gap between lifestyle and mentality in urban Nigeria, namely Lagos, and rural areas of the country. After several years living in Ireland, would you say that this urban/rural tension is somehow similar to the differences that one could find between Dublin and more rural areas of Ireland?

MO: I know in "Gathering Thoughts" the family went from the city to visit families in a village; and in "Shackles" Osita was based in Lagos before relocating to Ireland. In "If George Could Talk" Jumi left the village to live with her uncle at the death of her grandmother. So I see the movements in my stories and the differences between rural/urban lives, and I guess it will be the same to some level no matter where one is, but it's not something I've paid particular attention to since living in Ireland. I've recently moved to the rural part of Ireland from the city, but I'm yet to integrate deeply into the rural life. I suppose when I do, I'll be able to draw better comparison.

SMR: **You are very critical of the Irish State, and more specifically, of the Direct Provision system, in some of your stories. In "Shackles," as well as in "This Hostel Life," you portray the inhuman conditions under which asylum seekers are made to live in the Irish asylum system.[12] Do you think that the very political contents of your stories, which give visibility to a hidden reality in contemporary Ireland, might be one of your obstacles for having your work published in wider Irish media?**

MO: It is a strong possibility. But, I can only tell my truth. It doesn't mean that Ireland is bad, or that Irish people are bad, but that particular system is what is inhuman. I must point out that I have been shown kindness like I've never experienced before in my life in this country, and I have also felt the most isolated and a visible outsider here as well. And that's life.

SMR: **I would like to ask you some questions about "This Hostel Life." Though it maintains some of the usual traits of your stories, it also somehow departs from your previously published writing. I was especially struck by the comical aspects of the story.**

MO: Hmm, I think the only way to capture the whole asylum system is by satire. I can't picture an event that happened during my time in direct provision that does not have a comical nuance to it. There was always laughter. Despite the sadness, there was always laughter. That was how we coped. I couldn't have done that story any other way.

SMR: **Another trait which I would highlight from "This Hostel Life" is the very polyphonic vision of Direct Provision that you offer through the somehow comical narrative of Beverlée, together with the negative, stereotypical comments that Mummy Dayo gives about different nationalities (including Nigerians). It is as if you were trying to present the reader with a very diverse reality of different peoples living in DP, breaking the typical homogenization of "asylum seekers" in mainstream media.**

MO: If you've ever been inside a direct provision hostel, you would know that it's a condensation of the United Nations….the different languages, the different people…you learn so much, and you deal with so much prejudice as well. It's like you're thrown into a "Big Brother" house with these bunch of strangers so you have to be constantly aware and alert. I even learnt a lot about the different cultures which make up Nigeria, and other African countries than I had ever known in all my years, and I'm sure it's the same for everybody else who went through DP.

SMR: **Also, the style of this piece is really interesting, especially the use of language. Could you comment on this?**

MO: The language of the story is a completely made up one; by this, I mean the voice of the main character, Beverléé. It may come across to the reader as Pidgin English, but a study of the West African Pidgin English will show that the language of the story is different, and does not fit the construct of the Pidgin English, if there's any such thing! When writing the story I considered the fact that the main character, Beverléé, was Congolese, with little French and even less English. I needed to give her the right tool of communication. To do this, I had to coin out what I'll call a mixture of Englishes, made up of the Englishes that are being spoken around her: the West African Broken English, Standard English, the American English that she picks up from watching television - "I'm gonna" - and of course, Congolese pronunciations, as can be seen in the way she says certain words like, "Mamaa"...Her language is of course different from Mama Dayo's. With Mummy Dayo's character, I gave her the Pidgin English spoken on the rougher Streets of Lagos, while Mercy, Mama Bomboy, Ngozi and Franca have a variation of Nigerian standard English.

SMR: **As a final note... Chimamanda Ngozi Adichie is an Igbo writer whose books have become best sellers, not only in the States, but all around the world. Do you think that authors like her might perhaps open the door for other migrant women like yourself, writing about the struggles of trying to live in another country?**

MO: Ireland is a smaller country in comparison to the United States. I think what you're suggesting will happen, but how soon, I'm not sure.

Notes

1. Direct Provision (DP) is the system employed by the Irish State to deal with asylum seekers. It was established in November 1999 by the Dáil, without any vote or debate, as a temporary solution to deal with the relatively growing numbers of asylum seekers arriving to Celtic Tiger Ireland. However, 18 years later, the system is still working without any major changes. Under this scheme, asylum seekers are allocated in specific centres, often isolated from mainstream society, following a dispersal policy. Asylum seekers are not allowed to work. Instead, they receive 19.10 euros per week per adult, and 12.60 euros per week per child (the latter sum has recently been increased from 9.60 euros per week). They are not allowed to enter free third-level education. Asylum

seekers living in Direct Provision centres lack basic rights such as being able to choose when or what to eat, or having a proper private space in which to live safely. Direct Provision has been vocally criticised and opposed by several anti-racist platforms such as MASI (Movement of Asylum Seekers in Ireland), ADI (Anti-Deportation Ireland), or Anti Racism Network Ireland, as well as by academics such as Ronit Lentin (2003, 2004, 2006, 2016), Eithne Luibhéid (2013), Anne Mulhall (2014), Vukasin Nedeljković (2016a, 2016b, 2016c), or myself (Martín-Ruiz 2015a, 2015b, 2016a, 2016b, and forthcoming).

2. *Metro Éireann* is a migrant-led, migrant-focused newspaper based in Dublin. It was established in April 2000 by Nigerian-born journalists Chinedu Onyejelem and Abel Ugba.

3. Irish Writers' Exchange is a small publishing house established by Canadian-born Roslyn Fuller in 2008. Its catalogue mostly includes literature written by immigrant authors living in Ireland.

4. AkiDwa (*Akina Dada wa Africa*; Swahili for "sisterhood") is a non-governmental, minority ethnic-led national network of migrant women living in Ireland. It was officially established in 2001. AkiDwa's main objective is to offer support and solutions for migrant women living in Ireland, focusing on the areas of gender-based violence (including Genital Female Mutilation) and gender discrimination.

5. The interviewer has had the honor of accessing many of Okorie's unpublished stories, courtesy of the author. After the interview with Okorie had taken place, "Under the Awning" (2017) was published in *College Green Magazine* (www.collegegreenmagazine. com). This story deals with the various manifestations of racism experienced by a black female writer living in Ireland, including the problems she faces about the reception of her autobiographical writing.

6. In relation to "Gathering Thoughts," Doyle stated: "It's a shocking story, not only because of its subject, but because of the writing – the choice of words, the brilliance of the dialogue, the quality of the writing" (2009: 12).

7. As claimed by Pilar Villar-Argáiz in the "Introduction" to her edited volume *Literary Visions of Multicultural Ireland: The Immigrant in Contemporary Irish Literature* (15).

8. I offer a full analysis of this story in "Literature and Dissidence under Direct Provision: Melatu Uche Okorie and Ifedinma Dimbo," an article in the forthcoming book *Irishness on the Margins: Minority and Dissident Identities*, edited by Pilar Villar-Argáiz.

9. I offer a full analysis of this story in "'If George Could Talk': The Resignification of a Traditional Nigerian Cloth in Multicultural Ireland," a chapter in *Irish Migrant Adaptations: Memory, Performance and Place*, edited by Jason King, Charlotte McIvor and Matthew Spangler (forthcoming).

10. See my interview with Nigerian-born, Irish-based author Ifedinma Dimbo in *Estudios Irlandeses*.

11. Interestingly, in my interview with Dimbo, she also told me that she believed that the reception of her novel, *She Was Foolish?*, had been negatively affected by her not being Irish-born (Martín-Ruiz 2015a).

12. As the narrator Osita puts it himself: "I'm here, […] stuck in a system that does not care, living amongst people who speak to me with disdain and treat my family with a barely veiled contempt. And you know the funniest thing? […] I can't do anything about it, not one damn thing!" (2010: 151).

Works Cited

Barry, Kevin. "Foreword." *Alms on the Highway. New Writing from the Oscar Wilde Centre Trinity College Dublin.* Ed. Edel Corrigan. Dublin: Myrtle Press, 2011. xi–xii. Print.

Dimbo, Ifedinma. *She Was Foolish?* Malahide: Irish Writers' Exchange, 2012. Print.

Doyle, Roddy. "New Writers Crossing Borders". *Metro Éireann*, 15–21 October 2009: 12. Print.

Fuller, Roslyn (ed.). *Dublin: Ten Journeys, One Destination.* Malahide: Irish Writers' Exchange, 2010. Print.

Sinéad Gleeson. "Introduction." *The Art of the Glimpse: 100 Irish Short Stories.* Ed. Sinéad Gleeson Head of Zeus: London, 2020. ix–xii. Print.

Lentin, Ronit, and Robbie McVeigh. *After Optimism? Ireland, Racism and Globalisation.* Dublin: Metro Éireann Publications, 2006. Print.

_____. "Asylum Seekers, Ireland, and the Return of the Repressed." *Irish Studies Review* 24:1 (2016): 21–34. Print.

_____. "From Racial State to Racist State: Ireland on the Eve of the Citizenship Referendum." *Variant* 2:20 (2004): 7–8. Print.

_____. "Pregnant Silence: (En)gendering Ireland's Asylum Space." *Patterns of Prejudice* 37:3 (2003): 301–322. Print.

Luibhéid, Eithne. *Pregnant on Arrival. Making the Illegal Immigrant.* Minneapolis, London: University of Minnesota Press, 2013. Print.

Martín-Ruiz, Sara. "The way the Irish asylum system turns people into un-human is my problem': An Interview with Ifedinma Dimbo." *Estudios Irlandeses* 10 (2015a): 109–114. Print.

_____. "Forced to Migrate, Forced to Illegality: Literary Representations of Irish Immigration Law." Conference paper delivered at "Crisis, Migration and Performance" Symposium. National University of Ireland, Galway, 11th March 2016(a).

_____. "'If George Could Talk': The Resignification of a Traditional Nigerian Cloth in Multicultural Ireland." *Irish Migrant Adaptations: Memory, Performance and Place.* Eds. Jason King, Charlotte McIvor and Matthew Spangler. Forthcoming.

_____. "Literature and Dissidence under Direct Provision: Melatu Okorie and Ifedinma Dimbo." *Irishness on the Margins: Minority and Dissident Identities.* Ed. Pilar Villar-Argáiz. London: Palgrave MacMillan. Forthcoming.

_____. "Literature under Direct Provision: Ifedinma Dimbo and Melatu Okorie". Conference paper delivered at XIV AEDEI International Conference: "Discourses of Inclusion and Marginalisation: Minority, Dissident and Mainstream Irish Identities." University of Granada, 30th May 2015(b).

_____. "State of Homelessness: Asylum Seekers' Literature in Ireland." Conference paper delivered at "1916: HOME:2016." University College Dublin, 28th October2016(b).

Mulhall, Anne. "Dead Time: Queer Temporalities and the Deportation Regime". *Social Text: Periscope. Time Binds,* 2014. http://socialtextjournal.org/periscope_article/dead-time-queer-temporalities-and-the-deportation-regime/Accessed Sep 24 2016.

Nedeljkovic, Vukasin. "Asylum Archive: An Archive of Asylum and Direct Provision In Ireland". *Textshop Experiments, Tours and Detours,* 2016a. http://textshopexperiments.org/textshop02/asylum-archive. Accessed 07.12.2016.

_____. "Direct Provision Centres as Manifestations of Resistance". *Transactions* 1, 2016c. http://transactionspublication.com/. Accessed 31.03.2016.

_____. "The Spring in the Centre". *Broadsheet,* 2016b. http://www.broadsheet.ie/2016/03/31/postcards-fromdirect-provision/. Accessed 01.04.2016.

Okorie, Melatu Uche. "Gathering Thoughts." *Metro Éireann*, 15–21 October 2009: 12–13. Print.

_____. "BrownLady12345." *Being Various: New Irish Short Stories*. Ed. Lucy Caldwell. Faber & Faber: London, 2019. 104–112. Print.

_____. "If George Could Talk." *Alms on the Highway. New Writing from the Oscar Wilde Centre Trinity College Dublin*. Ed. Edel Corrigan. Dublin: Myrtle Press, 2011. 133–44. Print.

_____. "Shackles." *Dublin: Ten Journeys, One Destination*. Ed. Roslyn Fuller. Malahide: Irish Writers' Exchange, 2010. 138–51. Print.

_____. *This Hostel Life*. Dublin: Skein Press, 2018. Print.

_____. "Under the Awning." *College Green. Trinity's Postgraduate Arts and Humanities Magazine*. Winter 2016, 2017. Available online: http://www.collegegreenmagazine.com/

_____. "Under the Awning." *The Art of the Glimpse: 100 Irish Short Stories*. Ed. Sinéad Gleeson. Head of Zeus: London, 2020. 640–647. Print.

Rehnstrom, J.B. *Bebove*. Malahide: Irish Writers' Exchange, 2013. Print.

Villar-Argáiz, Pilar. "Introduction: The Immigrant in Contemporary Irish Literature." *Literary Visions of Multicultural Ireland: The Immigrant in Contemporary Irish Literature*. Ed. Pilar Villar-Argáiz. Manchester: Manchester University Press, 2014. 1–33. Print.

This Hostel Life

Melatu Uche Okorie

10:26am

From the window, me I can see everybody is here, and me I can see the place is also full. Mercy voice reach my ear before me I even go inside.

"Mehn," she say, "that grey hair really freaked me out this morning," and me I hear everybody laugh. Dis make me start to think if dey are talk about old age, and where Mercy see grey hair because she no too old like dat.

I use my back to push open the door because I hol buggy for my hand and the door is too heavy to open with my hand and hol the buggy at the same time. I am still try for turn around and face everybody when I hear my friend, Ngozi shout, "Yee!! Look, who is here."

"Craa-zy!" Her voice boom as she wave for me to come stand with her. I start to pass all the people and all the buggy, holing my own buggy.

"Too many people is here today, Mamaa," I say to Ngozi when I finally reach her side. "I hope you get number for me."

Then I start to hug everybody – Mercy, her friend, Mama Bomboy, Mummy Dayo, Franca.

"Ah, You know today is Monday naw, they won't let me collect number for someone who is not here."

Ngozi voice match her size. She is a big woman, and her voice is big and sound like man voice. She like to call everybody "Crazy" and I have hear some Nigerias complain behind her back dat their name is not "Crazy," and their Mama is not call them crazy and dey will tell her dat the very next time she try to call them "Crazy." Me I don't mind, I must tell you. But you know all this Nigerias, dey like to fight all the time.

Me I am here for collect my provision and toilet-tings for dis week. We collect only for Mondays and Tuesdays for the dining room for dis direct provision hostel. Dat is why there many humans and buggies. The first time my husband see me carry buggy like dis, he say: "Dis woman, why you carry buggy and you don have baby inside?"

"Dat is what everybody do here!" Me I tell him.

But dat is before. Now, if he ask me dat type of question again, me I'm gonna say to him: "How you gonna know what everybody do when you sit inside all time for watch football?"

For my last hostel, dey give you provision any day, but it's gonna be one month since you collect last. So if you get toilet paper today, it's gonna be one month before you get another. Dat is why me I happy when dey give me every week for here, but now, me I don feel happy again. Dis direct provision business is all the same, you see, because even if you collect provision for every week or you collect for every month, it is still somebody dat is give you the provision. Nothing is better than when you for decide something for yourself!

But me I still like dis hostel more than my last hostel. Because here, me I have my own kitchen, my own bathroom, my own toilet, my own sitting room, my own room with my husband, and my daughters have their own room. Before, all of us have to share one big room, and my husband have to use cloth to share the rooms for everybody. Dats why me I don like to complain too much for this hostel like some Nigerias.

Just last week, me I see Mummy Dayo outside her house on my way to laundry. I greet her and say: "Mummy Dayo, you no collect provision today?"

"Me I no dey bother myself to dey *waka* about on Mondays, *o jare*. From here to there, from there to here, for what!" She answer me like she angry.

Mummy Dayo is a small woman like dis, but she talk fight fight all the time. Me I know her now, but before, if I see her talking to somebody and shaking her head dat she always tie with scarf, I use to think she's gonna fight dem. Even now, she is roll her eyes and look me up and down as she is talk. "I just do the things I can do and leave the rest for God."

Me I agree Monday morning is crazy crazy for dis hostel because everybody like to go collect provision and toilet-tings. But you can go for Tuesday and they tell you, "We've run out of toiletries!" – and dat the end.

Everybody like to see GP for Monday too. Dey say the GP for Monday is better than the GP for Tuesday because he give better medicine. And sometimes, when you go to see GP, you remember dat you need to see Social for something, because dey share the same building and those Social people can put up sign anytime changing the time dey for see people. And as you do all of dis, you are washing clothes for the laundry too, because you don want to leave dirty clothes for house from weekend.

Sometimes, I tell myself, "it is not good to do everything for Monday because you stay like dis, nothing to do, for all the other days." But, it is not good to start week lazy too.

"Who is give number?" I ask Ngozi. She is my close Nigeria friend and me I like her very much. She talk free free like me and does not care about anybody. People tell me before, when I first come this hostel: "Be careful of

Nigerias; do not make friends with Nigerias; Nigerias like to make trouble and fight too much; the management don't like Nigerias."

It's not like dat for my last hostel; everybody do everything together. But me I still listen, and I go close to my own people, and make friends with only Congolese people and go only Congolese party. But now, me I know no one is good complete, and no one can do you bad like your own people. So me I start to make friends with Nigerias again. And if dey do me bad, I show them I don come Europe to take shit from anybody. Now, dey laugh and say, "Beverléé, you're crazy," and dey make my hair for free and give me good prize for sew my clothes. Now, all Congolese people come to me and start to say, "Please Beverléé," for connect dem to my Nigeria friends.

Mercy is one for answer me. She point for some place behind Ngozi and say to me, "You better go quickly and get your number. Then come back and I will tell you where I see grey hair for my body this morning."

Everybody laugh again. I look behind Ngozi and see one man. He is wear the uniform for the hostel security. "I never see dat man before," me I say.

"He new, my sister," Mummy Dayo tell me for sad voice and shake her head like something disappoint her. "I speak to am. He from one of those fake *Oyinbo* country. Me, I don't really like all those people! They racist pass Irish!" She look for where the man is stand holing something for his hand and hiss.

Ngozi laugh and push Mummy Dayo shoulder small. "This woman," she say, "you too funny."

Mercy look Mummy Dayo with no laugh for her face. She has tell me before dat Mummy Dayo is too old to be talking the way she talk.

I look at the man again and he look me and look away. Maybe he can tell we are talk about him. Even though I don like the way Mummy Dayo look the man like fight, I don say anything to her. Me I know Mummy Dayo don like anybody and always say something about everybody:

"Those Moslems, me I suspect dem too much o. I no follow dem do anything."

"Dat Cameroon girl, she can like to do *shakara*. I no know who she think she be."

"Congo? Dey crazy pass Nigeria o! We Nigerias, na only mouth we get, but Congo fit take knife fight you."

"Zimbabwe, Kenya, Uganda, South Africa – You better watch your husband around those women, their *toto* loose like anything."

"Eastern Europeans dem all be fake *oyinbo*."

"Irish people too dey cold. Whisper, whisper, all the time."

She have warn me about Ngozi many times. She say: "Be very careful. Igbo people na real scorpion. If you take your eye away from dem, anything you see, na you know. I like you, that is why I'm telling you all dis things."

But from everybody, me I know she hate Benin more. I know this because she don like Mercy. She say: "Benin people na the real best for everything. Dem be best liar, best criminal, best prostitute, best husband-snatcher." As she is tell me dis, she is count her finger…"all the bad bad things for this world, na dem be best for there. No let anybody you know marry Benin. Me, I be Nigeria, dat is why I know all dis things."

I leave Ngozi and the other women to go get ticket for collect provision. One, two, three, four people have reach the security man before me, so I wait for him to tear ticket one by one to give everybody. He no say anything to anyone. He just tear ticket and give, tear ticket and give. The ticket is small like this, like the one you get when you want to do raffle. It reach my turn and he tear ticket and give me. Me I look my number, it is 126.

Just then, the woman who give provision come out from the office where she give provision and stand for the door. She is wearing white coat, like the type the nurses for wear for hospital and me I can hear the sound of keys jiggle for inside the pocket of her coat. She is a fat woman like dis, and the manager for the dining room. She don say anything to the new security, but it look like he fear small to see her stand like dat. He look the ticket book for his hand and start to call out numbers quick quick. He is a very tall man and look like he can even be the father for the manager for the dining room.

"Number eighteen? Number eighteen?"

I no know why, but me I just start to feel sorry for the security man. I can see he no shout very well for the people to hear him, so me I start to help him to shout.

"Number aaeeteen!!!! Number aaeeteen!!!!!" I shout loud and loud because the noise for the dining room is too much and many people are talking for small small group. Soon, other people start to join me to shout the number. "Number aaeeteeeen!! Number aaeeteeeen!!!!"

The next thing me I see is the manager waving for the security man to come and I stop to shout to see what she's gonna do. The security man go for where she stand. He bend him head like dis because the noise is much. The Manager say small thing to him dat me I cannot hear before she turn and go back inside the office. It look from her face like she no happy with the new security man and the way everybody is shout. The security man fold the ticket book for him hand and put it for him coat pocket and he stop to shout number aaeeteen with us.

Just then, one small group of people start to clap. One man is start to walk to a window where he gonna collect provision. He has his hand up for air like this, holing the number aaeeteen ticket. He is a Somali man. He is wear glasses and is smiling like someone has catch him doing something dat is not good and he is sorry for dat. Quick, I look Mummy Dayo and she is look the Somali man up and down like dis as he walk pass her, and after he pass her, she turn and say something for the other women and everybody laugh. As soon as I see dis, me I hurry to go for join dem.

"Honest to God, naw, that is what I heard." I hear Ngozi say when I come back with my ticket.

"How you know it's true?" Mercy is ask her.

"Ah, ah, I hear the girl say it on the television with my own ears, naw!" Ngozi say like she is start to vex with Mercy small. She raise her hand which hol her ticket and shake it for me to show it is near her turn to collect provision and she leave.

"Most of my references these days are from reality television, too." Mercy friend, Mama Bomboy say with gentle voice like she is try to make peace.

"No be only you, my dear sister," Mummy Dayo cross her arms for her chest and sigh. "How man for do? No work, no nothing. Na so so television person go dey watch now."

"Try to understand me," Mercy say, touching her friend, Mama Bomboy for arm. "Why is Ngozi saying something she hear from television like she hear it from the doctor?"

"What the matter?" Me I ask Mercy. "You talk about the grey hair?"

"Ah beg, make we no talk about that grey hair matter again," Mummy Dayo say, shaking her head.

"Ngozi just told us that she heard from a woman on the Real Housewives that eating Yam helps with fertility." Mama Bomboy is the one to answer me. "You know that show, don't you?" She ask me with worry face.

"Oh, me I know the show" I answer Mama Bomboy. I like her very much because she talk different from everybody. "But I don watch it all the time. I don understand all the things for there."

"Ah, me too oh! The kin' English dey speak, me I don't understand at all," Mummy Dayo say and hiss.

Mama Bomboy look Mercy quick, like she is sorry for what Mummy Dayo is saying. Ngozi has tell me many times dat Mama Bomboy no get confident and dat her husband bully her for house. But me I no agree with Ngozi. Mama Bomboy is gentle and she respect people and she no like to fight. Beside of dat, me I can tell dat Mama Bomboy go correct school, so me I don think any man can bully her.

"But what dat mean? Fertility?" I ask Mama Bomboy.

Mama Bomboy wait small, like she want to sure Mercy is not gonna talk before she start to answer me. "Fertility means a woman can have a baby........I think." She look for Mercy again like she want to see if Mercy want to say something but Mercy no look her.

"Aeh, so Ngozi know this Yam for help woman get baby and she no tell me? And she know me I am try to find boy baby for my husband."

"Maybe Ngozi not sure!" Franca shout for me like me I am say something bad about Ngozi and dat make me angry.

"No, no, no, Mamaa," me I shout back for Franca. "Ngozi is my friend, OK? I just say it for play!"

"You see what I mean?" Mercy say, holing me for shoulder like she want me to stop to be angry. "Beverléé has bought into the Yam story without asking question."

"Aeh, the woman for television no eat the Yam?"

Mercy put her other hand for her mouth like dis, like she want to use the hand to stop the laugh from come out, but her shoulder is shake small small. "See Beverléé," she say after small time. "Not everyone on the television knows what they're talking about."

"The television is our modern day pop culture," Mama Bomboy say and smile for me.

Me I smile back for her. I no understand her but me I just like way she talk.

"Do you know that same woman on Real Housewives, yeah…?" Mercy stop to look all of us for face one by one like she want to tell us something big. "She said they have 265 days in a year."

"OMG! Imagine that!" Franca shout, like what Mercy talk is real bad something. She like for act like small girl sometime, and for copy Mercy and Mama Bomboy because Mercy have live for London before and Mama Bomboy speak correct English.

Me I have hear she about my age just dat she no get children and she no get husband, and when woman no get children or get husband, it is hard for tell her age.

"How many days it suppose be?" Mummy Dayo ask the question for my mind.

"365" Mama Bomboy tell her.

"Or 366, depending…" Mercy say, and Mama Bomboy nod her head quick like dis.

"Why it depend?" Me I ask and look Franca straight. Me I want to see if she even know the answer the way she shout, "OMG" but she no look me at all. She just keep her head down like dis, like she busy for something.

"February is sometimes 29 days," Mama Bomboy answer me.

"Na true, na true," Mummy Dayo nod her head and twist her mouth. Dis make me start to think for my head dat maybe she is tired of dis television talk.

"Do you know?" Mercy say again, like she just remember something. "I think that same woman in Real Housewives has never heard of Gandhi."

"Who dat?" Me I ask her. "All dis name we don't have for Congo."

"Na one man!" Mummy Dayo answer me quick as she use her shoulder to push my own like she don want me to continue the talk with Mercy.

"What of that boy in Big Brother, what's his name again? He has never heard of Shakespeare!" Everybody look at Mercy quiet. Mummy Dayo roll her eyes. Me I can see she is now real tired for Mercy talk.

"What?!!"

Ngozi shout make all of us for jump. She is back from collect provision and she is carry a big Lidl bag. A man who is stand near for us move away. He is not happy for the shout.

"Which kind stupid boy be that?" Ngozi say. "You no hear of Shakespeare for Congo, Beverléé?" she ask me.

"Aeh, it's long time me I hear about this Shakespeare man, long time for Congo."

Everybody start to talk for same time, except for Mummy Dayo. She is busy for look inside Ngozi Lidl bag, and she is count all the provision for inside. Me I have to say dat I look small, and I see two box for Rice Krispie, two box for Cornflakes, one packet for Sugar, one packet for Lyons tea. Me I cannot see the things under but I see Mummy Dayo is try to see dat. Maybe she want to know if Ngozi is get more provision than she. Me I know some people come for dining room sometime just to see what provision dis person or dat person collect, and after, dey use it for fight staff. Me I have complain about dis to Ngozi, but she see it different. She say why staff not give everybody the same because everybody for equal. She say to give some persons special things is quick way for cause trouble for a place like dis.

"Guess what?" Ngozi say, "My husband say he was watching one programme…"

Mercy raise her hand for Ngozi to stop. Everybody quiet and listen. The security man have start to shout another ticket number. Everybody look their hand but nobody is hol the number.

"I better go," Mercy point for her ticket. "It go soon be my turn."

"Eh-ehe, like I was saying," Ngozi start her story again. "My husband was watching this programme…"

"Dis number just dey move small small." Mummy Dayo is the one for cut what Ngozi is talk about dis time.

"What you expect?" Franca say in her small voice, pointing for the provision window. "Only two people is serving." Me I follow Franca hand and see dat only the manager and one staff is stand for window. Nobody is there for the other two windows.

"Only two people is serve all dis number of people?!" Me I shout for surprise.

"Dem dey outside dey smoke," Mummy Dayo nod her head like she is know many things we don know. "After dat, dem go take break. Dats Irish people for you!"

"But why dey take person for play here?" I ask with small anger.

"My husband say one nineteen year old boy did not know his alphabets," Ngozi start her story again. Me I am not listen very well to her because I am think of all the things I am gonna do dis morning.

"Nineteen years old!" Ngozi say shaking her head like it hard for her to understand. "And my husband say the presenters were laughing. They think it funny."

When I see nobody is answer Ngozi, me I start to feel small bad.

"All dis children for here, they don know nothing, Mamaa," Me I tell her.

"They are crazy!" Ngozi say and laugh.

"Dey real crazy, Mamaa," I say and join her for laugh.

Just then, Ngozi see one man holing a jar of honey coming from provision window. "Ehen, Beverléé," she say, "I forget to collect something. I'm coming." She hurry back to the provision office window. Mercy is also stand there. Me I see Ngozi say something for Mercy and Mercy shift aside for her. The staff come for the window and me I see Ngozi tell her something. She look down for the paper for her front and tell Ngozi something. Then Ngozi say something back for her.

"Who do you think you are?" Me I hear the staff shout for Ngozi. Everybody is quiet now and is listen. Even Mercy is look at Ngozi like she wait for her answer to the question.

"And who do you think you are too?" Ngozi is ask back, and she is point at the staff as she is talk. Me I see the manager leave her window and come for the window where Ngozi and the staff is stand and argue.

"Is Ngozi fighting?" Franca ask like all of us are no seeing the same thing.

"Listen Ngozi, we are not allowed to give honey to anyone," the manager tell Ngozi like she not in the mood for too much talk.

"Then why did she give that man honey just now when I ask for it first? This is what you people do all the time! You always pick people you want to give this or that. Why?" Ngozi voice is loud now as she is talk.

The new security man come and stand for the back of Ngozi but he no say or do anything. That make me I know he really new. The other securities will hol and carry anybody they see for argue with staff.

"Well, that is the last honey we have and we've just given it out," the manager answer Ngozi in a way everybody can tell she is lying but there is nothing Ngozi can do about it.

"You better find one for me oh, because I'm not leaving this place until I get one." Ngozi tell her and fold her hands. Me I wait to hear what the manager gonna say to Ngozi but she just move back. She push away the paper where people for sign their name for provision out of the way, then she take one side of the window and close it. She do the same for the other side of the window too.

Ngozi run to the second window but the manager come there and close dat window too. Then she and the staff come out of the provision office and she take the bunch of key for her coat pocket and start to lock the door.

As soon as all the people see dis, dey start to shout. "You can't just lock up because of one person. We've been waiting here for long. What do you mean?"

But the Manager no say anything to anybody. Dis make all the people angry more and dey start to shout for Ngozi.

"If there's no honey, why not take sugar?"

"Is sugar and honey not the same thing?"

"All these women that like to make trouble."

12:01 pm

Small small, all the people have start to go as dey see the manager is not gonna change her mind and open the office to give provision. Mercy and Mama Bomboy, then Franca and Mama Dayo, all go. Now me I can see new people have start to line up outside the dining room for lunch. I take my empty buggy and open the dining room door. I am quiet and sad as I go. Ngozi is my best friend for dis hostel but I have to leave her. From the window outside, me I can still see her stand alone for the dining room, fighting for her honey.

Index

Note: Page numbers followed by "n" denote endnotes.

For Product Safety Concerns and Information please contact our
EU representative GPSR@taylorandfrancis.com Taylor & Francis
Verlag GmbH, Kaufingerstraße 24, 80331 München, Germany